Savannah

JIM MOREKIS

Contents

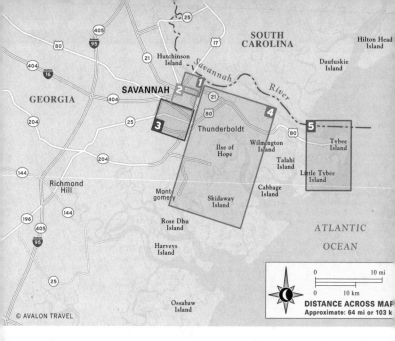

Maps

SIGHTS

- 6 WORLD WAR II MEMORIAL
- 12 CITY HALL
- 13 CHATHAM ARTILLERY GUNS
- 18 SAVANNAH COTTON EXCHANGE
- 19 ROUSAKIS PLAZA
- 21 FACTOR'S WALK
- 23 EMMET PARK
- 25 THE BRICE
- 27 THE WAVING GIRL
- 29 FIRST AFRICAN BAPTIST CHURCH
- 31 HAITIAN MONUMENT
- 32 SHIPS OF THE SEA MARITIME MUSEUM
- 41 U.S. CUSTOM HOUSE
- 42 CHRIST EPISCOPAL CHURCH
- 43 OLDE PINK HOUSE
- 45 OLIVER STURGIS HOUSE
- 46 LUCAS THEATRE FOR THE ARTS
- 49 HAMPTON LILLIBRIDGE HOUSE AND CHARLES ODDINGSELLS HOUSE
- 50 TRUSTEES GARDEN
- 64 TRUSTEES THEATRE
- 65 JEN LIBRARY
- 69 TELFAIR ACADEMY OF ARTS AND SCIENCES
- 70 TRINITY UNITED METHODIST CHURCH
- 71 FEDERAL COURTHOUSE AND POST OFFICE
- 73 EVANGELICAL LUTHERAN CHURCH OF THE ASCENSION
- 75 OWENS-THOMAS HOUSE
- 76 KEHOE HOUSE
- 78 ISAIAH DAVENPORT HOUSE MUSEUM
- 79 SECOND AFRICAN BAPTIST CHURCH
- 80 CUNNINGHAM HOUSE
- 82 JEPSON CENTER FOR THE ARTS
- 83 JULIETTE GORDON LOW BIRTHPLACE

RESTAURANTS

- 14 OLYMPIA CAFÉ
- 17 VIC'S ON THE RIVER
- 24 B. MATTHEW'S EATERY
- 30 VINNIE VANGOGO'S
- 33 LULU'S CHOCOLATE BAR
- 37 SAPPHIRE GRILL
- 38 THE LADY & SONS
- 44 OLDE PINK HOUSE
- 54 THE COFFEE FOX
- 59 KAYAK KAFE
- 63 LEOPOLD'S ICE CREAM
- 68 TEQUILA'S TOWN
- 72 WRIGHT SQUARE CAFE
- 74 ZUNZI'S

NIGHTLIFE

- 2 CHUCK'S BAR
- 4 CLUB ONE JEFFERSON
- 7 KEVIN BARRY'S IRISH PUB
- 8 ROCKS ON THE ROOF
- 11 MOON RIVER BREWING COMPANY
- 34 RAIL PUB
- 35 22 SQUARE
- 39 THE JINX
- 40 HANG FIRE
- 48 ABE'S ON LINCOLN
- 52 CIRCA 1875
- 57 CHIVE SEA BAR AND LOUNGE
- 62 O'CONNELL'S

ARTS AND CULTURE

- 47 LUCAS THEATRE FOR THE ARTS
- 55 SAVANNAH PHILHARMONIC

SPORTS AND ACTIVITIES

- 15 SAVANNAH RIVERBOAT CRUISES
- 28 SAVANNAH BELLES
- 67 SAVANNAH BIKE TOURS

WILLIAMSON ST
MONTGOMERY ST

World War II Memorial 6

W RIVER ST

2
3
7 8 9
10
14 15 16 17
Rousakis Plaza 19

RIVER FACTORS WY
E LOWER FACTORS WALK

W BAY ST
City Hall 12
Chatham Artillery Guns 13
18

4 5
W BAY LN
11
41
U.S. Custom House

Franklin Square

First African Baptist Church 29
31 Haitian Monument
30
Ellis Square
W BRYAN ST
35 36
37 38
Johnson Square
Olde Pink House 43 44
42
Christ Episcopal Church
45 Oliver Sturgis House

32
Ships of the Sea Maritime Museum
33 34
W CONGRESS ST
39 40
52
W CONGRESS LN

57
58
62
59 60 61

W BROUGHTON ST
51
W BROUGHTON LN

53 54 55 56

68
W STATE ST
Federal Courthouse and Post Office 71

Telfair Academy of Arts and Sciences 69
Telfair Square
W PRESIDENT ST
Trinity United Methodist Church 70
ALTON ST

Wright Square
Evangelical Lutheran Church of the Ascension 73
E PRESIDENT ST
74

W YORK ST
72

Jepson Center for the Arts 82
W YORK LN

Juliette Gordon Low Birthplace 83 84

W OGLETHORPE AVE
W OGLETHORPE LN

HISTORIC DISTRICT

W HULL ST

Chippewa Square

MARTIN LUTHER KING JR BLVD
MONTGOMERY ST
JEFFERSON ST
BARNARD ST
WHITAKER ST
BULL ST
DRAYTON ST

© AVALON TRAVEL

SEE MAP 2

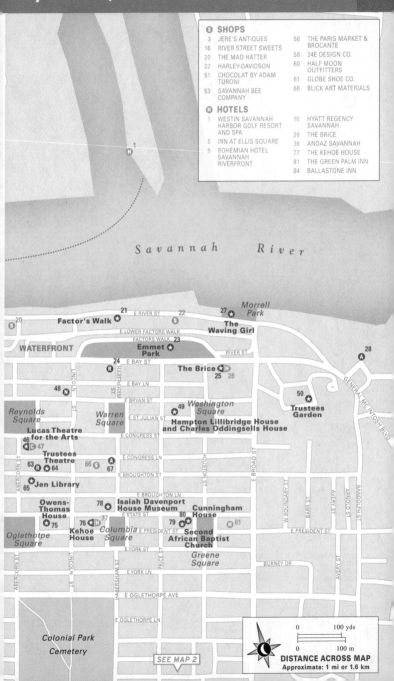

S SHOPS

3 JERE'S ANTIQUES
16 RIVER STREET SWEETS
20 THE MAD HATTER
22 HARLEY-DAVIDSON
51 CHOCOLAT BY ADAM TURONI
53 SAVANNAH BEE COMPANY

56 THE PARIS MARKET & BROCANTE
58 24E DESIGN CO.
60 HALF MOON OUTFITTERS
61 GLOBE SHOE CO.
66 BLICK ART MATERIALS

H HOTELS

1 WESTIN SAVANNAH HARBOR GOLF RESORT AND SPA
5 INN AT ELLIS SQUARE
9 BOHEMIAN HOTEL SAVANNAH RIVERFRONT

10 HYATT REGENCY SAVANNAH
26 THE BRICE
36 ANDAZ SAVANNAH
77 THE KEHOE HOUSE
81 THE GREEN PALM INN
84 BALLASTONE INN

Savannah River

Morrell Park

21 E RIVER ST 22
Factor's Walk

27 The Waving Girl

20 S
E LOWER FACTORS WALK
FACTORS WALK 23
WATERFRONT
Emmet Park
RIVER ST

28 A

24 E BAY ST
The Brice
25 26

48 N
E BAY LN

E BRYAN ST

Reynolds Square
Warren Square
E ST JULIAN ST
49 Washington Square
Hampton Lillibridge House and Charles Oddingsells House

50
Trustees Garden

Lucas Theatre for the Arts
46
E CONGRESS ST

GENERAL MCINTOSH BLVD

E CONGRESS LN
Trustees Theatre
63 64 66 67
65 Jen Library

E BROUGHTON ST

E BROUGHTON LN

Owens-Thomas House
78 Isaiah Davenport House Museum
80 Cunningham House
75 76 77 79 81 N
E STATE ST
Kehoe House
Columbia Square
E PRESIDENT ST
Second African Baptist Church
Oglethorpe Square
E PRESIDENT ST
Greene Square
E YORK ST

BURNEY DR

E YORK LN

E OGLETHORPE AVE

E OGLETHORPE LN

Colonial Park Cemetery

SEE MAP 2

0   100 yds
0   100 m
DISTANCE ACROSS MAP
Approximate: 1 mi or 1.6 km

SEE MAP 1

Orleans Square

SCAD Museum of Art

Savannah History Museum

To Muse Arts Warehouse

Battlefield Park

Pulaski Square

Georgia State Railroad Museum

Savannah Children's Museum

Chatham Square

Ralph Mark Gilbert Civil Rights Museum

SEE MAP 3

SIGHTS

2 SCAD MUSEUM OF ART
4 SAVANNAH HISTORY MUSEUM
7 BATTLEFIELD PARK
8 GEORGIA STATE RAILROAD MUSEUM
9 SAVANNAH CHILDREN'S MUSEUM
10 INDEPENDENT PRESBYTERIAN CHURCH
13 FIRST BAPTIST CHURCH
15 HISTORIC SAVANNAH THEATRE
18 COLONIAL CEMETERY
21 HILTON SAVANNAH DESOTO
23 CATHEDRAL OF ST. JOHN THE BAPTIST
24 BEACH INSTITUTE
25 GREEN-MELDRIM HOUSE

27 UNITARIAN UNIVERSALIST CHURCH OF SAVANNAH
28 ANDREW LOW HOUSE MUSEUM
29 HAMILTON-TURNER INN
30 FLANNERY O'CONNOR CHILDHOOD HOME
31 SCOTTISH RITE TEMPLE
33 POETTER HALL
34 JONES STREET
44 RALPH MARK GILBERT CIVIL RIGHTS MUSEUM
45 MERCER-WILLIAMS HOUSE MUSEUM
48 TEMPLE MICKVE ISRAEL
49 WESLEY MONUMENTAL UNITED METHODIST CHURCH
50 MASSIE HERITAGE CENTER

RESTAURANTS

11 ANGEL'S BBQ
37 MRS. WILKES' DINING ROOM

NIGHTLIFE

6 THE DISTILLERY
17 MCDONOUGH'S
22 PINKIE MASTERS

© AVALON TRAVEL

Independent Presbyterian Church 10

11 12

Historic Savannah Theatre

13 Chippewa Square 15 16

First Baptist Church 14

W HULL ST

E MC DONOUGH ST

17

E PERRY ST

E PERRY LN

19

HISTORIC DISTRICT

E PERRY LN

E LIBERTY

20 21

Hilton Savannah DeSoto

E LIBERTY LN

22

Cathedral of St. John the Baptist

23

Beach Institute

24

Green-Meldrim House

E HARRIS ST

25 Madison Square 26

E MACON ST

27 Unitarian Universalist Church of Savannah

29 E MACON ST

Hamilton-Turner Inn

E CHARLTON ST

Lafayette Square

28

Andrew Low House Museum

W CHARLTON ST

31 32

Scottish Rite Temple

33 Poetter Hall

E CHARLTON ST

Flannery O'Connor Childhood Home

30

34 Jones Street

37

38

35

E JONES ST

36

E JONES LN

39 40

34

42 43

41

E TAYLOR ST

45

Monterey Square

E WAYNE ST

48

49

Wesley Monumental United Methodist Church

Calhoun Square

Whitefield Square

Mercer-Williams House Museum

46 47

Temple Mickve Israel

E GORDON ST

50 Massie Heritage Center

E GORDON LN

51

E GASTON ST

MARINE MEMORIAL

Forsyth Fountain

Forsyth

Park

CONFEDERATE MEMORIAL

VICTORIAN DISTRICT

0   100 yds
0   100 m

DISTANCE ACROSS MAP
Approximate: 1.1 mi or 1.7 km

ARTS AND CULTURE

3   MUSE ARTS WAREHOUSE

16 HISTORIC SAVANNAH THEATRE

SPORTS AND ACTIVITIES

1   SAVANNAH DERBY DEVILS

5   SAVANNAH MOVIE TOUR

14 SAVANNAH'S UNCOMMON WALK

36 SIXTH SENSE SAVANNAH GHOST TOUR

51 SAVANNAH TOURS BY FOOT

SHOPS

19 THE BOOK LADY

20 SAINTS AND SHAMROCKS

26 E. SHAVER BOOKSELLER

32 SHOPSCAD

38 ONE FISH TWO FISH

39 THE CORNER DOOR

40 SMALL PLEASURES

41 V&J DUNCAN

42 MADAME CHRYSANTHEMUM

43 CUSTARD BOUTIQUE

46 ALEX RASKIN ANTIQUES

47 FOLKLORICO

HOTELS

12 FOLEY HOUSE INN

35 ELIZA THOMPSON HOUSE

SEE MAP 2

SIGHTS
5 FORSYTH PARK
9 CARNEGIE BRANCH LIBRARY
10 LAUREL GROVE CEMETERY

RESTAURANTS
3 LEOCI'S TRATTORIA
7 THE SENTIENT BEAN
11 BUTTERHEAD GREENS
12 FOXY LOXY
13 ELIZABETH ON 37TH
14 BACK IN THE DAY BAKERY
15 GREEN TRUCK NEIGHBORHOOD PUB
16 THE FLORENCE

NIGHTLIFE
8 AMERICAN LEGION BAR

SPORTS AND ACTIVITIES
6 FORSYTH PARK
17 WILDERNESS SOUTHEAST

HOTELS
1 THE GASTONIAN
2 DRESSER-PALMER HOUSE
4 MANSION ON FORSYTH PARK

Laurel Grove Cemetery
10

Laurel Grove Cemetery
10

0   250 yds
0   250 m
DISTANCE ACROSS MAP
Approximate: 2.2 mi or 3.5 km

Chatham Square
Monterey Square
Calhoun Square

E TAYLOR ST

SEE MAP 2

Mother Matilda Beasley Park

W GORDON ST
E GORDON LN

W GASTON ST

1 H

H 2
E GASTON LN

MARINE MEMORIAL

R 3
E HUNTINGDON ST
E HUNTINGDON LN

Forsyth Fountain

E HALL ST
E HALL LN

4 H
E GWINNETT ST

VICTORIAN DISTRICT

CONFEDERATE MEMORIAL

E BOLTON ST

Forsyth Park

5 6

E WALDBURG ST

THE HIKER

E PARK AVENUE LN

R 7
N 8
E DUFFY ST

E HENRY ST

9
Carnegie Branch Library

E ANDERSON ST

E 31ST ST

W 32ND ST
W 33RD ST

W 34TH ST

11 R
E 36TH ST

12 R

SOFO

204
E 37TH ST

R 13
W 38TH ST
E 38TH ST
E 39TH ST

W 39TH ST
E 40TH ST

W 40TH ST
204

14 R
W 41ST ST
E 41ST ST
E 41ST LN

W 42ND ST

R 15

E VICTORY DR
80

R 16
E 44TH ST

E 45TH ST

E 46TH ST

CHATHAM CRES

17 A
WASHINGTON AVE

BARNARD ST
WHITAKER ST
DRAYTON ST
ABERCORN ST
LINCOLN ST
HABERSHAM ST
PRICE ST
EAST BROAD ST
REYNOLDS ST
ATLANTIC AVE
PAULSEN ST
BULL ST

© AVALON TRAVEL

SEE MAP 1

SEE MAP 2

SEE MAP 3

1 Old Fort Jackson

2

3 Oatland Island Wildlife Center

4 Bonaventure Cemetery

5

6

Daffin Park

7 8 9

Thunderbolt Museum
10 11

Thunderbolt

12 Savannah State University

Whitemarsh Island

Dutch Island

Skidaway Island

Wilmington Island

13

14

15 University of Georgia Marine Educational Center and Aquarium

EISENHOWER DR

16

To 17 Oglethorpe Mall

18

Isle of Hope
20

19 Wormsloe State Historic Site

Isle of Hope

Skidaway Island State Park
25 26

To 21 Armstrong State University Masquers

Pin Point Heritage Museum
22

24
23

Savannah River

St. Augustine Creek

Wilmington River

SIGHTS
1 OLD FORT JACKSON
3 OATLAND ISLAND WILDLIFE CENTER
4 BONAVENTURE CEMETERY
7 DAFFIN PARK
10 THUNDERBOLT MUSEUM
12 SAVANNAH STATE UNIVERSITY

15 UNIVERSITY OF GEORGIA MARINE EDUCATIONAL CENTER AND AQUARIUM
19 WORMSLOE STATE HISTORIC SITE
20 ISLE OF HOPE
22 PIN POINT HERITAGE MUSEUM
25 SKIDAWAY ISLAND STATE PARK

RESTAURANTS
6 DESPOSITO'S
18 SANDFLY BBQ

ARTS AND CULTURE
21 ARMSTRONG STATE UNIVERSITY MASQUERS

SPORTS AND ACTIVITIES
2 SAVANNAH FLY FISHING CHARTERS
5 SAVANNAH CANOE & KAYAK
8 DAFFIN PARK
9 SAVANNAH SAND GNATS
11 TELECASTER CHARTERS
13 MISS JUDY CHARTERS
14 WILMINGTON ISLAND CLUB
16 BACON PARK
23 MOON RIVER KAYAK TOURS
24 SKIDAWAY NARROWS
26 SKIDAWAY ISLAND STATE PARK

SHOPPING
17 OGLETHORPE MALL

0   1 mi
0   1 km
DISTANCE ACROSS MAP
Approximate: 6.3 mi or 10.1 km

© AVALON TRAVEL

SOUTH CAROLINA

GEORGIA

Savannah River

Fort Pulaski National Monument

 1 2

Cockspur Island

A 3

Lazaretto

4 A

A 5,6

Creek

Tybee Island Light Station and Museum

10 R 11

SOLOMON AVE

8 R

A 9

VAN HORNE ST

80

1ST ST

12 A

3RD ST

13 A

DAVIS ISLAND RD

7

8TH ST

BUTTER AVE

SIGHTS

1 FORT PULASKI NATIONAL MONUMENT
10 TYBEE ISLAND LIGHT STATION AND MUSEUM

16 SOUTH END
20 TYBEE ISLAND MARINE SCIENCE CENTER

RESTAURANTS

7 THE CRAB SHACK
8 HUC-A-POO'S BITES & BOOZE
11 NORTH BEACH GRILL

17 TYBEE ISLAND SOCIAL CLUB
19 THE BREAKFAST CLUB

SPORTS AND ACTIVITIES

2 FORT PULASKI NATIONAL MONUMENT
3 MCQUEEN'S ISLAND TRAIL
4 LAZARETTO CREEK
5 AMICK'S DEEP SEA FISHING
6 NORTH ISLAND SURF AND KAYAK

9 SEA KAYAK GEORGIA
12 HIGH TIDES SURF SHOP
13 TYBEE ISLAND MEMORIAL PARK
14 LITTLE TYBEE ISLAND
15 NORTH BEACH

HOTELS

18 THE GEORGIANNE INN
21 ATLANTIS INN

SEE DETAIL

A 14

Little Tybee Island

0   750 yds

0   750 m

DISTANCE ACROSS MAP
Approximate: 3.8 mi or 6.1 km

© AVALON TRAVEL

9TH ST
2ND AVE
LOVELL AVE
15 A
10TH ST

South End
16
11TH ST
JONES AVE
12TH ST

13TH ST
BUTLER AVE

17 R
14TH ST
18

15TH ST

Marine Science Center
19 R
20

TABRISA ST

21

16TH ST

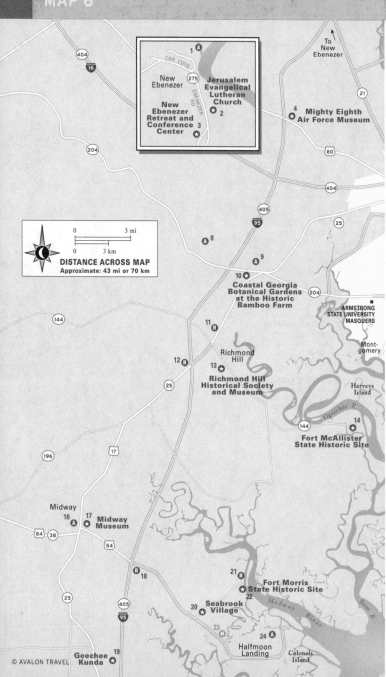

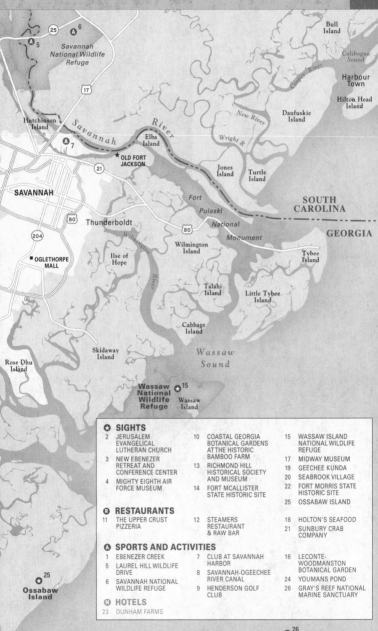

⊙ SIGHTS

2 JERUSALEM EVANGELICAL LUTHERAN CHURCH

3 NEW EBENEZER RETREAT AND CONFERENCE CENTER

4 MIGHTY EIGHTH AIR FORCE MUSEUM

10 COASTAL GEORGIA BOTANICAL GARDENS AT THE HISTORIC BAMBOO FARM

13 RICHMOND HILL HISTORICAL SOCIETY AND MUSEUM

14 FORT MCALLISTER STATE HISTORIC SITE

15 WASSAW ISLAND NATIONAL WILDLIFE REFUGE

17 MIDWAY MUSEUM

19 GEECHEE KUNDA

20 SEABROOK VILLAGE

22 FORT MORRIS STATE HISTORIC SITE

25 OSSABAW ISLAND

ⓡ RESTAURANTS

11 THE UPPER CRUST PIZZERIA

12 STEAMERS RESTAURANT & RAW BAR

18 HOLTON'S SEAFOOD

21 SUNBURY CRAB COMPANY

ⓐ SPORTS AND ACTIVITIES

1 EBENEZER CREEK

5 LAUREL HILL WILDLIFE DRIVE

6 SAVANNAH NATIONAL WILDLIFE REFUGE

7 CLUB AT SAVANNAH HARBOR

8 SAVANNAH-OGEECHEE RIVER CANAL

9 HENDERSON GOLF CLUB

16 LECONTE-WOODMANSTON BOTANICAL GARDEN

24 YOUMANS POND

26 GRAY'S REEF NATIONAL MARINE SANCTUARY

ⓗ HOTELS

23 DUNHAM FARMS

DISCOVER
Savannah

Surprisingly cosmopolitan for a Deep South city, Savannah's quirky hedonism permeates any visit. The brainchild of General James Oglethorpe, the city's layout is studied even today as a masterpiece of urban design. Rarely has a city owed so much to the vision of one person as Savannah owes to Oglethorpe.

Today, Savannah is also known for being able to show you a rowdy good time, and not only during its massive, world-famous St. Patrick's Day celebration. Savannahians will use any excuse for a party and any excuse to drink in the full flavor of natural beauty here. Whether you're admiring an antebellum home from the cotton era or enjoying the sea breeze and a cocktail out on Tybee Island, a sense of fun imbues all parts of life here.

Savannah's outskirts are generally self-contained. Despite the fact that Tybee Island is largely dependent on Savannah's economy, it has willfully kept its own fun and funky persona. Rural areas outside town, such as New Ebenezer and Midway, are reflective of a wholly different side of the state—a Georgia of country churches and tight-knit descendants of original plantation owners.

Clockwise from top left: the Cathedral of St. John the Baptist; old Southern house; Gracie sculpture in the Bonaventure Cemetery; River Street.

Planning Your Trip

Neighborhoods

WATERFRONT
It's only natural to start one's adventures in Savannah where Oglethorpe's adventures themselves began: on the waterfront, now dominated by scenic and historic River Street. Once the bustling center of Savannah's thriving cotton and naval stores export industry, the waterfront also includes Factor's Walk and Bay Street.

CITY MARKET
In local parlance, the phrase "City Market" refers not only to the refurbished warehouses that make up this tourist-friendly area of shops and restaurants in the historic district's western portion but also to its bookends, Franklin and Ellis Squares.

HISTORIC DISTRICT
Life in the bulk of downtown revolves around Savannah's many historic squares, legacies of the colony's founding. Churches, homes, shops, and businesses abound in this sizable but very walkable National Landmark Historic District.

SOFO DISTRICT
The name means "South of Forsyth Park," and this pretty, quiet, but up-and-coming area includes Savannah's Victorian district as well as turn-of-the-20th-century "streetcar suburbs." It also has many of Savannah's foodie gems.

fountain at Savannah Cotton Exchange

garden of a Victorian District home

Tybee Island Light Station

VICTORIAN DISTRICT

Boasting 50 blocks of fine Victorian and Queen Anne frame houses, Savannah's Victorian district is truly magnificent. The city's first suburb, it was built between 1870 and 1910. In addition to the glories of Forsyth Park, some key areas for connoisseurs of truly grand Victorian architecture are the residential blocks of East Hall Street between Lincoln and Price Streets—one of the few street sections in town with the original paving. Some other nice examples are in the 1900-2000 blocks of Bull Street near the large Bull Street Public Library, including the famous "Gingerbread House" at 1917 Bull Street.

EASTSIDE

Eastside includes many areas that are technically islands, but you'll sense little difference from the mainland. Marshland, Spanish moss, and outdoor scenery are the draws.

SOUTHSIDE

To most locals, "Southside" refers to the generic strip-mall sprawl below Derenne Avenue, but for our purposes, the term also includes some outlying islands. They are among the most scenic areas in Savannah.

TYBEE ISLAND

Its name means "salt" in the old Euchee tongue, indicative of the island's chief export in those days. And Tybee Island—"Tybee" to locals—is indeed one of the essential seasonings of life in Savannah. Tybee is part and parcel of the city's social and cultural fabric. Many of the island's 3,000 full-time residents, known for their boozy bonhomie and quirky personal style, commute to work in the city. And those living "in town" often reciprocate by visiting Tybee to dine in its few but excellent restaurants, drink in its casual and crazy watering holes, and frolic on its wide, beautiful beaches lined with rare sea oats waving in the Atlantic breeze.

GREATER SAVANNAH

Outlying areas of Savannah differ in character, ranging from the bustling new growth of West Chatham County, featuring the Mighty Eighth National Air Force Museum, to the Henry Ford-related history of the bedroom community of Richmond Hill, to the blackwater ecosystem of New Ebenezer, to the quaint and quiet Liberty County, home of two out of three of Georgia's signers of the Declaration of Independence.

When to Go

Springtime is for lovers, and it's no coincidence that springtime is when most love affairs with the region begin. Unless you have severe pollen allergies—not a trivial concern given the explosion of plant life at this time—you should try to experience this area at its peak of natural beauty during the magical period from mid-March to mid-May. Not surprisingly, lodging is the most expensive and most difficult to secure at that time. Hilton Head's busiest time is during the RBC Heritage golf tournament in mid-April. While last-minute cancellations are always possible, the only real guarantee is to secure reservations as far in advance as possible (a full year in advance is not unusual for peak times).

Activity here slows down noticeably in July and August. But overall, summertime in the South gets a bad rap and is often not appreciably worse than summers north of the Mason-Dixon Line—though it's certainly more humid.

My favorite time of year on the southeastern coast is the middle of November, when the tourist crush noticeably subsides. Not only are the days delightful and the nights crisp (but not frigid), but you can get a room at a good price.

What to Take

Unless you're coming in the winter to take advantage of lower rates or to enjoy the copious seasonal cheer, there's not much need for a heavy jacket. A sweater or windbreaker will do fine for chillier days. Also note that the ocean and the larger rivers can generate some surprisingly crisp breezes, even on what otherwise might be a warm day.

Because of the area's temperate climate, perspiration is likely to be a constant travel companion; pack accordingly. Whatever you wear, stay with natural fabrics such as cotton. The humidity and generally warm weather combine for a miserable experience with polyester and other synthetic fabrics.

Unless you're coming in the hottest days of summer or the coldest part of winter—both unlikely scenarios—plan on a trip to a drugstore or supermarket to buy some bug spray or Skin So Soft, an Avon product that also keeps away the gnats.

The Best of Savannah

Downtown Savannah comprises one of the largest historic districts in the country, and is certainly among the most walkable and friendly. This itinerary also takes you to outlying areas around Savannah and down the beautiful Georgia coast, where you can experience the area's natural beauty and pleasant climate.

Day 1

Hit downtown Savannah hard today, starting with a walk down River Street. Then enjoy the aesthetic charms of two adjacent museums, one traditional and one modern: the Telfair Academy of Arts and Sciences and the Jepson Center for the Arts. Tour the exquisite Owens-Thomas House and then take a walk through the squares, visiting the Cathedral of St. John the Baptist in Lafayette Square and the Mercer-Williams House Museum on Monterey Square.

Day 2

On your way out to Tybee Island, stop for a walk through amazing Bonaventure Cemetery—about 15 minutes outside of downtown—and pay your respects to native son Johnny Mercer. A half-hour drive takes you to scenic and historically important Fort Pulaski National Monument. Scoot on into Tybee (another 10 minutes) and take a climb to the top of the Tybee Light Station before dinner.

Day 3

Drive down scenic U.S. 17 through the Altamaha River estuary, about

lilies in the Okefenokee Swamp

Bonaventure Cemetery

an hour and a half south of Savannah, and stop by historic Hofwyl-Broadfield Plantation, near Brunswick, for an authentic glimpse at an old rice plantation. Make the five-minute trip over the causeway and enjoy the afternoon at The Village on St. Simons Island, with a visit to historic Fort Frederica National Monument.

Day 4

This morning, a 20-minute drive takes you into the Jekyll Island Historic District. Tour the grounds and have lunch at any of the great restaurants on-site. Rent a bike and pedal up to the Clam Creek Picnic Area, checking out the Horton House tabby ruins along the way. Ride on the sand to Driftwood Beach and relax awhile.

Day 5

This morning, drive an hour south to St. Marys and have a walk around the cute little downtown area before heading out on the ferry to Cumberland Island National Seashore. The 45-minute ferry ride takes you to a full day of biking or hiking the many trails among the ruins and dunes.

Day 6

Make the half-hour drive into Folkston and the Suwanee Canal Recreation Area at Okefenokee National Wildlife Refuge. Take a guided tour up and down the blackwater canal, or walk the trails out to the swamp's prairie vistas and drink in this unique natural beauty.

African American Heritage

The cities and Sea Islands of the Georgia coast are integral to a full understanding of the experience of African Americans in the South. More than that, they are living legacies, with a thriving culture—called Gullah in South Carolina and Geechee in Georgia—whose roots can be traced directly back to West Africa.

Waterfront

Check out the African American Monument in Rousakis Plaza on River Street.

Historic District

Head over to the former center of black life in Savannah, Martin Luther King Jr. Boulevard (once West Broad St.), and see the Ralph Mark Gilbert Civil Rights Museum.

Southern Cooking: High Style and Homestyle

Elizabeth on 37th

Fresh Seafood

The best seafood places put a premium on freshly harvested fish and shellfish.

- **Desposito's,** Savannah—Shrimp and oysters dockside.
- **Red Fish,** Hilton Head Island—Stylish but always fresh.
- **Speed's Kitchen,** Shellman Bluff—Delicacies right off the boat.

New Southern

Savannah is home to some adventurous chefs offering an updated take on Lowcountry classics.

- **Elizabeth on 37th,** Savannah—Still Savannah's premier fine-dining spot.
- **Sapphire Grill,** Savannah—Closest thing to a Manhattan restaurant in Savannah.

Classic Southern

Your best bet for fine old-school Southern cooking:

- **Mrs. Wilkes' Dining Room,** Savannah—Old-school "pass the plate" community seating in a historic home.

Barbecue

The pleasures of the pig are never far away in this region. Here is the best coastal 'cue joint:

- **Angel's BBQ,** Savannah—Hipsters do 'cue too.

The Second African Baptist Church is where Sherman announced the famous "40 acres and a mule" field order.

The Beach Institute is a repository of African American art, culture, and history. Check out the restored schoolroom at Massie Heritage Center, Savannah's first African American school.

Coastal Cruising on U.S. 17

Fans of retro Americana and roadside kitsch will find a treasure trove of down-home sites along the old Coastal Highway, now known as U.S. 17. Before the arrival of the interstate highway system, U.S. 17 was by far the most-traveled route in the region. While now just a shadow of its former self, it is still a vital roadway and contains a lot of interesting, little-known history. Here's a look at some of the highlights, beginning just south of Savannah and ending at Brunswick, Georgia. This is a fun road trip you could easily accomplish in a day, just checking out the sights along the way.

- **Keller's Flea Market:** South of Savannah and about a half-hour from Hardeeville on U.S. 17, at the intersection with Highway 204 (Abercorn Extension), you'll find this classic rambling and friendly Southern flea market. Look for the statue of the hat-wearing cow out front.

- **Midway Church:** Forty-five minutes south of Savannah in the Liberty County town of Midway is this beautiful 1792 church, whose congregation once boasted two of Georgia's signers of the Declaration of Independence. Don't miss the historic cemetery across the street.

- **Smallest Church in North America:** About 15 minutes south of Midway on the side of the road near South Newport is the minuscule and charming Memory Park Christ Chapel, erected in 1950.

- **Butler Island Plantation Ruins:** In another 15 or so minutes, just south of Darien, Georgia, on the west side of U.S. 17, you'll find this tall chimney—the only remnant of the Butler plantation. English actress Fanny Kemble, who married a Butler heir, wrote the influential abolitionist work *Journal of a Residence on a Georgian Plantation* after witnessing the miserable life of the slaves who worked here. (Strangely, the nearby historical marker makes no mention of this.)

- **Brunswick Stewpot:** Allegedly the container in which the first batch of Brunswick stew was cooked up, this cast-iron pot can be found in Brunswick, Georgia, at the corner of U.S. 17 and the Torras Causeway to St. Simons Island, about 20 minutes south of Butler Island.

Keller's Flea Market

City Market

Tour the First African Baptist Church in City Market, the oldest black congregation in North America. Nearby is the Haitian Monument, a nod to the volunteers who helped the cause of independence in the Revolutionary War.

Victorian District

Supreme Court Justice Clarence Thomas once studied at the Carnegie Branch Library, Savannah's first black library.

Westside

Pay your respects at Laurel Grove South, a historic African American cemetery with stirring memorials to some of Savannah's most notable black figures.

The Golden Isles

Harris Neck National Wildlife Refuge was once the site of an African American community, displaced for a World War II airfield. Be sure to visit the vernacular Gould Cemetery near the landing within the refuge.

If you drive all the way down to little Meridian near Darien and ride the ferry out to Sapelo Island, you can take a guided day tour of the island and its rich Gullah/Geechee history, including the community of Hog Hammock.

Hilton Head

On Hilton Head, stop by the Coastal Discovery Museum and take an African American heritage tour, visiting the site of Mitchelville, the first community of freed slaves in the United States.

Kayaking Southern Swamps

The Savannah area is framed by the largest contiguous salt marsh in the world and is just a short drive from Okefenokee National Wildlife Refuge. These places are not only a kayaker's paradise, but amazing natural habitats for indigenous and migratory birds. This five-day trip hits the green highlights.

Day 1

Head down to Tybee Island outside Savannah for a day trip across the Back River to undeveloped Little Tybee Island, where wilderness camping is allowed, or a kayak run at Skidaway Narrows, near Skidaway

Seaside Romance

Spanish moss, friendly beaches, sunsets over the water, sultry weather, moonlit carriage rides—what more could you ask for? The Lowcountry and Georgia coast pretty much wrote the book on romantic getaways. Here's a starter list of the most romantic spots.

Savannah

- Relax on the grass at vast, scenic **Forsyth Park,** surrounded by Victorian architecture.

- Yes, cemeteries can be romantic—especially gorgeous **Bonaventure Cemetery.**

- Avoid the lines at The Lady & Sons and instead have a delightful dinner at **Sapphire Grill.** Share a coffee, sweet treat, or perhaps a signature martini at **Lulu's Chocolate Bar.**

the Jekyll Island Club Hotel

- Have a nightcap at **Rocks on the Roof** on top of the Bohemian Hotel Savannah Riverfront and watch the big cargo ships roll in and out on the river.

- Up for a crazy night of dancing? **Club One Jefferson**'s the ticket.

The Golden Isles

- Stay at the **Jekyll Island Club Hotel,** former stomping ground of the world's richest people. Rent a bike and crisscross the whole island in the late afternoon, coming back to the club to enjoy a romantic dinner by the fireplace at the **Courtyard at Crane.**

- Take the ferry to **Cumberland Island National Seashore,** surely one of the most romantic locations on earth. Rent a bike on arrival and take your time pedaling among the ruins of the old mansions, making sure to visit the chapel at the **First African Baptist Church,** site of the wedding of John F. Kennedy Jr. and Carolyn Bessette. Before you board the ferry to conclude your journey, maybe you'll get lucky and encounter some of the island's famous wild horses, fitting symbols of passion and romance.

State Park, which also offers great camping. If you opt not to camp out under the stars, enjoy a great dinner in Savannah's historic district.

Day 2

Today, head west of town to the undeveloped blackwater Ebenezer Creek, amid the cypress swamps and crisscrossed by old rice paddy field dikes. Later visit the nearby Savannah National Wildlife Refuge, with parts in both South Carolina and Georgia and an excellent bird-watching (and gator-watching!) area.

the Altamaha River

Day 3

Bird-watchers mustn't miss a trip to Harris Neck National Wildlife Refuge, world-renowned for its colonies of wood storks and other waterfowl. Have a meal at nearby Shellman Bluff, a picturesque shrimping village with a couple of excellent, authentic down-home seafood restaurants.

Day 4

This morning, make a run down the hybrid blackwater Altamaha River, Georgia's largest. Amid the remnants of what were once some of America's largest rice and cotton plantations, you'll see a stunning display of waterfowl and migratory birds. Tonight have a nice dinner on relaxing St. Simons Island, or make it onto Jekyll Island in time to see the birds on the north-side beaches. There's a nifty little campground on Jekyll's north end.

Day 5

This is a full day at Okefenokee National Wildlife Refuge, a vast natural wonderland that belies the name "swamp." On its broad "prairies" bird-watchers will see a nearly unmatched variety of species for this region, and kayakers can paddle down several blackwater runs amid the cypress. Extend your trip an extra night by camping out in the middle of the swamp on one of the refuge's special raised platforms, or at one of two great state parks east and west of the Okefenokee. Look out for the alligators!

Life's a Beach

Not far from Savannah, there are plenty of beaches, many of them are made even more enjoyable by the fact that they tend to get much less traffic than more touristy areas. Here's a quick guide to match the beach to the trip:

Family-Friendly

- Hilton Head Island's beaches are roomy and spotlessly maintained. And because no alcohol is allowed on them, they're more geared toward families with children.

- A playground for the people of Georgia by order of the state legislature, Jekyll Island is a safe, roomy, and friendly getaway.

Sportin' Life

- You can ride your bike for 12 miles on the expansive, hard-packed sand all around Hilton Head Island, as well as enjoy more strenuous adventures such as parasailing.

- Tybee Island offers kayak adventures, parasailing, and boogie boarding. Enjoy a nice bike ride on a converted railbed that takes you into the grounds of historic Fort Pulaski.

Peace and Quiet

- Romantic and isolated, Cumberland Island is virtually the mossy picture of the old Sea Island South.

- Low-traffic Sapelo Island offers friendly folks and a really beautiful beach.

Dog-Friendly

- Easily the most dog-friendly beach in the area is Jekyll Island. Just keep 'em on a leash and you're fine year-round.

- Hilton Head doesn't allow canines at all Memorial Day-Labor Day, but you can take them on a leash 10am-5pm from April 1 until the day before Memorial Day.

- Sorry, Rover can't come over to Tybee Island at all.

kayaks on Hilton Head Island

Sights

Look for ★ to find
recommended sights.

Highlights

★ **Best Place to See Enormous Ships Up Close:** There's still nothing like strolling the cobblestones of **River Street** amid the old cotton warehouses, enjoying the cool breeze off the river, and watching the huge cargo ships on their way to and from the bustling port (page 30).

★ **Most Unusual Church:** The oldest black congregation in the United States, **First African Baptist Church** still meets in its historic sanctuary, a key stop on the Underground Railroad (page 34).

★ **Oldest Public Art Museum in the South:** Old school meets new school in a museum complex that comprises the traditional collection of the ultramodern **Jepson Center for the Arts** and the **Telfair Academy of Arts and Sciences,** located within a stone's throw of each other (page 44).

★ **If There's Only Time for One House Museum Tour:** Possibly the country's best example of Regency architecture and definitely an example of state-of-the-art historic preservation in action, **Owens-Thomas House** is Savannah's single greatest historic home (page 46).

★ **Most Inspirational Sight:** The soaring Gothic Revival edifice of the **Cathedral of St. John the Baptist** is complemented by its ornate interior and its matchless location on verdant Lafayette Square, stomping ground of the young Flannery O'Connor (page 51).

★ **Most Iconic Square:** Quintessential **Monterey Square** has some of the best examples of local architecture and world-class ironwork all around its periphery (page 54).

★ **Savannah's Version of Central Park:** A verdant expanse ringed by old live oaks and chockablock with memorials, **Forsyth Park** is the true center of downtown life. It is also Savannah's backyard (page 59).

★ **Most Oddly Romantic Burial Ground:** The moss-draped **Bonaventure Cemetery** is the final resting place for some of Savannah's favorite citizens, including the great Johnny Mercer, and makes great use of its setting on the banks of the Wilmington River (page 66).

★ **Best History Site for the Whole Family:** The well-run **Fort Pulaski National Monument,** built with the help of a young Robert E. Lee, is not only historically significant, its beautiful setting makes it a great place for the entire family (page 70).

Assigned by King George II of England to buffer Charleston from the Spanish, General James Edward Oglethorpe laid out his settlement in a deceptively simple plan that is still studied the world over as a model of nearly perfect urban design. Savannah was built as a series of rectangular "wards,"

each constructed around a central square. As the city grew, each square took on its own characteristics, depending on who lived on the square and how they made their livelihood.

It's best to introduce yourself to the sights of Savannah by traveling from the river southward. It's no small task to navigate the nation's largest contiguous historic district, but when in doubt it's best to follow James Oglethorpe's original plan of using the five "monumental" squares on Bull Street (Johnson, Wright, Chippewa, Madison, and Monterey) as focal points.

Originally known as West Broad Street (you'll still hear old-timers refer to it that way), Martin Luther King Jr. Boulevard is the spiritual home of Savannah's African American community, though it has gone through several transformations. In the early 1800s, West Broad was a fashionable address, but during the middle of that century its north end got a bad reputation for crime and blight as thousands of Irish immigrants packed in right beside the area's poor black population.

Several important sites are clustered together on MLK Jr. Boulevard under the auspices of the Coastal Heritage Society: the Savannah History

Museum, the Georgia State Railroad Museum, the Savannah Children's Museum, and Battlefield Park.

Savannah's outlying areas still bear the indelible marks of the plantation era. While history is no less prominent, it is more subtle in these largely semirural areas, and the tourist infrastructure is much less developed than in Savannah proper.

This area contains some of the most impoverished communities in Georgia, so keep in mind that the locals may have more on their minds than keeping you entertained—though certainly at no point will their Southern manners fail them. And also keep in mind that you are traveling in one of the most unique ecosystems in the country, and natural beauty is never far away.

In Savannah, you don't need a car to have a great time and see most sights worth enjoying. A strong walker can easily traverse the length and breadth of downtown in a day, although less energetic travelers should consider a central location or make use of the free downtown shuttle. To fully enjoy the city, however, you'll need access to a vehicle so you can go east to Tybee Island and south to various historic sites with spottier public transportation. You'll appreciate downtown all the more when you can get away and smell the salt air.

Waterfront   Map 1

★ River Street

It's much tamer than it was 30 years ago—when muscle cars cruised its cobblestones and a volatile mix of local teenagers, sailors on shore leave, and soldiers on liberty made things less than family-friendly after dark—but River Street still has more than enough edginess to keep things interesting. Families are safe and welcome here, but energetic pub crawling remains a favorite pastime for locals and visitors alike.

If you have a car, park it somewhere else and walk. The cobblestones—actually old ballast stones from some of the innumerable ships that docked here over the years—are tough on the suspension, and much of River Street is dedicated to pedestrian traffic anyway. If you do find yourself driving here, keep in mind that the north-south "ramps" leading up and off River Street are all extensions of major downtown streets, so you can easily drive or walk up them and find yourself in the middle of bustling Bay Street and on to points beyond.

Factor's Walk

One level up from River Street, Factor's Walk has nothing to do with math, though a lot of money has been counted here. In arcane usage, a "factor" was a broker, i.e., a middleman for the sale of cotton, Savannah's chief export during most of the 1800s. Factors mostly worked in Factor's Row, the traditional phrase for the actual buildings on River Street, most all of

Clockwise from top left: *The Waving Girl*; First African Baptist Church; cargo ships off River Street.

which were used in various import-export activities before their current transformation into a mélange of shops, hotels, restaurants, and taverns. Factor's Walk is divided into Lower Factor's Walk, comprising the alleys and back entrances behind Factor's Row, and Upper Factor's Walk, the system of crosswalks at the upper levels of Factor's Row that lead directly to Bay Street.

MAP 1: E. River St.

Rousakis Plaza

Rousakis Plaza is a focal point for local festivals. It's a great place to sit, feed the pigeons, and watch the huge container ships go back and forth from the Georgia Ports Authority's sprawling complex farther upriver (you can see the huge Panamax cranes in the distance). The **African American Monument** at the edge of Rousakis Plaza was erected in 2002 to controversy for its stark tableau of a dazed-looking African American family with broken shackles around their feet. Adding to the controversy was the graphic content of the inscription at the base of the 12-foot statue, written especially for the monument by famed poet Maya Angelou. It reads:

> We were stolen, sold and bought together from the African continent.
> We got on the slave ships together. We lay back to belly in the holds of
> the slave ships in each other's excrement and urine together, some-
> times died together, and our lifeless bodies thrown overboard together.
> Today, we are standing up together, with faith and even some joy.

Nearby you can't miss the huge, vaguely cubist Hyatt Regency Savannah, another controversial local landmark. The modern architecture of the Hyatt caused quite a stir when it was first built in 1981, not only because it's so contrary to the area's historic architecture but because its superstructure effectively cuts off one end of River Street from the other. "Underneath" the Hyatt—actually still River Street—you'll find elevators to the hotel lobby, the best way to get up off the waterfront if you're not up for a walk up the cobblestones. Immediately outside the west side of the Hyatt up toward Bay Street is another exit and entry point, a steep and solid set of antebellum stairs that, despite its decidedly pre-Americans with Disabilities Act aspect, is nonetheless one of the quicker ways to leave River Street for those with strong legs and good knees.

MAP 1: E. River St., behind City Hall

The Waving Girl

At the east end of River Street is the statue of Florence Martus, aka *The Waving Girl*, set in the emerald-green expanse of little Morrell Park. Beginning in 1887 at the age of 19, Martus—who actually lived several miles downriver on Elba Island—took to greeting every passing ship with a wave of a handkerchief by day and a lantern at night, without fail for the next 40 years. Ship captains returned the greeting with a salute of their own on the ship's whistle, and word spread all over the world of the beguiling woman who waited on the balcony of that lonely house. Was she looking for a sign of a long-lost love who went to sea and never returned? Was she trying to get a handsome sea captain to sweep her off her feet and take her off that little island? No one knows for sure, but the truth is probably more prosaic. Martus was a lifelong spinster who lived with her brother, the lighthouse keeper, and was by most accounts an eccentric, if delightful, person—which of course makes her an ideal Savannah character. After her brother died, Martus moved into a house on the Wilmington River, whiling away the hours by—you guessed it—waving at passing cars. Martus became such an enduring symbol of the personality and spirit of Savannah that a U.S. Liberty ship was named for her in 1943. She died a few months after the ship's christening at the age of 75.

MAP 1: Morrell Park, E. River St. and E. Broad St.

World War II Memorial

Near the foot of the Bohemian Hotel Savannah Riverfront on River Street is a 21st-century addition to Savannah's public monuments. Installed in 2010, the World War II Memorial—fairly modernist by local standards—features a copper-and-bronze globe torn in half to represent the European and Pacific theaters of the war. The more than 500 local people who gave their lives in that conflict are memorialized by name.

MAP 1: W. River St., near Bohemian Hotel Savannah Riverfront, 102 W. Bay St.

Bay Street

Because so few downtown streets can accommodate 18-wheelers, Bay Street unfortunately has become the default route for industrial traffic in the area on its way to and from the industrial west side of town. In front of the Hyatt Regency Savannah is a concrete bench marking the spot on which Oglethorpe pitched his first tent.

Chatham Artillery Guns

Directly adjacent to City Hall on the east is a small canopy sheltering two cannons, which together compose the oldest monument in Savannah. These are the Chatham Artillery Guns, presented to the local militia group of the same name by President George Washington during his one and only visit to town in 1791. Today, locals use the phrase "Chatham Artillery" differently, to refer to a particularly potent local punch recipe that mixes several hard liquors.

MAP 1: Adjacent to City Hall, 2 E. Bay St.

City Hall

Dominating Bay Street is City Hall, with its gold-leaf dome. The 1907 building was designed by acclaimed architect Hyman Witcover and erected on the site of Savannah's first town hall.

MAP 1: 2 E. Bay St.

Savannah Cotton Exchange

Directly behind the Chatham Artillery Guns is the ornate Savannah Cotton Exchange, built in 1886 to facilitate the city's huge cotton export business. Once nicknamed "King Cotton's Palace" but now a Masonic lodge, this delightful building by William Gibbons Preston is one of Savannah's many great examples of the Romanesque style. You'll become well acquainted with Preston's handiwork during your stay in Savannah, as the Boston architect built many of Savannah's finest buildings. The fanciful lion figure in front—sometimes mistakenly referred to as a griffin—represents Mark the Evangelist. However, it isn't original—the first lion was destroyed in 2009 in a bizarre traffic accident.

MAP 1: 100 E. Bay St.

U.S. Custom House

The large gray Greek Revival building directly across from City Hall is the U.S. Custom House (not "customs," regardless of what the tour guides may say). Built on the spot of Georgia's first public building in 1852, the Custom House was also Georgia's first federal building and was the first local commission for renowned New York architect John Norris, who went on to design 22 other buildings in Savannah. Within its walls was held the trial of the captain and crew of the notorious slave ship *Wanderer,* which illegally plied its trade after a national ban on the importation of slaves. Local newspaper publisher and educator John H. DeVeaux worked here after his appointment as the first African American U.S. Collector of Customs.

MAP 1: 1 E. Bay St.

City Market

Map 1

Franklin Square

Just west of City Market is Franklin Square, once known simply as "Water Tank Square" because that's where the city reservoir was back in the day. Don't be alarmed by the numbers of men hanging out in the square. Scruffy heirs to an old Savannah tradition, most of them are day laborers for hire. Until recently, Franklin Square was, like Ellis Square, a victim of "progress," this time in the form of a highway going right through the middle of it. But as part of the city's effort to reclaim its history, Franklin Square was returned to its original state in the mid-1980s.

★ First African Baptist Church

Without a doubt the premier historic attraction on Franklin Square—and indeed one of the most significant historic sites in Savannah—is the First African Baptist Church. It's the oldest black congregation in North America, dating from 1777. The church also hosted the first African American Sunday school, begun in 1826. The church's founding pastor,

The Rebirth of Ellis Square

Ellis Square has been completely reimagined.

Ellis Square's history as Savannah's main open-air marketplace goes back to 1755, when there was a single City Market building in the square itself. The fourth City Market was built in 1872, an ornate Romanesque affair with a 50-foot roofline. In 1954, the city decided to build a parking garage in the square. So the magnificent City Market building—and Ellis Square—simply ceased to exist.

Several large warehouses surrounding City Market survived. Now a hub of tourism, City Market encompasses working art studios, hip bars, cute cafés, live music in the east end of the courtyard, cutting-edge art galleries, gift shops, and restaurants.

The eyesore that was the Ellis Square parking garage is gone, and the square has been rebuilt as a pedestrian hangout, complete with a fountain, all atop a huge underground parking garage. Be sure to check out the smallish bronze of native Savannahian and Oscar-winning lyricist Johnny Mercer on the square's western edge.

George Liele, was the first black Baptist in Georgia and perhaps the first black missionary in the country. He baptized his successor, Andrew Bryan, a slave who opted to stay in Savannah and preach instead of leaving with many other blacks after the British vacated the city in 1782. Third pastor Andrew Marshall was an ardent supporter of American independence and purchased his freedom shortly after the end of the Revolution. He served as George Washington's personal servant during his visit here. This founding trio is immortalized in stained glass windows in the sanctuary.

The present building dates from 1859 and was built almost entirely by members of the congregation themselves, some of whom redirected savings intended to purchase their freedom toward the building of the church. It houses the oldest church organ in Georgia. A key staging area for the fabled Underground Railroad, First African Baptist still bears the scars of that turbulent time. In the floor of the fellowship hall—where many civil rights meetings were held, because it was safer for white citizens to go there instead of black activists going outside the church—you'll see breathing holes, drilled for use by escaped slaves hiding in a cramped crawlspace.

MAP 1: 23 Montgomery St., 912/233-2244, http://firstafricanbc.com; tours Tues.-Sat. 11am and 2pm, Sun. 1pm; $7 adults, $6 students/seniors

Haitian Monument
The Haitian Monument in the center of the square commemorates the sacrifice and service of "Les Chasseurs Volontaires de Saint-Dominigue," the 750 Haitian volunteers who fought for American independence and lost many of their number during the unsuccessful attempt to wrest Savannah back from the British in 1779.

MAP 1: Franklin Square

Historic District North   Map 1

Johnson Square
Due east of City Market, Johnson Square, Oglethorpe's very first square, is named for Robert Johnson, governor of South Carolina at the time of Georgia's founding. It was here that one of Georgia's first "liberty poles" was erected to urge citizens to rally for independence. And it was here that a gathering in 1861 celebrated Georgia's secession, ironically with a huge banner draped over the Greene Monument bearing the words "Don't Tread on Me"—a slogan used in the founding of the very union the secessionists sought to dissolve.

The roomy, shaded square, ringed with major bank branches and insurance firms, is dominated by the **Nathanael Greene Monument** in honor of George Washington's second-in-command, who was granted nearby Mulberry Grove plantation for his efforts. Marquis de Lafayette dedicated the towering obelisk during his one and only visit to Savannah in 1825. At the time it did not honor any one person. Its dedication to Greene came in 1886, followed by the reinterment of Greene's remains directly underneath the monument in 1901. In typically maddening Savannah fashion, there is a separate square named for Greene, and which has no monument to him at all.

Christ Episcopal Church
The southeast corner of Johnson Square is dominated by Christ Episcopal Church, aka Christ Church, a historic house of worship also known as the "Mother Church of Georgia" because its congregation traces its roots to that first Anglican service in Savannah, held the same day Oglethorpe landed. While this spot on Johnson Square was reserved for the congregation from the very beginning, this is actually the third building on the site, dating from 1838. Much of the interior is more recent than that, however, since a fire gutted the inside of the church in 1895. In the northeast bell tower is a bell forged in 1919 by Revere and Sons of Boston.

MAP 1: 28 Bull St., 912/236-2500, www.christchurchsavannah.org

Reynolds Square

Walk directly east of Johnson Square to find yourself at Reynolds Square, named for John Reynolds, the first (and exceedingly unpopular) royal governor of Georgia. First called "Lower New Square," Reynolds Square originally served as site of the filature, or cocoon storage warehouse, during the fledgling colony's ill-fated flirtation with the silk industry (a federal building now occupies the site). As with Johnson Square, the monument in Reynolds Square has nothing to do with its namesake, but is instead a likeness of John Wesley dedicated in 1969 near the spot believed to have been his home. On the northeast corner of the square is the parish house of Christ Church, Wesley's congregation during his stay in Savannah.

Lucas Theatre for the Arts

The other major Savannah landmark on Reynolds Square is the Lucas Theatre for the Arts. Built in 1921 as part of Arthur Lucas's regional chain of movie houses, the Lucas also featured a stage for road shows. Ornate and stately but with cozy warmth to spare, the venue was a hit with Savannahians for four decades, until the advent of TV and residential flight from downtown led to financial disaster. In 1976, the Lucas closed after a screening of *The Exorcist*. When the building faced demolition in 1986, a group of citizens created a nonprofit to save it. Despite numerous starts and stops, the 14-year campaign finally paid off in a grand reopening in 2000, an event helped immeasurably by timely donations from *Midnight* star Kevin Spacey and the cast and crew of the locally shot *Forrest Gump*. The theater's schedule stays pretty busy, so it should be easy to check out a show while you're in town.
MAP 1: 32 Abercorn St., 912/525-5040, www.lucastheatre.com

Olde Pink House

A Reynolds Square landmark, the Olde Pink House is not only one of Savannah's most romantic restaurants but quite a historic site as well. It's the oldest Savannah mansion from the 18th century still standing as well as the first place in Savannah where the Declaration of Independence was read aloud. Pink inside as well as out, the Georgian mansion was built in 1771 for rice planter James Habersham Jr., one of America's richest men at the time and a member of the notorious "Liberty Boys" who plotted revolution. The building's pink exterior was a matter of serendipity, resulting from its core redbrick seeping through the formerly white stucco outer covering.
MAP 1: 23 Abercorn St.

Oliver Sturgis House

At the southwest corner of Reynolds Square is the understated Oliver Sturgis House, former home of the partner with William Scarbrough in the launching of the SS *Savannah*. This is one of the few Savannah buildings to feature the stabilizing earthquake rods that are much more common in Charleston. Don't miss the dolphin downpour spouts at ground level.
MAP 1: 27 Abercorn St.

Columbia Square

Named for the mythical patroness of America, Columbia Square features at its center not an expected portrait of that female warrior figure but the original fountain from Noble Jones's Wormsloe Plantation, placed there in 1970.

Isaiah Davenport House Museum

Columbia Square is primarily known as the home of the Isaiah Davenport House Museum. The house museum is a delightful stop in and of itself because of its elegant simplicity, sweeping double staircase, and near-perfect representation of the Federalist style. But the Davenport House occupies an exalted place in Savannah history as well, because the fight to save it began the preservation movement in Savannah. In 1955 the Davenport House, then a tenement, was to be demolished for a parking lot. But Emma Adler and six other Savannah women, angered by the recent destruction of Ellis Square, refused to let it go down quietly. Together they formed the Historic Savannah Foundation in order to raise the $22,500 needed to purchase the Davenport House. By 1963 the Davenport House—built in 1820 for his own family by master builder Isaiah Davenport—was open to the public as a museum.

Most Octobers, the Davenport House hosts living history dramatizations based on Savannah's yellow fever plague of the 1820s. Despite the grim subject matter, the little playlets are usually quite entertaining. Other special seasonal tours include a Madeira wine tour and "Tea with Mrs. Davenport."
MAP 1: 324 E. State St., 912/236-8097, www.davenporthousemuseum.org; Mon.-Sat. 10am-4pm, Sun. 1pm-4pm; $9 adults, $5 children

Kehoe House

Across the corner from the Davenport House is the Classical Revival masterpiece Kehoe House, designed for local ironworks owner William Kehoe in 1892 by DeWitt Bruyn. Sadly, the proof of Kehoe's self-described "weakness for cupolas" no longer exists, the cupola having rotted away. Once a funeral home, the Kehoe House is now one of Savannah's premier bed-and-breakfasts. It's unique not only in its exuberantly Victorian architecture but in its twin fireplaces and ubiquitous rococo ironwork, courtesy of the irrepressible Kehoe himself.
MAP 1: 123 Habersham St.

Warren and Washington Squares

Warren Square and its neighbor Washington Square formed the first extension of Oglethorpe's original four and still boast some of the oldest houses in the historic district. Both squares are lovely little garden spots, ideal for a picnic in the shade.

The Brice

Now a hotel, The Brice on Washington Square was once a cotton ware-house and subsequently one of the nation's first Coca-Cola bottling plants.
MAP 1: 601 E. Bay St.

Hampton Lillibridge House and Charles Oddingsells House

Two houses near Washington Square were restored by the late Jim Williams of *Midnight* fame: the Hampton Lillibridge House, which once hosted an Episcopal exorcism, and the Charles Oddingsells House.
MAP 1: 507 E. St. Julian St. and 510 E. St. Julian St.

SIGHTS
HISTORIC DISTRICT NORTH

Greene Square

Named for Revolutionary War hero Nathanael Greene, but bearing no monument to him whatsoever, Greene Square is of particular impor-tance to local African American history. In 1818, the residence at 542 East State Street was constructed for free blacks Charlotte and William Wall. The property at 513 East York Street was built for the estate of Catherine DeVeaux, part of a prominent African American family.

Cunningham House

At the corner of Houston (pronounced "HOUSE-ton") and East State Streets is the 1810 Cunningham House, built for Henry Cunningham, former slave and founding pastor of the Second African Baptist Church.
MAP 1: Houston St. and State St.

Second African Baptist Church

The Second African Baptist Church, on the west side of the square, is where General Sherman made his famous promise of "40 acres and a mule." The founding pastor of the church was Henry Cunningham, whose home, the Cunningham House, is also on Green Square.
MAP 1: 124 Houston St., 912/233-6163, www.secondafrican.org

Old Fort

One of the lesser-known aspects of Savannah history is this well-trod neighborhood at the east end of Bay Street, once the site of groundbreak-ing experiments and piratical intrigue, and then a diverse melting pot of Savannah citizenry.

Emmet Park

Just north of Reynolds Square on the north side of Bay Street you'll come to Emmet Park, first a Native American burial ground and then known as "the Strand" or "Irish Green" because of its proximity to the Irish slums of the Old Fort. In 1902 the park was named for Robert Emmet, an Irish patriot of the early 1800s, who was executed by the British for treason. Within it is the eight-foot **Celtic Cross,** erected in 1983 and carved of Irish limestone.

The Celtic Cross is at the center of a key ceremony for local Irish Catholics during the week prior to St. Patrick's Day.

Close by is one of Savannah's more recent monuments, the **Vietnam War Memorial** at East Bay Street and Rossiter Lane. The reflecting pool is in the shape of Vietnam itself, and the names of all 106 Savannahians killed in the conflict are carved into an adjacent marble tablet.

Walk a little farther east and you'll find my favorite little chapter of Bay Street history, the **Beacon Range Light,** tucked into a shady corner. Few visitors bother to check out this masterfully crafted 1858 navigation aid, intended to warn approaching ships of the old wrecks sunk in the river as a defense during the Revolutionary War.

MAP 1: E. Bay St. west of E. Broad St.

Trustees' Garden

At the east end of Bay Street where it meets East Broad Street rises a bluff behind a masonry wall—at 40 feet off the river, still the highest point in Chatham County. This is Trustees' Garden, the nation's first experimental garden. Modeled on the Chelsea Botanical Garden in London, it was intended to be the epicenter of Savannah's silk industry. Alas, the colonists had little knowledge of native soils or climate—they thought the winters would be milder—and the experiment was not as successful as hoped. Soon Trustees' Garden became the site of Fort Wayne, named after General "Mad Anthony" Wayne of Revolutionary War fame, who retired to a plantation near Savannah. The Fort Wayne area—still called the "Old Fort" neighborhood by old-timers—fell from grace and became associated with the "lowest elements" of Savannah society, which in the 19th and early 20th centuries were Irish and African Americans. It also became known for its illegal activity and as the haunt of sea salts such as the ones who frequented what is now the delightfully schlocky **Pirates' House** restaurant. That building began life in 1753 as a seamen's inn and was later chronicled by Robert Louis Stevenson in *Treasure Island* as a rogue's gallery of pirates and nautical ne'er-do-wells.

Find the **Herb House** on East Broad Street, the older-looking clapboard structure next to the Pirates' House entrance. You're looking at what is considered the single oldest building in Georgia and one of the oldest in the United States. Constructed in 1734, it was originally the home of Trustees' Garden's chief gardener.

To the rear of Trustees' Garden is the 1881 Hillyer building, now the **Charles H. Morris Center,** a mixed-use performing arts and meeting space that is heavily used during the springtime Savannah Music Festival.

MAP 1: 10 E. Broad St., 912/443-3277, http://trusteesgarden.com

Broughton Street

Downtown's main shopping district for most of the 20th century, Broughton Street once dazzled shoppers with decorated gaslights, ornate window displays, and fine examples of terrazzo, a form of mosaic that still

A Southern St. Paddy's Day

St. Patrick's Day Parade

Savannah hosts the second-largest St. Patrick's Day celebration in the world, second only to New York City's. With its fine spring weather and walkability—not to mention its liberal rules allowing you to carry an adult beverage on the street—Savannah is tailor-made for a boisterous outdoor celebration.

Ironically, given St. Patrick's Day's current close association with the Catholic faith, the first parade in Savannah was organized by Irish Protestants. Thirteen members of the local Hibernian Society—the country's oldest Irish society—took part in a private procession to Independent Presbyterian Church in 1813. The first public procession was in 1824, when the Hibernians invited all local Irishmen to parade through the streets. The first recognizably modern parade, with bands and a "grand marshal," happened in 1870.

Organized by a "committee" of about 700 local Irishmen—with but a tiny sprinkling of women—today's three-hour procession includes marchers from all the local Irish organizations, in addition to marching bands and floats representing many local groups. The assembled clans wear kelly green blazers, brandishing their walking canes and to-go cups, some pushing future committee members in strollers.

adorns many shop entrances. Postwar suburbs and white flight brought neglect to the area by the 1960s, and many thought Broughton was gone for good. But with the downtown renaissance brought about largely by the Savannah College of Art and Design (SCAD), Broughton was able not only to get back on its feet but to thrive as a commercial center once again.

Jen Library

The Savannah College of Art and Design's Jen Library is a state-of-the-art facility set in the circa-1890 Levy and Maas Brothers department stores. An important piece of Broughton Street history happened farther west at its intersection with Whitaker Street. Tondee's Tavern was where the infamous "Liberty Boys" met over ale and planned Savannah's role in the American

Revolution. Only a plaque marks the site's contribution to Savannah's colonial history.

MAP 1: 201 E. Broughton St.

Trustees Theater

Around the corner from the Lucas Theatre on Reynolds Square is the art moderne Trustees Theater, a Savannah College of Art and Design (SCAD) operation that seats 1,200 and hosts concerts, film screenings, and the school's much-anticipated spring fashion show. It began life in the postwar boom of 1946 as the Weis Theatre, another one of those ornate Southern movie houses that took full commercial advantage of being the only buildings at the time to have air-conditioning. But by the end of the 1970s it had followed the fate of Broughton Street, lying dormant and neglected until its purchase and renovation by SCAD in 1989.

This block of Broughton in front of Trustees Theater is usually blocked off to mark the gala opening of the Savannah Film Festival each fall. Searchlights crisscross the sky, limos idle in wait, and Hollywood guests strike poses for the photographers.

MAP 1: 216 E. Broughton St., 912/525-5051, www.trusteestheater.com

Wright Square

The big monument in Wright Square, Oglethorpe's second square, has nothing to do with James Wright, royal governor of Georgia before the Revolution, for whom it's named. Instead the monument honors William Gordon, former mayor and founder of the Central of Georgia Railway, which upon completion of the Savannah-Macon run was the longest railroad in the world. Gordon is in fact the only native Savannahian honored in a city square. But more importantly, Wright Square is the final resting place for the great Yamacraw chief Tomochichi, buried in 1737 in an elaborate state funeral at James Oglethorpe's insistence. A huge boulder of north Georgia granite honoring the chief was placed in a corner of the square in 1899 under the auspices of William Gordon's daughter-in-law. However, Tomochichi is not buried under the boulder, but rather somewhere underneath the Gordon monument. So why not rename it Tomochichi Square? Old ways die hard down here, my friend.

Evangelical Lutheran Church of the Ascension

Next to the old courthouse is the historic Evangelical Lutheran Church of the Ascension, built in the 1870s for a congregation that traced its roots to some of the first Austrian Salzburgers to come to Savannah in 1734.

MAP 1: 120 Bull St., 912/232-4151, www.elcota.org

Federal Courthouse and Post Office

On the west side of Wright Square is the Federal Courthouse and Post Office, built in 1898 out of Georgia marble. The building's stately facade

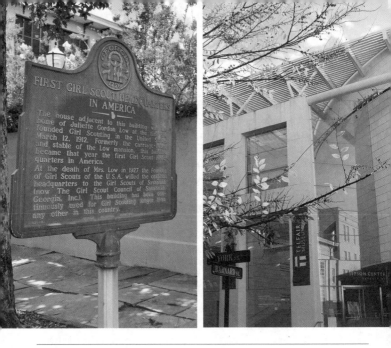

Clockwise from top left: plaque at Juliette Gordon Low Birthplace; Jepson Center for the Arts; the Telfair Academy of Arts and Sciences.

makes an appearance in several films, including the original *Cape Fear* and *Midnight in the Garden of Good and Evil*.

MAP 1: 125-127 Bull St.

Telfair Square

One of the few Savannah squares to show consistency in nomenclature, Telfair Square was indeed named for Mary Telfair, last heir of a family that was one of the most important in Savannah history. Mary bequeathed the family mansion to the Georgia Historical Society upon her death in 1875 to serve as a museum. Originally called St. James Square after a similar square in London, Telfair was the last of Oglethorpe's original four squares.

Telfair Square hosts two of the three buildings operated by **Telfair Museums,** an umbrella organization that relies on a combination of private and public funding and has driven much of the arts agenda in Savannah for the last 125 years. The third component of Telfair Museums is the **Owens-Thomas House** on Oglethorpe Square.

Get a triple site pass to the Jepson Center, the Telfair Academy, and the Owens-Thomas House for $20 per person.

★ Jepson Center for the Arts

The latest and proudest addition to the Telfair Museums group is the striking, 64,000-square-foot Jepson Center for the Arts, whose ultramodern exterior sits catty-corner from the Telfair Academy of Arts and Sciences. Promoting a massive, daringly designed new facility devoted to nothing but modern art was a hard sell in this traditional town, especially when renowned architect Moshe Safdie insisted on building a glassed-in flyover across a lane between two buildings. After a few delays in construction, the Jepson opened its doors in 2006 and has since wowed locals and visitors alike with its cutting-edge traveling exhibits and rotating assortment of late-20th-century and 21st-century modern art. If you get hungry, you can enjoy lunch in the expansive atrium café, and, of course, there's a nice gift shop.

Each late January-early February the Jepson Center hosts most events of the unique Pulse Art + Technology Festival, a celebration of the intersection of cutting-edge technology and performing and visual arts.

MAP 1: 207 W. York Ln., 912/790-8800, www.telfair.org; Tues.-Sat. 10am-5pm, Sun.-Mon. noon-5pm; $12 adults, $5 students

★ Telfair Academy of Arts and Sciences

The oldest public art museum in the South, the Telfair Academy of Arts and Sciences was built in 1821 by the great William Jay for Alexander Telfair, scion of that famous Georgia family. The five statues in front are of Phidias, Raphael, Rubens, Michelangelo, and Rembrandt. As well as displaying Sylvia Judson Shaw's now-famous *Bird Girl* sculpture, which originally stood in Bonaventure Cemetery (actually the third of four casts by the sculptor), the Telfair Academy features an outstanding collection of primarily 18th- and 20th-century works, most notably the largest public collection of visual art by Khalil Gibran. Major paintings include work by Childe Hassam, Frederick Frieseke, Gari Melchers, and the massive *Black Prince of Crécy* by Julian Story.

MAP 1: 121 Barnard St., 912/790-8800, www.telfair.org; Tues.-Sat. 10am-5pm, Sun.-Mon. noon-5pm; $12 adults, $5 students

Trinity United Methodist Church

Directly between the Telfair and the Jepson stands Trinity United Methodist Church, Savannah's first Methodist church. Built in 1848 on the site of the Telfair family garden, its masonry walls are of famous "Savannah Gray" bricks—a lighter, more porous and elegant variety—under stucco. Virgin longleaf pine was used for most of the interior, fully restored in 1969. Call ahead for a tour.

MAP 1: 225 W. President St., 912/233-4766, www.trinitychurch1848.org, sanctuary daily 9am-5pm, services Sun. 8:45am and 11am

Oglethorpe Square

Don't look for a monument to Georgia's founder in the square named for him. That would be way too easy, so of course his monument is in Chippewa Square. Originally called "Upper New Square," Oglethorpe Square was created in 1742.

Juliette Gordon Low Birthplace

Around the corner from Wright Square at Oglethorpe and Bull is the Juliette Gordon Low Birthplace, declared the city's very first National Historic Landmark in 1965. The founder of the Girl Scouts of the USA lived here from her birth in 1860 until her marriage. The house was completed in 1821 for Mayor James Moore Wayne, future Supreme Court justice, but the current furnishings, many original, are intended to reflect the home during the 1880s.

Also called the Girl Scout National Center, the Low birthplace is probably Savannah's most festive historic site because of the heavy traffic of Girl Scout troops from across the United States. They flock here year-round to take part in programs and learn more about their organization's founder, whose family sold the house to the Girl Scouts in 1953. You don't have to be affiliated with the Girl Scouts to tour the home. Tours are given every 15 minutes, and tickets are available at the Oglethorpe Avenue entrance. Be aware the site is closed most holidays, sometimes for extended periods; be sure to check the website for details.

MAP 1: 10 E. Oglethorpe Ave., 912/233-4501, www.juliettegordonlowbirthplace.org; Mar.-Oct. Mon.-Sat. 10am-4pm, Sun. 11am-4pm, Nov.-Feb. Mon.-Tues. and Thurs.-Sat. 10am-4pm, Sun. 11am-4pm; $10 adults, $9 children, $8 Girl Scouts under age 19

Scout's Honor:
Juliette Gordon Low

Known as "Daisy" to family and friends, Juliette Magill Kinzie Gordon was born to be a pioneer. Her father's family took part in the original settlement of Georgia, and her mother's kin were among the founders of Chicago. Mostly known as the founder of the Girl Scouts of the USA, Daisy was also an artist, adventurer, and healer. Born and raised in the house on Oglethorpe Avenue in Savannah known to Girl Scouts as simply "The Birthplace," she was an animal lover with an early penchant for theater, drawing, and poetry.

In 1911 while in England, Daisy met Robert Baden-Powell, founder of the Boy Scouts and Girl Guides in Britain. Struck by the simplicity and usefulness of his project, she carried the seeds of a similar idea back with her to the United States. "I've got something for the girls of Savannah, and all of America, and all the world, and we're going to start it tonight," were her famous words in a phone call to a cousin after meeting Baden-Powell. So on March 12, 1912, Daisy gathered 18 girls to register the first troop of American Girl Guides, later the Girl Scouts of the USA.

Juliette "Daisy" Gordon Low died of breast cancer in her bed in the Andrew Low House on January 17, 1927. She was buried in Laurel Grove Cemetery. Girl Scout troops from all over the United States visit her birthplace, the Andrew Low House, and her gravesite to this day, often leaving flowers and small personal objects near her tombstone as tokens of respect and gratitude.

★ Owens-Thomas House

The square's main claim to fame, the Owens-Thomas House, lies on the northeast corner. Widely known as the finest example of Regency architecture in the United States, the Owens-Thomas House was designed by brilliant young English architect William Jay. One of the first professionally trained architects in the United States, Jay was only 24 when he designed the home for cotton merchant or "factor" Richard Richardson, who lost the house in the depression of 1820 (all that remains of Richardson's tenure are three marble-top tables). The house's current name is derived from Savannah mayor George Owens, who bought the house in 1830. It remained in his family until 1951, when his granddaughter Margaret Thomas bequeathed it to the Telfair Academy of Arts and Sciences, which currently operates the site.

Several things about the Owens-Thomas House stand out. First, it's constructed mostly of tabby, a mixture of lime, oyster shells, and sand. Its exterior is English stucco while the front garden balustrade is a type of artificial stone called Coade stone. Perhaps most interestingly, a complex plumbing system features rain-fed cisterns, flushing toilets, sinks, bathtubs, and a shower. When built, the Owens-Thomas House in fact had the first indoor plumbing in Savannah.

While inside the house, notice the little touches like the unusual curved walls, with doors bowed to match, and the recessed skylights. While many Owens family furnishings are part of the collection, much of it is representative of American and European work from 1750 to 1830. On the south facade is a beautiful cast-iron veranda from which Revolutionary War hero Marquis de Lafayette addressed a crowd of starstruck Savannahians during his visit in 1825. The 1990s marked the most intensive phase of restoration for the home, which began with a careful renovation of the carriage house and the associated slave quarters—discovered in a surprisingly intact state, including the original "haint blue" paint. The carriage house, where all tours begin, is now the home's gift shop.

The Owens-Thomas House is owned and operated by the Telfair Museums. Get a combination pass to all Telfair sites—the Jepson Center for the Arts, the Telfair Academy of Arts and Sciences, and the Owens-Thomas House—for $20 per person.

MAP 1: 124 Abercorn St., 912/233-9743, www.telfair.org; Tues.-Sat. 10am-5pm, Sun.-Mon. noon-5pm, last tour 4:30pm; $15 adults, $5 children, $20 multi-site ticket

Martin Luther King Jr. Boulevard
Ships of the Sea Maritime Museum

One of Savannah's more unique museums is the quirky Ships of the Sea Maritime Museum. The stunning Greek Revival building in which it resides is known as the Scarbrough House because it was initially built in 1819 by the great William Jay for local shipping merchant William Scarbrough, co-owner of the SS *Savannah,* the first steamship to cross the Atlantic. After the Scarbroughs sold the property, it became the West Broad School for African Americans from Reconstruction through integration.

One of the Historic Savannah Foundation's key restoration projects in the 1970s, the museum got another major facelift in 1998, including a roof based on the original Jay design, an outdoor performance space, and a delightful enlargement of the mansion's garden out back. Inside, children, maritime buffs, and crafts connoisseurs can find intricate and detailed scale models of various historic vessels, such as Oglethorpe's *Anne,* the SS *Savannah,* and the NS *Savannah,* the world's first nuclear-powered surface vessel. There's even a model of the *Titanic.*

MAP 1: 41 MLK Jr. Blvd., 912/232-1511, http://shipsofthesea.org; Tues.-Sun. 10am-5pm; $8.50 adults, $6.50 students

Chippewa Square

Named for a battle in the War of 1812, Chippewa Square has a large monument not to the battle, natch, but to James Oglethorpe, clad in full soldier's regalia. Notice the general is still facing south, toward the Spanish.

Yes, the bench on the square's north side is in the same location as the one Tom Hanks occupied in *Forrest Gump,* but it's not the same bench that hosted the two-time Oscar winner's backside—that one was donated by Paramount Pictures to be displayed in the Savannah History Museum on MLK Jr. Boulevard.

From Chippewa Square look south for the huge rectangular steel-and-glass structure dominating the skyline along Liberty Street. That's the infamous **Drayton Tower,** an outstanding, nearly pure example of the internationalist architecture style nonetheless loathed by traditionalists since its construction in 1955. Until recently it served as low-cost housing for students and seniors. They've since been kicked out, as now the building is subdivided into high-end condos with retail on the ground floor.

Colonial Cemetery

Just north of Chippewa Square is Oglethorpe Avenue, originally called South Broad and the southern boundary of the original colony. At Oglethorpe and Abercorn Streets is Colonial Cemetery, first active in 1750. You'd be forgiven for assuming it's the "DAR" cemetery; the Daughters of the American Revolution contributed the ornate iron entranceway in 1913, thoughtfully dedicating it to themselves instead of the cemetery itself.

Unlike the picturesque beauty of Bonaventure and Laurel Grove Cemeteries, Colonial Cemetery has a morbid feel. The fact that burials stopped here in 1853 plays into that desolation, but maybe another reason is because it's the final resting ground of many of Savannah's yellow fever victims. Famous people buried here include Button Gwinnett, one of Georgia's three signers of the Declaration of Independence. The man who reluctantly killed Gwinnett in a duel, General Lachlan McIntosh, is also buried here. The original burial vault of Nathanael Greene is in the cemetery, although the Revolutionary War hero's remains were moved to Johnson Square over a century ago.

Vandalism through the years, mostly by Union troops, took a toll on the old gravestones. Many line the east wall of the cemetery, with no one alive able to remember where they originally stood.

MAP 2: Oglethorpe St. and Abercorn St., www.savannahga.gov; daily 8am-dusk

First Baptist Church

The nearby First Baptist Church—not to be confused with the more famous First African Baptist Church on Franklin Square—claims to be the oldest original church building in Savannah, with a cornerstone dating from 1830. Services were held here throughout the Civil War, with Union troops attending during the occupation. The church was renovated by renowned local architect Henrik Wallin in 1922. Call ahead for a tour.

MAP 2: 223 Bull St., 912/234-2671; service Sun. 11am

Historic Savannah Theatre

At the square's northeast corner is the Historic Savannah Theatre, which claims to be the oldest continuously operating theater in the United States. Designed by William Jay, it opened in 1818 with a production of *The Soldier's Daughter*. In the glory days of gaslight theater in the 1800s, some of the nation's best actors, including Edwin Booth, brother to Lincoln's assassin, regularly trod the boards of its stage. Other notable visitors were Sarah Bernhardt, W. C. Fields, and Oscar Wilde. Due to a fire in 1948, little remains of Jay's original design except a small section of exterior wall. The building is currently home to a semiprofessional revue company specializing in oldies shows.

MAP 2: 222 Bull St., 912/233-7764, www.savannahtheatre.com

Independent Presbyterian Church

Built in 1818, possibly by William Jay—scholars are unsure of the scope of his involvement—Independent Presbyterian Church is called the "mother of Georgia Presbyterianism." A fire destroyed most of Independent Presbyterian's original structure in 1889, but the subsequent rebuilding was a very faithful rendering of the original design, based on London's St. Martin-in-the-Fields. The marble baptism font survived the fire and is still used today. Note also the huge mahogany pulpit, another original feature. The church's steeple made a cameo appearance in *Forrest Gump* as a white feather floated by.

Lowell Mason, composer of the hymn "Nearer My God to Thee," was organist at Independent Presbyterian. In 1885 President Woodrow Wilson married local parishioner Ellen Louise Axson in the manse to the rear of the church. Presiding was her grandfather, minister at the time. During the Great Awakening in 1896, almost 3,000 people jammed the sanctuary to hear famous evangelist D. L. Moody preach. Call ahead for a tour.

MAP 2: 207 Bull St., 912/236-3346, www.ipcsav.org; services Sun. 11am, Wed. noon

Madison Square

Named for the nation's fourth president, Madison Square memorializes a local hero who gave his life for his city during the American Revolution. Irish immigrant Sergeant William Jasper, hero of the Battle of Fort Moultrie in Charleston three years earlier, was killed leading the American charge during the 1779 Siege of Savannah, when an allied army failed to retake the city from the British. The monument in the square honors Jasper, but he isn't buried here; his body was interred in a mass grave near the battlefield along with other colonists and soldier-immigrants killed in the one-sided battle.

The two small, suitably warlike cannons in the square have nothing to do with the Siege of Savannah. They commemorate the first two highways in Georgia, today known as Augusta Road and Ogeechee Road.

Green-Meldrim House

Given the house's beauty and history, visitors will be forgiven for not immediately realizing that the Green-Meldrim House is also the rectory of the adjacent St. John's Episcopal Church, which acquired it in 1892. Though it's known primarily for serving as General William T. Sherman's headquarters during his occupation of Savannah, visitors find the Green-Meldrim House a remarkably calming, serene location in and of itself, quite apart from its role as the place where Sherman formulated his ill-fated "40 acres and a mule" Field Order No. 15, giving most of the Sea Islands of Georgia and South Carolina to freed blacks. A tasteful example of Gothic Revival architecture, this 1850 design by John Norris features a beautiful external gallery of filigree ironwork. The interior is decorated with a keen and rare eye for elegant minimalism in this sometimes rococo-minded town.

MAP 2: 1 W. Macon St., 912/232-1251, www.stjohnssav.org; tours every 30 minutes Tues. and Thurs.-Fri. 10am-4pm, Sat. 10am-1pm; $8 adults, $5 students and children

Hilton Savannah DeSoto

At the north side of Madison Square is the Hilton Savannah DeSoto. Imagine occupying that same space the most glorious, opulent, regal building you can think of, a paradise of brick, mortar, and buff-colored terra-cotta. That would have been the old DeSoto Hotel, which from its opening in 1890 was known as one of the world's most beautiful hotels and the clear masterpiece in Boston architect William Gibbons Preston's already-impressive Savannah portfolio. Alas, it didn't have air-conditioning, so the Hilton chain demolished it in 1968 to build the current nondescript box.

MAP 2: 15 E. Liberty St., 912/232-9000, www.desotohilton.com

Poetter Hall

The Savannah College of Art and Design's first building, Poetter Hall, known to old-timers as the Savannah Volunteer Guards Armory, is directly across from the Scottish Rite Temple. With its imposing but somewhat whimsical facade right out of a Harry Potter movie, this brick and terra-cotta gem of a Romanesque Revival building was built in 1893 by William Gibbons Preston. It housed National Guard units (as well as a high school) until World War II, when the USO occupied the building during its tenant unit's service in Europe.

MAP 2: 342 Bull St., www.scad.edu

Scottish Rite Temple

The old Scottish Rite Temple at Charlton and Bull Streets was designed by Hyman Witcover, who also designed City Hall. A popular drugstore with a soda fountain for many years, it currently houses the **Gryphon Tea Room**, run by the Savannah College of Art and Design.

Lafayette Square

Truly one of Savannah's favorite squares, especially on St. Patrick's Day, verdant Lafayette Square boasts a number of important sights and attractions.

Andrew Low House Museum

A major landmark on Lafayette Square is the Andrew Low House Museum, once the home of Juliette "Daisy" Gordon Low, the founder of the Girl Scouts of the USA, who was married to cotton heir William "Billow" Low, Andrew Low's son. Despite their happy-go-lucky nicknames, the union of Daisy and Billow was a notably unhappy one. Still, divorce was out of the question, so the couple lived separate lives until William's death in 1905. The one good thing that came out of the marriage was the germ for the idea for the Girl Scouts, which Juliette got from England's "Girl Guides" while living there with her husband, Savannah being the couple's winter residence.

Designed by the great New York architect John Norris, the Low House is a magnificent example of the Italianate style. Check out the cast-iron balconies on the long porch, a fairly rare feature in historic Savannah homes. Antiques junkies will go nuts over the furnishings, especially the massive secretary in the parlor, one of only four of this type in existence (a sibling is in the Metropolitan Museum of Art). Author William Makepeace Thackeray ate in the dining room, now sporting full French porcelain service, and slept in an upstairs room; he also wrote at the desk by the bed. Also on the second floor you'll see the room where Robert E. Lee stayed during his visit and the bed where Juliette Gordon Low died.

MAP 2: 329 Abercorn St., 912/233-6854, www.andrewlowhouse.com; Mon.-Sat. 10am-4pm, Sun. noon-4pm; $10 adults, $8 children

★ Cathedral of St. John the Baptist

Spiritual home to Savannah's Irish community and the oldest Catholic church in Georgia, the Cathedral of St. John the Baptist was initially known as Our Lady of Perpetual Help. It's the place to be for mass the morning of March 17 at 8am, as the clans gather in their green jackets and white dresses to take a sip of communion wine before moving on to harder stuff in honor of St. Patrick.

Despite its overt Celtic character today, the parish was originally founded by French émigrés from Haiti who arrived after the successful overthrow of the colonial government by a slave uprising on the island in the late 1700s. They were joined by other Gallic Catholics when some nobles fled from the French Revolution. The first sanctuary on the site was built in 1873, after the diocese traded a lot at Taylor and Lincoln Streets to the Sisters of Mercy in exchange for this locale. In a distressingly common event back then in Savannah, fire swept through the edifice in 1898, leaving only two spires and the external walls. In an amazing story of determination and skill, the cathedral was completely rebuilt within a year and a half. In the years since, many renovations have been undertaken, including an interior renovation following the Second Vatican Council to incorporate some of that body's sweeping reforms (for example, a new altar allowing the celebrant to face the congregation). The most recent renovation, from 1998 to 2000, involved the intricate removal, cleaning, and releading of more than 50 of the cathedral's stained glass windows, a roof replacement, and an interior makeover.

When inside the magnificent interior, look for the new 9,000-pound altar and the 8,000-pound baptismal font, both made of Italian marble.

In 2003 an armed man entered the cathedral and set the pulpit and bishop's chair on fire, resulting in nearly $400,000 of damage. The pulpit you see now is an exact replica carved in Italy. The arsonist claimed he did it as a statement against organized religion.

MAP 2: 222. E. Harris St., 912/233-4709, www.savannahcathedral.org; daily 9am-noon and 12:30pm-5pm, mass Sun. 8am, 10am, 11:30am, Mon.-Sat. noon, Latin mass Sun. 1pm

Flannery O'Connor Childhood Home

On a corner of Lafayette Square stands the rather Spartan facade of the Flannery O'Connor Childhood Home. The Savannah-born novelist lived in this three-story townhome from her birth in 1925 until 1938 and attended church at the cathedral across the square. Once a fairly nondescript attraction for so favorite a native daughter, a recent round of renovations has returned the two main floors to the state Flannery would have known, including an extensive library. A nonprofit association sponsors O'Connor-related readings and signings. While the current backyard garden dates to 1993, it's the place where five-year-old Flannery is said to have taught a chicken to walk backward, foreshadowing the eccentric, Gothic flavor of her writing.

MAP 2: 207 E. Charlton St., 912/233-6014, www.flanneryoconnorhome.org; Fri.-Tues. 1pm-4pm; $6 adults, $5 students, free under age 15

Hamilton-Turner Inn

Across from the O'Connor house is the Hamilton-Turner Inn. Now a privately owned bed-and-breakfast, this 1873 Second Empire mansion is best known for the showmanship of its over-the-top Victorian appointments and its role in *Midnight in the Garden of Good and Evil* as the home of Joe Odom's girlfriend "Mandy Nichols" (real name Nancy Hillis). In 1883 it was reportedly the first house in Savannah to have electricity.

MAP 2: 330 Abercorn St., 912/233-1833, www.hamilton-turnerinn.com

Troup Square

Low-key Troup Square boasts the most modern-looking monument downtown, the **Armillary Sphere.** Essentially an elaborate sundial, the sphere is a series of astrologically themed rings with an arrow that marks the time by shadow. It is supported by six tortoises.

James Pierpont wrote "Jingle Bells" while in the congregation of the Unitarian Church.

Boston and Savannah vie over bragging rights as to where the classic Christmas song "Jingle Bells" was written. The song's composer, James L. Pierpont, led a life at times as carefree as the song itself. Born in Boston, Pierpont ventured from his wife and young children in 1849 to follow the gold rush to San Francisco. When his brother John was named minister of the new Unitarian congregation in Savannah in 1853, Pierpont followed him, becoming music director and organist, again leaving behind his wife and children in Boston. During this time Pierpont became a prolific composer of secular tunes, including polkas, ballads, and minstrel songs.

In August 1857, a Boston-based publisher, Oliver Ditson and Co., published Pierpont's song "One Horse Open Sleigh." Two years later it was re-released with the current title, "Jingle Bells." At neither time, however, was the song a popular hit. It took action by his son Juriah in 1880 to renew the copyright to what would become one of the most famous songs of all time.

In Massachusetts, they swear Pierpont wrote the song while at the home of one Mrs. Otis Waterman. In Georgia, scholars assure us a homesick Pierpont wrote the tune during a winter at a house at Oglethorpe and Whitaker Streets, long since demolished. The Savannah contingent's ace in the hole is the fact that "Jingle Bells" was first performed in public at a Thanksgiving program at the local Unitarian Universalist Church in 1857. And despite persistent claims in Massachusetts that he wrote the song there in 1850, Southern scholars point out that Pierpont was actually in California in 1850.

Beach Institute

Just east of Troup Square, near the intersection of Harris and Price Streets, is the Beach Institute. Built as a school by the Freedmen's Bureau soon after the Civil War, it was named after its prime benefactor, Alfred Beach, editor of *Scientific American.* It served as an African American school through 1919. Restored by SCAD and given back to the city to serve as a museum, the Beach Institute houses the permanent Ulysses Davis collection and a rotating calendar of art events with a connection to black history.

MAP 2: 502 E. Harris St., 912/234-8000; Tues.-Sun. noon-5pm; $4

Jones Street

There aren't a lot of individual attractions on Jones Street, the east-west avenue between Taylor and Charlton Streets just north of Monterey Square. Rather, it's the small-scale, throwback feel of the place and its tasteful, dignified homes, including the former home of **Joe Odom** (16 E. Jones St.), that are the attraction. The **Eliza Thompson House** (5 W. Jones St.), now a bed-and-breakfast, was the first home on Jones Street. Cotton factor Joseph Thompson built the house for his wife, Eliza, in 1847. The carriage house is not original to the structure, having been built almost from scratch in 1980.

MAP 2: Jones St. between Taylor St. and Charlton St.

Unitarian Universalist Church of Savannah

Troup Square is the home of the historic Unitarian Universalist Church of Savannah. This original home of Savannah's Unitarians, who sold the church when the Civil War came, was recently reacquired by the congregation. It is where James L. Pierpont first performed his immortal tune "Jingle Bells." When he did so, however, the church was actually on Oglethorpe Square. The entire building was moved to Troup Square in the mid-1800s.

MAP 2: 313 E. Harris St., 912/234-0980, www.jinglebellschurch.org; service Sun. 11am

★ Monterey Square

Originally named "Monterrey Square" to commemorate the local Irish Jasper Greens' participation in a victorious Mexican-American War battle in 1846, the spelling morphed into its current version somewhere along the way. But Monterey Square remains one of the most visually beautiful and serene spots in all of Savannah. At the center of the square is a monument not to the victory for which it is named but to Count Casimir Pulaski, killed while attempting to retake the city from the British, and whose remains supposedly lie under the 55-foot monument. As early as 1912, people began noticing the disintegration of the monument due to substandard marble used in some key parts, but it wasn't until the 1990s that a full restoration was accomplished. The restoration company discovered that one of the monument's 34 sections had been accidentally installed upside down. In the true spirit of preservation, they dutifully put the section back—upside down. The *Goddess of Liberty* atop the monument, however, is not original; you can see her in the Savannah History Museum. Fans of ironwork will enjoy the ornate masterpieces in wrought iron featured at many houses on the periphery of the square.

Mercer-Williams House Museum

Many visitors come to see the Mercer-Williams House Museum. While locals never begrudge the business Savannah has enjoyed since the publishing of "The Book," *Midnight in the Garden of Good and Evil*, it's a shame that this grand John Norris building is now primarily known as a crime scene involving antiques dealer Jim Williams and his lover. Therefore it might come as no surprise that if you take a tour of the home, you might hear

Clockwise from top left: inside the Massie Heritage Center; building on Monterey Square; Mercer-Williams House Museum.

less about "The Book" than you may have expected. Now proudly owned by Jim Williams's sister Dorothy Kingery, an established academic in her own right, the Mercer-Williams House deliberately concentrates on the early history of the home and Jim Williams's prodigious talent as a collector and conservator of fine art and antiques. That said, Dr. Kingery's mama didn't raise no fool, as we say down here. The house was known to generations of Savannahians as simply the Mercer House until *Midnight in the Garden of Good and Evil* took off, at which time the eponymous nod to the late Mr. Williams was added.

The house was built for General Hugh W. Mercer, Johnny Mercer's great-grandfather, in 1860, but the war interrupted construction. General Mercer—descendant of the Revolutionary War general and George Washington's close friend Hugh Mercer—survived the war, in which he was charged with the defense of Savannah. But he soon fell on hard times and was forced to sell the house to John Wilder, who moved in after completion in 1868. Just so you know, and despite what any tour guide might tell you, the great Johnny Mercer himself never lived in the house. Technically, no member of his family ever did either.

Tours of the home's four main rooms begin in the carriage house to the rear of the mansion. They're worth it for art aficionados even though the upstairs, Dr. Kingery's residence, is off-limits. Be forewarned that if you're coming just to see things about the book or movie, you might be disappointed.

MAP 2: 429 Bull St., 912/236-6352, www.mercerhouse.com; Mon.-Sat. 10:30am-4pm, Sun. noon-4pm; $12.50 adults, $8 students

Temple Mickve Israel

Directly across Monterey Square from the Mercer House is Temple Mickve Israel, a notable structure for many reasons: It's Georgia's first synagogue; it's the only Gothic synagogue in the country; and it's the third-oldest Jewish congregation in North America (following those in New York and Newport, Rhode Island). Notable congregants have included Dr. Samuel Nunes Ribeiro, who helped stop an epidemic in 1733; his descendant Raphael Moses, considered the father of the peach industry in the Peach State; and current Mickve Israel Rabbi Arnold Mark Belzer, one of Savannah's most beloved community leaders. A specialist in the study of small, often-persecuted Jewish communities around the world, Belzer met Pope John Paul II in 2005 as a part of that pontiff's historic rapprochement between the Catholic Church and Judaism.

Mickve Israel offers 30- to 45-minute tours of the sanctuary and museum. No reservations are necessary for tours.

MAP 2: 20 E. Gordon St., 912/233-1547, www.mickveisrael.org; Mon.-Fri. 10am-1pm and 2pm-4pm, closed Jewish holidays; $4 suggested donation

Calhoun Square

The last of the 24 squares in Savannah's original grid, Calhoun Square is also the only square with all its original buildings intact—a rarity indeed in a city ravaged by fire so many times in its history.

Massie Heritage Center

Dominating the south side of Calhoun Square is Savannah's first public elementary school and the spiritual home of Savannah educators, the Massie Heritage Center. In 1841, Peter Massie, a Scots planter with a populist streak, endowed the school to give poor children as good an education as the children of rich families, like Massie's own, received. Another of Savannah's masterpieces by John Norris—whose impressive oeuvre includes the Andrew Low House, the Mercer-Williams House, and the Green-Meldrim House—the central portion of the trifold building was completed in 1856. After the Civil War, the "Massie School," as it's known locally, was designated as the area's African American public school. Classes ceased in 1974, and it now operates as a living-history museum, centering on the period-appointed one-room "heritage classroom" but with several other exhibit spaces of note.

A million-dollar renovation in 2012 added an interactive model of Oglethorpe's urban design and several interesting exhibits on aspects of Savannah architecture and history. In all Massie provides possibly the best one-stop tour for an all-encompassing look at Savannah history and culture. You can either do a self-guided tour or take the very informative guided tour at 11am or 2pm for the same admission price. Call ahead to double-check tour availability; lots of school groups come through here and sometimes the schedule is shifted.

MAP 2: 207 E. Gordon St., 912/201-5070, www.massieschool.com; Mon.-Sat. 10am-4pm, Sun. noon-4pm; $7 adults, $5 youth

Wesley Monumental United Methodist Church

Catty-corner to the Massie School is the Wesley Monumental United Methodist Church. This home of Savannah's first Methodist parish was named not only for movement founder John Wesley but also for his musical younger brother Charles. Built in 1875 on the model of Queen's Kirk in Amsterdam and the fourth incarnation of the parish home, this is another great example of Savannah's Gothic churches. Its acoustically wonderful sanctuary features a magnificent Noack organ, which would no doubt please the picky ears of Charles Wesley himself, author of the lyrics to "Hark! The Herald Angels Sing."

MAP 2: 429 Abercorn St., 912/232-0191, www.wesleymonumental.org; sanctuary daily 9am-5pm, services Sun. 8:45am and 11am

Martin Luther King Jr. Boulevard

Battlefield Park

Right off MLK Jr. Boulevard is Battlefield Park, aka the Spring Hill Redoubt, a reconstruction of the British fortifications at the Siege of Savannah with an interpretive site. Note that the redoubt is not at the actual location of the original fort; that lies underneath the nearby Sons of the Revolution marker. Eight hundred granite markers signify the battle's casualties, most of whom were buried in mass graves soon afterward. Sadly, most of the remains of these brave men were simply bulldozed up and discarded without ceremony during later construction projects.

MAP 2: Corner of MLK Jr. Blvd. and Louisville Rd.; dawn-dusk; free

Georgia State Railroad Museum

The Georgia State Railroad Museum, aka "The Roundhouse," is an ongoing homage to the deep and strangely underreported influence of the railroad industry on Savannah. Constructed in 1830 for the brand-new Central of Georgia line, the Roundhouse's design was cutting-edge for the time, the first building to put all the railroad's key facilities in one place. Spared by Sherman, the site saw its real heyday after the Civil War. But as technology changed, so did the Roundhouse, which gradually fell further into neglect until the 1960s, when preservation-minded buffs banded together to raise enough money to save it. The real highlight of the Roundhouse is the thing in the middle that gave the structure its name, a huge central turntable for positioning rolling stock for repair and maintenance. Frequent demonstrations occur with an actual steam locomotive firing up and taking a spin on the turntable.

MAP 2: 601 W. Harris St., 912/651-6823, www.chsgeorgia.org; daily 9am-5pm; $10 adults, $6 students

Ralph Mark Gilbert Civil Rights Museum

One of the former black-owned bank buildings on MLK Jr. Boulevard is now home to the Ralph Mark Gilbert Civil Rights Museum. Named for a pastor of the First African Baptist Church and a key early civil rights organizer, the building was also the local NAACP headquarters for a time. Three floors of exhibits here include photos and interactive displays, the highlight for historians being a fiber-optic map of nearly 100 significant civil rights sites. The first floor features a re-creation of the Azalea Room of the local Levy's department store, an early boycott diner where blacks were not allowed to eat, though they could buy goods from the store. The second floor is more for hands-on education, with classrooms, a computer room, and a video and reading room. A film chronicles mass meetings, voter registration drives, boycotts, sit-ins, kneel-ins (the integration of churches), and wade-ins (the integration of beaches).

MAP 2: 460 MLK Jr. Blvd., 912/231-8900; Tues.-Sat. 10am-4pm; $10

Savannah Children's Museum

Next to the Railroad Museum is the Savannah Children's Museum, open since 2012. The children's museum is a work in progress that currently has an outdoor "Exploration Station" and a pending, larger facility.

MAP 2: 655 Louisville Rd., 912/651-6823, www.savannahchildrensmuseum.org; Tues.-Sat. 10am-4pm, Sun. 11am-4pm; $7.50

Savannah History Museum

The Savannah History Museum, first stop for many a visitor to town because it's in the same restored Central of Georgia passenger shed as the visitors center, contains many interesting exhibits on local history, concentrating mostly on colonial times. Toward the rear of the museum is a room for rotating exhibits, as well as one of Johnny Mercer's four Oscars and, of course, the historic "*Forrest Gump* bench" that Tom Hanks sat on during his scenes in Chippewa Square.

MAP 2: 303 MLK Jr. Blvd., 912/651-6825, www.chsgeorgia.org; Mon.-Fri. 8:30am-5pm, Sat.-Sun. 9am-5pm; $7 adults, $4 children

SCAD Museum of Art

In 2011, the Savannah College of Art and Design (SCAD) expanded this handsome building into an old railroad facility immediately behind it, more than doubling exhibition space and adding the impressive Walter O. Evans Collection of African American Art. The SCAD Museum of Art now hosts a rotating series of exhibits, from standard painting to video installations, many of them commissioned by the school itself.

MAP 2: 601 Turner Blvd., 912/525-5220, www.scadmoa.org; Tues.-Wed. and Fri. 10am-5pm, Thurs. 10am-8pm, Sat.-Sun. noon-5pm; $10 adults, $5 students

Victorian District Map 3

Carnegie Branch Library

The Carnegie Branch Library is the only example of prairie architecture in town, designed by Savannah architect Julian de Bruyn Kops and built, as the name implies, with funding from tycoon-philanthropist Andrew Carnegie in 1914. But more importantly, the Carnegie Library was for decades the only public library for African Americans in Savannah. One of its patrons was a young Clarence Thomas, who would of course grow up to be a U.S. Supreme Court justice.

MAP 3: 537 E. Henry St., 912/652-3600, www.liveoakpl.org; Mon. 10am-8pm, Tues.-Thurs. 10am-6pm, Fri. 2pm-6pm, Sat. 10am-6pm

★ Forsyth Park

A favorite with locals and visitors alike, the vast, lush expanse of Forsyth Park is a center of local life, abuzz with activity and events year-round.

A Walking Tour of Forsyth Park

As you approach the park, don't miss the ornate ironwork on the west side of Bull Street marking the **Armstrong House,** designed by Henrik Wallin. Featured in the 1962 film *Cape Fear* as well as 1997's *Midnight in the Garden of Good and Evil,* this Italianate mansion was once home to Armstrong Junior College before its move to the south side. Directly across Bull Street is another site of *Midnight* fame, the **Oglethorpe Club,** one of the many brick and terra-cotta designs by local architect Alfred Eichberg.

It's easy to miss, but as you enter the park's north side, you encounter the **Marine Memorial,** erected in 1947 to honor the 24 Chatham County Marines killed in World War II. Subsequently, the names of Marines killed in Korea and Vietnam were added. Look west at the corner of Whitaker and Gaston Streets; that's **Hodgson Hall,** home of the Georgia Historical Society. This 1876 building was commissioned by Margaret Telfair to honor her late husband, William Hodgson.

Looking east at the corner of Drayton and Gaston Streets, you'll see the old **Poor House and Hospital,** in use until 1854, when it was converted to serve as the headquarters for the Medical College of Georgia. During the Civil War, General Sherman used the hospital to treat Federal soldiers. From 1930 to 1980 the building was the site of Candler Hospital. Behind the old hospital's cast-iron fence is Savannah's most famous tree, the 300-year-old **Candler Oak.** During Sherman's occupation, wounded Confederate prisoners were treated within a barricade around the oak. The tree is in the National Register of Historic Trees and was the maiden preservation project of the Savannah Tree Foundation, which secured the country's first-ever conservation easement on a single tree.

Walking south into the park proper, you can't miss the world-famous **Forsyth Fountain,** an iconic Savannah sight. Cast in iron on a French model, the fountain was dedicated in 1858. Two other versions of this fountain exist—one in Poughkeepsie, New York, and the other in, of all places, the central plaza in Cusco, Peru.

The park owes its existence to William B. Hodgson, who donated its core 10 acres to the city for use as a park. Deeply influenced by the then-trendy design of green-space areas in France, Forsyth Park's landscape design by William Bischoff dates to 1851. Named for Georgia governor John Forsyth, the park covers 30 acres, and its perimeter is about a mile.

Near the center of the park is the "fort," actually a revitalized version of an old dummy fort used for military drills in the early 20th century. Now managed by the nearby Mansion on Forsyth hotel, it's a good place to stop in and get a snack or use the public restroom.

The park is a center of activities all year long, from free festivals to concerts to Ultimate Frisbee games to the constant circuit around the periphery of walkers, joggers, dog owners, and bicyclists. The only time you shouldn't venture into the park is after midnight; otherwise, enjoy.

MAP 3: Bordered by Drayton St., Gaston St., Whitaker St., and Park Ave., 912/351-3850; daily 8am-dusk

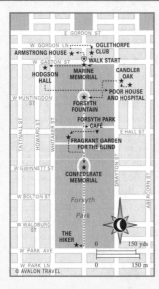

Café (daily 7am-dusk). To the west is the charming **Fragrant Garden for the Blind.** One of those precious little Savannah gems that is too often overlooked, the Fragrant Garden was initially sponsored by the local Garden Club and based on others of its type throughout the United States.

The tall monument dominating Forsyth Park's central mall is the **Confederate Memorial.** Dedicated in 1875, it wasn't finished until several years later. A New York sculptor carved the Confederate soldier atop the monument.

My favorite Forsyth Park landmark is at the extreme southern end. It's the Memorial to Georgia Veterans of the Spanish-American War, more commonly known as *The Hiker* because of the subject's casual demeanor and confident stride. Savannah was a major staging area for the 1898 conflict, and many troops were bivouacked in the park. Sculpted in 1902 by Alice Ruggles Kitson, more than 50 replicas of The Hiker were made and put up all over the United States.

Continuing south, you'll encounter two low buildings in the center of the park. The one on the east side is the so-called "Dummy Fort," circa 1909, formerly a training ground for local militia. Now it's the **Forsyth Park**

SoFo District

Map 3

Laurel Grove Cemetery

Its natural vista isn't as alluring as Bonaventure Cemetery's, but Laurel Grove Cemetery boasts its own exquisitely carved memorials and a distinctly Victorian type of surreal beauty that not even Bonaventure can match. In keeping with the racial apartheid of Savannah's early days, there are actually two cemeteries: **Laurel Grove North** (802 W. Anderson St.) for whites, and **Laurel Grove South** (2101 Kollock St.) for blacks. Both are well worth visiting.

By far the most high-profile plot in the North Cemetery is that of Juliette Gordon Low, founder of the Girl Scouts of the USA. Other historically significant sites there include the graves of 8th Air Force founder Frank O. Hunter, Central of Georgia Railway founder William Gordon, and "Jingle Bells" composer James Pierpont. But it's the graves of the anonymous and near-anonymous that are the most poignant sights. The various sections for infants, known as "babylands," cannot fail to move. "Mr. Bones," a former Savannah police dog, is the only animal buried at Laurel Grove. There's an entire site reserved for victims of the great yellow fever epidemic. And don't blink or you'll miss the small rock pile, or cairn, near Governor James Jackson's tomb, the origin and purpose of which remains a mystery. Make sure to view the otherworldly display of Victorian statuary, originally from the grand Greenwich Plantation, which burned in the early 20th century. As with Bonaventure, throughout Laurel Grove you'll find examples of so-called "slave tiles," actually Victorian garden tiles, lining gravesites.

Laurel Grove South features the graves of Savannah's early black Baptist ministers, such as Andrew Bryan and Andrew Cox Marshall. Some of the most evocative gravesites are those of African Americans who obtained their freedom and built prosperous lives for themselves and their families. The vast majority of local firefighters in the 1800s were African Americans, and their simple graves are among the most touching, such as the headstone for one known simply as "August," who died fighting a fire.

To get to Laurel Grove North, take MLK Jr. Boulevard to Anderson Street and turn west. To get to Laurel Grove South, take Victory Drive (U.S. 80) west to Ogeechee Road. Take a right onto Ogeechee, then a right onto West 36th Street. Continue on to Kollock Street.

MAP 3: 802 W. Anderson St. and 2101 Kollock St.; daily 8am-5pm; free

Southside

Map 4

Isle of Hope

A charming, friendly seaside community and National Historic District, Isle of Hope is one of a dwindling number of places where parents still let their kids ride around all day on bikes, calling them in at dinnertime. It doesn't boast many shops or restaurants—indeed, the marina is the only real business—but the row of waterfront cottages on Bluff Drive should not be missed. You might recognize some of them from movies such as *Forrest Gump* and *Glory*. Built from 1880 to 1920, they reflect Isle of Hope's reputation as a healing area and serene Wilmington River getaway from Savannah's capitalist hustle.

To get to Isle of Hope, take Victory Drive (U.S. 80) east and take a right on Skidaway Road. Continue south on Skidaway Road and take a left on Laroche Avenue. Continue until you hit Bluff Drive.

MAP 4: 10 miles south of Savannah

Wormsloe State Historic Site

The one-of-a-kind Wormsloe State Historic Site was first settled by Noble Jones, who landed with Oglethorpe on the *Anne* and fought beside him in the War of Jenkins' Ear. One of the great renaissance men of history, this soldier was also an accomplished carpenter, surveyor, forester, botanist, and physician. Wormsloe became famous for its bountiful gardens, so much so that the famed naturalist William Bartram mentioned them in his diary after a visit in 1765 with father John Bartram. After his death, Noble Jones was originally buried in the family plot on the waterfront, but now his remains are at Bonaventure Cemetery. Jones's descendants donated 822 acres of Wormsloe to The Nature Conservancy, which transferred the property to the state. The house, dating from 1828, and 65.5 acres of land are still owned by his family, and no, you can't visit them.

The stunning entrance canopy of 400 live oaks, Spanish moss dripping down the entire length, is one of those iconic images of Savannah that will stay with you forever. A small interpretive museum, a one-mile nature walk, and occasional living-history demonstrations make this a great site for the entire family. Walk all the way to the Jones Narrows to see the ruins of the site's original 1739 fortification, one of the oldest and finest examples of tabby construction in the United States. No doubt the area's abundance of Native American shell middens, where early inhabitants discarded their oyster shells, came in handy for its construction. You can see one nearby.

To get to Wormsloe, take Victory Drive (U.S. 80) to Skidaway Road. Go south on Skidaway Road for about 10 miles and follow the signs; you'll see the grand entrance on the right.

MAP 4: 7601 Skidaway Rd., 912/353-3023, www.gastateparks.org/info/wormsloe; Tues.-Sun. 9am-5pm; $10 adults, $4.50 children

Pin Point

Off Whitfield Avenue (Diamond Causeway) on the route to Skidaway Island is tiny Pin Point, a predominantly African American township better known as the boyhood home of Supreme Court Justice Clarence Thomas. Pin Point traces its roots to a community of former slaves on Ossabaw Island. Displaced by a hurricane, they settled at this idyllic site overlooking the Moon River, itself a former plantation.

Pin Point Heritage Museum

Many Pin Point residents made their living by shucking oysters at the Varn Oyster Company, the central shed of which still remains and forms the basis of the Pin Point Heritage Museum, opened in 2012. The museum tells the story of the Pin Point community through exhibits, a film, and demonstrations of some of the maritime activities at the Varn Oyster Company through the decades, such as crabbing, canning, shucking, and shrimp net-making.

MAP 4: 9924 Pin Point Ave., www.pinpointheritagemuseum.com; Thurs. and Sat. 9am-5pm; free

Skidaway Island

Skidaway Island is notable for two beautiful and educational nature-oriented sites.

Pin Point on the Moon River

On Ossabaw Island, former slaves had settled into freedom as subsistence farmers after the Civil War. But when a massive hurricane devastated the island in 1893, many moved to the mainland, south of Savannah along what would later be known as Moon River, to a place called Pin Point. While many continued farming, plenty gained employment at local factories, where crabs and oysters were packed and sold. The largest and longest-lived of those factories was A. S. Varn & Son, which employed nearly 100 Pin Point residents—about half of the adult population.

Because so many local people worked at the same place, Pin Point developed a strong community bond, one that was instrumental in forging the life and career of future Supreme Court Justice Clarence Thomas, who was born at Pin Point in 1948. Until he was seven, Thomas lived in a tiny house there with his parents, one without plumbing and insulated with newspapers. After a house fire, Thomas moved to Savannah with his grandparents.

While times have certainly changed here—paved roads finally came in the 1970s, and most of the old shotgun shacks have been re-placed with mobile homes—Pin Point remains a small, close-knit community of about 300 people, with most property still owned by descendants of the freedmen who bought it after Reconstruction. The Varn factory remained the economic heart of Pin Point until it shut down in 1985. Today, the old factory forms the heart of an ambitious new project, the **Pin Point Heritage Museum** (www.pinpointheritage-museum.com), which conveys the spirit and history of that community, including its most famous native son, through a series of exhibits and demonstrations.

Skidaway Island State Park

A site of interest to visitors is Skidaway Island State Park. Yeah, you can camp here ($25-28), but the awesome nature trails leading out to the marsh—featuring an ancient Native American shell midden and an old whiskey still—are worth a trip just on their own, especially when combined with the Marine Educational Center and Aquarium. To get here, take Victory Drive (U.S. 80) until you get to Waters Avenue and continue south as it turns into Whitefield Avenue and then the Diamond Causeway. The park is on your left after the drawbridge. An alternative route from down-town is to take the Truman Parkway all the way to its dead end at Whitefield Avenue; take a left and continue as it turns into Diamond Causeway as it enters Skidaway.

MAP 4: 52 Diamond Causeway, 912/598-2300, www.gastateparks.org/info/skidaway; daily 7am-10pm; parking $5

University of Georgia Marine Educational Center and Aquarium

The University of Georgia Marine Educational Center and Aquarium shares a picturesque 700-acre campus on the scenic Skidaway River with the research-oriented **Skidaway Institute of Oceanography,** also

Clockwise from top left: Forsyth Fountain; beautiful Bonaventure Cemetery; Wormsloe State Historic Site.

University of Georgia (UGA) affiliated. It hosts scientists and grad students from around the nation, often for trips on its research vessel, the RV *Sea Dawg*. The main attraction of the Marine Center is the small but well-done and recently upgraded aquarium featuring 14 tanks with 200 live animals.

MAP 4: 30 Ocean Science Circle, 912/598-3474, www.marex.uga.edu; Mon.-Fri. 9am-4pm, Sat. 10am-5pm; $6 adults, $3 children, cash only

Eastside
Map 4

★ Bonaventure Cemetery

On the banks of the Wilmington River just east of town lies one of Savannah's most unique sights, Bonaventure Cemetery. John Muir, who went on to found the Sierra Club, wrote of Bonaventure's Spanish moss-bedecked beauty in his 1867 book *A Thousand-mile Walk to the Gulf*, marveling at the screaming bald eagles that then frequented the area. The bald eagles are long gone, but, like Muir, Savannahians to this day reserve a special place in their hearts for Bonaventure. While its pedigree as Savannah's premier public cemetery goes back 100 years, it was used as a burial ground as early as 1794. In the years since, this achingly poignant vista of live oaks and azaleas has been the final resting place of such local and national luminaries as Johnny Mercer, Conrad Aiken, Wormsloe Historic Site founder Noble Jones, and, of course, the Trosdal plot, former home of the famous *Bird Girl* statue (the original is now in the Telfair Academy of Arts and Sciences). Fittingly, the late, great Jack Leigh, who took the *Bird Girl* photo for the cover of *Midnight in the Garden of Good and Evil*, is interred here as well.

Go to Section K to see the Greek cemetery, a veritable stone chronicle of that local community's history from the late 1800s. Section K also holds many memorials to Spanish-American War veterans, commemorated by a special cross. Close by is the Jewish section, established by congregants of Temple Mickve Israel, with many evocative inscriptions on the tombs of the numerous Holocaust survivors buried here. Closer to the river is an interesting plot set aside for railroad conductors.

Several local tour companies offer options that include a visit to Bonaventure. If you're doing a self-guided tour, go by the small visitors center at the entrance and pick up one of the free guides to the cemetery, assembled by the local volunteer Bonaventure Historical Society. By all means, do the tourist thing and pay your respects at Johnny Mercer's final resting place, and go visit beautiful little "Gracie" in Section E, Lot 99. But I also suggest doing as the locals do: Bring a picnic lunch and a blanket and set yourself beside the breezy banks of the Wilmington River, taking in all the lazy beauty and evocative bygone history surrounding you.

To get here from downtown, take the President Street Extension east and take a right on Pennsylvania Avenue, then a left on Bonaventure Road.

Johnny Mercer's Black Magic

The great Johnny Mercer is not only without a doubt Savannah's most noteworthy progeny, he is also one of the greatest lyricists music has ever known. Born in 1909, he grew up in southside Savannah on a small river then called the Back River but since renamed Moon River in honor of his best-known song.

Armed with an innate talent for rhythm and a curious ear for dialogue—both qualities honed by his frequent boyhood contact with Savannah African American culture and musicians during the Jazz Age, Mercer wrote what is arguably his greatest song, "Moon River," in 1961. The song, debuted by Audrey Hepburn in the film *Breakfast at Tiffany's*, won an Academy Award for Best Original Song. In addition to "Moon River," Mercer won three other Oscars, for "On the Atchinson, Topeka and the Santa Fe" (1946), "In the Cool, Cool, Cool of the Evening" (1951), and "Days of Wine and Roses" (1962).

Today you can pay your respects to Mercer in three places: his boyhood home (509 E. Gwinnett St., look for the historical marker in front of

the statue of Johnny Mercer at Ellis Square, sculpted by Susie Chisholm

this private residence); the bronze sculpture of Mercer in the newly revitalized Ellis Square near City Market; and at his gravesite in beautiful Bonaventure Cemetery. And regardless of what anyone tells you, neither Johnny Mercer nor any member of his family ever lived in the Mercer-Williams House on Monterey Square, of *Midnight in the Garden of Good and Evil* fame. Although it was built for his great-grandfather, the home was sold to someone else before it was completed.

Alternatively, go east on Victory Drive (U.S. 80) and take a left on Whatley Road in the town of Thunderbolt. Veer left onto Bonaventure Road. The cemetery is one mile ahead on the right.

MAP 4: 330 Bonaventure Rd., 912/651-6843; daily 8am-5pm; free

Daffin Park

A century spent in Forsyth Park's more genteel shadow doesn't diminish the importance of Daffin Park as Savannah's second major green space. Daffin not only hosts a large variety of local athletes on its fields and courts, but the park's east end is the setting for Historic Grayson Stadium, home of the minor league Savannah Sand Gnats. One of the great old ballparks of America, this venue dates from 1941 and has hosted greats such as Babe Ruth, Jackie Robinson, and Mickey Mantle.

Most picturesque for the visitor, however, is the massive fountain set in the middle of the expansive central pond on the park's west side. Originally built in the shape of the continental United States, the pond was the backdrop for a presidential visit by Franklin D. Roosevelt in 1933 that included a speech to an African American crowd. On the far west end of Daffin Park along Waters Avenue is a marker commemorating the site of the grandstand for the Great Savannah Races of 1911.

MAP 4: 1500 E. Victory Dr.; daily dawn-dusk

Oatland Island Wildlife Center

The closest thing Savannah has to a zoo is the vast, multipurpose Oatland Island Wildlife Center. Set on a former Centers for Disease Control site, it has undergone an extensive environmental cleanup and is now owned by the local school system, although supported purely by donations. Families by the hundreds come here for a number of special Saturdays throughout the year, including an old-fashioned cane-grinding in November and a day of sheep-shearing in April.

The main attractions here are the critters, located at various points along a meandering two-mile nature trail through the woods and along the marsh. All animals at Oatland are there because they're somehow unable to return to the wild. Highlights include a tight-knit pack of eastern wolves, a pair of bison, cougars (once indigenous to the region), some really cute foxes, and an extensive raptor aviary. Kids will love the petting zoo of farm animals, some of which are free to roam the grounds at will.

The massive central building was designed by noted local architect Henrik Wallin as a retirement home for railroad conductors. Inside, check out the display of a huge set of whalebones, the remains of a 50-foot-long endangered fin whale that washed ashore on Tybee Island in 1989.

To get here from downtown, take the President Street Extension (Islands Expressway) about five miles. Begin looking for the Oatland Island sign on the right. You'll go through part of a residential neighborhood until you take a bend to the right; Oatland's gate is then on the left. To get here from Bonaventure Cemetery, go straight out the gate on Bonaventure Road and take a right on Pennsylvania Avenue. As you dead-end on Islands Expressway, take a right and look for the entrance farther along on the right.

MAP 4: 711 Sandtown Rd., 912/898-3980, www.oatlandisland.org; daily 10am-5pm; $5 adults, $3 children

Old Fort Jackson

The oldest standing brick fort in Georgia, Old Fort Jackson, named for Georgia governor James Jackson, is also one of eight remaining examples of the so-called Second System of American forts built prior to the War of 1812. Its main claim to fame is its supporting role in the saga of the CSS *Georgia*, a Confederate ironclad now resting under 40 feet of water directly in front of the fort. Built with $115,000 in funds raised by the Ladies

Gunboat Society, the *Georgia*—wrapped in an armor girdle of rails—proved too heavy for its engine. So it was simply anchored in the channel opposite Fort Jackson as a floating battery. With General Sherman's arrival in 1864, Confederate forces evacuating to South Carolina scuttled the vessel where it lay to keep it out of Yankee hands.

Operated by the nonprofit Coastal Heritage Society, Fort Jackson is in an excellent state of preservation and provides loads of information for history buffs as well as for kids, who will enjoy climbing the parapets and running on the large parade ground (this area was once a rice field). Inside the fort's casemates underneath the ramparts you'll find well-organized exhibits on the fort's construction and history. Most visitors especially love the daily cannon firings during the summer. If you're really lucky, you'll be around when Fort Jackson fires a salute to passing military vessels on the river—the only historic fort in the United States that does so.

To get to Fort Jackson, take the President Street Extension (Islands Expressway) east out of downtown. The entrance is several miles down on the left.

MAP 4: Fort Jackson Rd., 912/232-3945, http://chsgeorgia.org; daily 9am-5pm; $7 adults, $4 children

Thunderbolt

Near the Bonaventure Cemetery is the little fishing village of Thunderbolt, almost as old as Savannah itself. According to Oglethorpe, the town was named after "a rock which was here shattered by a thunderbolt, causing a spring to gush from the ground, which continued ever afterward to emit the odor of brimstone."

Savannah State University

Continue on River Road and you'll soon be at the entrance to Savannah State University. This historically black university began life in 1890 as the Georgia State Industrial College for Colored Youth. Famous graduates include NFL great Shannon Sharpe. The main landmark is the newly restored Hill Hall, a 1901 building featured in the film *The General's Daughter*.

MAP 4: 3219 College St., 912/356-2186, www.savstate.edu

Thunderbolt Museum

Just off Victory Drive is the Thunderbolt Museum, housed in the humble former town hall. Cross Victory Drive onto River Road and notice how the road is built around the live oak tree in the middle of it. Most of the nice views of the river have been obscured by high-rise condos, but there's a cute public fishing pier.

MAP 4: Victory Dr. and Mechanics Ave., 912/351-0836, http://thunderboltmuseum.org; Wed.-Thurs. 9:30am-2:30pm, Sat. 1pm-5pm; free

Its name means "salt" in the old Euchee tongue, indicative of the island's chief export in those days. And Tybee Island—"Tybee" to locals—is indeed one of the essential seasonings of life in Savannah. First incorporated as Ocean City and then Savannah Beach, the island has since reclaimed its original name. Eighteen miles and about a half-hour drive from Savannah, in truth Tybee is part and parcel of the city's social and cultural fabric. Many of the island's 3,000 full-time residents, known for their boozy bonhomie and quirky personal style, commute to work in the city. And those living "in town" often reciprocate by visiting Tybee to dine in its few but excellent restaurants, drink in its casual and crazy watering holes, and frolic on its wide, beautiful beaches lined with rare sea oats waving in the Atlantic breeze.

★ Fort Pulaski National Monument

There's one must-see before you get to Tybee Island proper. On Cockspur Island you'll find Fort Pulaski National Monument. Not only a delight for any history buff, the fort's also a fantastic place to take the kids. They can climb on the parapets, earthworks, and cannons, and burn off calories on the great nature trail nearby. Along the way they'll no doubt learn a few things as well.

The Siege of Fort Pulaski

Fort Pulaski's construction was part of a broader initiative by President James Madison in the wake of the disastrous War of 1812, which dramatically revealed the shortcomings of U.S. coastal defense. Based on state-of-the-art European design forged in the cauldron of the Napoleonic Wars, Fort Pulaski's thick masonry construction used 25 million bricks, many of them of the famous "Savannah Gray" variety handmade at the nearby Hermitage Plantation.

When Georgia seceded from the Union in January 1861, a small force of Confederates immediately took control of Fort Pulaski and Fort Jackson. In early 1862 a Union sea-land force came to covertly lay the groundwork for a siege of Fort Pulaski. The siege would rely on several batteries secretly set up across the Savannah River. Some of the Union guns utilized new rifled-chamber technology, which dramatically increased the accuracy, muzzle velocity, and penetrating power of their shells. The Union barrage began at 8:15am on April 10, 1862, and Fort Pulaski's walls crumbled under the withering fire. At least one shell struck a powder magazine, igniting an enormous explosion. After 30 hours, Confederate general Charles Olmstead surrendered the fortress.

It was not only Fort Pulaski that was rendered obsolete—it was the whole concept of masonry fortification. From that point forward, military forts would rely on earthwork rather than brick. The section of earthwork you see as you enter Fort Pulaski, the "demilune," was added after the Civil War.

By all means, stop by the visitors center, a few hundred yards from the fort itself—but the palpable pleasure starts when you cross the drawbridge over the moat and see a cannon pointed at you from a narrow gun port. Enter the inside of the fort and take in just how big it is—Union occupiers regularly played baseball on the huge, grassy parade ground. Take a walk around the perimeter, underneath the ramparts. This is where the soldiers lived and worked, and you'll see re-creations of officers' quarters, meeting areas, sick rooms, and prisoners' bunks among the cannons, where Confederate prisoners of war were held after the fort's surrender. Cannon firings happen most Saturdays.

And now for the pièce de résistance: Take the steep corkscrew staircase up to the ramparts themselves and take in the jaw-dropping view of the lush marsh, with the Savannah River and Tybee Island spreading out in the distance. Stop and sit near one of the several remaining cannons and contemplate what went on here a century and a half ago. (Warning: There's no railing of any kind on the inboard side of the ramparts. Keep the kids well back from the edge, because it's a lethal fall to the fort interior.) Afterward, take a stroll all the way around the walls and see the power of those Yankee guns. Though much of the devastation was soon repaired, some sections of the wall remain in their damaged state. You can even pick out a few cannonballs still stuck in the masonry, like blueberries in a pie.

Save some time and energy for the extensive palmetto-lined nature trail through the sandy upland of Cockspur Island on which the fort is located. There are informative markers, a picnic area, and, as a bonus, a coastal defense facility from the Spanish-American War, Battery Hambright.

Continue east on U.S. 80, passing over Lazaretto Creek, named for the quarantine or "lazaretto" built in the late 1700s to make sure newcomers, mostly slaves, were free of disease. As you cross, look to your left over the river's wide south channel. On a tiny oyster shell islet, find the little **Cockspur Beacon** lighthouse, in use from 1848 to 1909, when major shipping was routed through the deeper north channel of the river. The site is now preserved by the National Park Service and is accessible only by boat or kayak. You have to time your arrival with the right tide; check with a local rental place for advice.

MAP 5: U.S. 80 E., 912/786-5787, www.nps.gov/fopu; June-Aug. daily 9am-6:30pm, Sept.-May daily 9am-5pm; $5, free under age 16

South End

Butler Avenue is Tybee's main drag, the beach fully public and accessible from any of the numbered side streets on the left. Go all the way down to **Tybrisa Street** (formerly 16th St.) to get a flavor of old Tybee. Here's where you'll find the old five-and-dimes like T. S. Chu's, still a staple of local life, and little diners, ice cream spots, and taverns. The new pride of the island is the large, long pier structure called the **Tybrisa Pavilion II,** built in 1996 in an attempt to recreate the lost glory of the Tybrisa Pavilion, social and spiritual center of the island's gregarious resort days. Built in 1891 by the

Clockwise from top left: art gallery on Tybee Island; view from the beach at Tybee Island; Fort Pulaski National Monument.

The Tybee Bomb

On a dark night in 1958 at the height of the Cold War, a USAF B-47 Stratojet bomber made a simulated nuclear bombing run over southeast Georgia. A Charleston-based F-86 fighter on a mock intercept came too close, clipping the bomber's wing. Before bringing down the wounded B-47 at Savannah's Hunter Airfield, Commander Howard Richardson decided to jettison his lethal cargo: a 7,000-pound Mark 15 hydrogen bomb, serial number 47782. Richardson, who won the Distinguished Flying Cross for his efforts that night, jettisoned the bomb over water. What no one knows is exactly where. And thus began the legend of "the Tybee Bomb." Speculation ran wild, with some locals fearing a nuclear explosion, radioactive contamination, or even that a team of scuba-diving terrorists would secretly retrieve the ancient weapon.

Former Army colonel Derek Duke has taken it as his personal mission to find the bomb. Duke claims to have found a radiation-emitting object off Little Tybee Island during a search in 2004.

Commander Richardson, now retired, says the bomb wasn't armed when he jettisoned it. Environmentalists say that doesn't matter, because the enriched uranium the Air Force admits was in the bomb is toxic whether or not there's the risk of a nuclear detonation. People who work in the fishing industry on Tybee say the fact that the bomb also had 400 pounds of high explosive "nuclear trigger" is reason enough to get it out of the waterways.

And what of the Air Force? In 2000, they sent a team to Savannah to find the bomb, concluding it was buried somewhere off the coast in 5-15 feet of mud. In 2005, in another attempt to find the weapon, they sent another team of experts down to look one last time. Their verdict: The bomb's still lost.

Central of Georgia Railway, the Tybrisa hosted name entertainers and big bands on its expansive dance floor. Sadly, fire destroyed it in 1967, an enormous blow to area morale.

MAP 5: Butler Ave.

Tybee Island Light Station and Museum

At North Campbell Avenue is the entrance to the less-populated, more historically significant north end of Tybee Island, once almost entirely taken up by Fort Screven, a coastal defense fortification of the early 1900s. Rebuilt several times in its history, the Tybee Island Light Station traces its construction to the first year of the colony, based on a design by the multi-talented Noble Jones. At its completion in 1736, it was the tallest structure in the United States. One of a handful of working 18th-century lighthouses today, the facility has been restored to its 1916-1964 incarnation, featuring a nine-foot-tall first-order Fresnel lens installed in 1867.

The entrance fee gives you admission to the lighthouse, the lighthouse museum, and the nearby Tybee Island Museum. All the outbuildings on the lighthouse grounds are original, including the residence of the lighthouse keeper, also the oldest building on the island. If you've got the legs and the lungs, definitely take all 178 steps up to the top of the lighthouse for a stunning view of Tybee, the Atlantic, and Hilton Head Island.

To get to the lighthouse, take a left onto North Campbell Avenue then left again on Van Horne Street. Take an immediate right onto Meddin Drive. Continue until you see a lighthouse on the left and a parking lot on the right.

All around the area of the north end around the lighthouse complex you'll see low-lying concrete bunkers. These are remains of Fort Screven's coastal defense batteries, and many are in private hands. Battery Garland is open to tours, and also houses the **Tybee Island Museum** (30 Meddin Ave., 912/786-5801, Wed.-Mon. 9am-5:30pm, last ticket sold 4:30pm, $9 adults, $7 children, includes admission to lighthouse and lighthouse museum), a charming, almost whimsical little collection of exhibits from various eras of local history.

MAP 5: 30 Meddin Ave., 912/786-5801, www.tybeelighthouse.org; Wed.-Mon. 9am-5:30pm, last ticket sold 4:30pm; $9 adults, $7 children

Tybee Island Marine Science Center

Literally at the foot of the Tybrisa Pavilion you'll find the little Tybee Island Marine Science Center, with nine aquariums and a touch tank featuring native species. Here is the nerve center for the Tybee Island Sea Turtle Project, an ongoing effort to document and preserve the local comings and goings of the island's most beloved inhabitant and unofficial mascot, the endangered sea turtle.

MAP 5: 1510 Strand Ave., 912/786-5917, www.tybeemarinescience.org; daily 10am-5pm; $4 adults, $3 children

Greater Savannah

Map 6

MIDWAY AND LIBERTY COUNTY

Locals will tell you that Midway is named because it's equidistant from the Savannah and Altamaha Rivers on Oglethorpe's old "river road," which it certainly is, but others say the small but very historic town is actually named after the Medway River in England. In seeking to pacify the local Creek people, the Council of Georgia in 1752 granted a group of Massachusetts Puritans then residing in Dorchester, South Carolina, a 32,000-acre land grant as incentive to move south. After moving into Georgia and establishing New Dorchester, they soon founded a nearby settlement that would later take on the modern spelling of Midway. Midway's citizens were very aggressive early on in the cause for American independence, which is why the area's three original parishes were combined and named Liberty County in 1777—the only Georgia county named for a concept rather than a person. Two of Georgia's three signers of the Declaration of Independence, Lyman Hall and Button Gwinnett, resided primarily in Midway, and both attended the historic Midway Church. A key part of which formerly challenged Savannah for economic supremacy in the region, no longer exists.

Tourism in this area has been made much more user-friendly by the liberal addition of signage for the "Liberty Trail," a collection of key attractions. When in doubt, follow the signs. The main highways in Midway are I-95, U.S. 17, and U.S. 84, also called Oglethorpe Highway, which becomes Highway 38 (Islands Hwy.) east of I-95.

Fort Morris State Historic Site

Built to defend the once-proud port of Sunbury, Fort Morris State Historic Site was reconstructed during the War of 1812 and was an encampment during the Civil War. It was here that Colonel John McIntosh gave his famous reply to the British demand for his surrender: "Come and take it." The museum has displays of military and everyday life of the era. Reenactments and cannon firings are highlights. There's a visitors center and a nature trail. The site is about 50 minutes from Savannah. To get here, take exit 76 off I-95 south. Go east on Islands Highway and take a left on Fort Morris Road; the site is two miles down.

MAP 6: 2559 Ft. Morris Rd., 912/884-5999, www.gastateparks.org/info/ftmorris; Thurs.-Sat. 9am-5pm; $4.50 adults, $3 children

Geechee Kunda

A little way south of Midway on the Liberty Trail in tiny Riceboro is Geechee Kunda, a combination museum-outreach center on the site of the former Retreat rice and indigo plantation. It's now dedicated to explaining and exploring the culture of Sea Island African Americans on the Georgia coast. (Don't be confused: *Geechee* is the Georgia word for the Gullah people. Both groups share similar folkways and history, and the terms are virtually interchangeable.) There are artifacts from slavery and Reconstruction, including authentic Geechee/Gullah relics. Geechee Kunda is about 40 minutes from Savannah. Take exit 67 off I-95 and head north about two miles on U.S. 17.

MAP 6: 622 Ways Temple Rd., Riceboro, 912/884-4440, www.geecheekunda.com; Tues.-Sat. 11am-5pm

Midway Museum

In Midway proper is the charming Midway Museum and the adjacent **Midway Church,** sometimes called the Midway Meetinghouse. The museum contains a variety of artifacts, most from the 18th and 19th centuries, and an extensive genealogy collection. The Midway Church, built in 1756, was burned during the Revolution but rebuilt in 1792. Both Button Gwinnett and Lyman Hall attended services here, and during the Civil War some of Sherman's cavalry set up camp on the grounds. The cemetery across the street is wonderfully poignant and is the final resting place of two Revolutionary War generals; Union cavalry kept horses within its walls.

Sunbury: Gone But Not Forgotten

If you spend much time in Liberty County, you'll probably hear someone mention that a certain place or person is "over near Sunbury." Such is the legacy of this long-gone piece of Georgia history that locals still refer to it in the present tense, though the old town itself is no more.

Founded soon after Midway in 1758, Sunbury rivaled Savannah as Georgia's main commercial port by 1761, with a thriving trade in lumber, rice, indigo, corn, and, unfortunately, slaves. At one time, seven square-rigged vessels called on the port in a single day.

At various times, all three of Georgia's signers of the Declaration of Independence—Button Gwinnett, Lyman Hall, and George Walton—had connections to Sunbury. The beginning of the end came with those heady days of revolution, however, when Sunbury was the scene of much fighting between colonists and the British army. A British siege in 1778 culminated in this immortal reply from the colonial commander, Colonel John McIntosh, to a redcoat demand for surrender: "Come and take it." By the beginning of 1779, a separate British assault did so.

After U.S. independence, Sunbury remained the Liberty County seat until 1797, but it was never the same, beset by decay, hurricanes, and yellow fever outbreaks. By 1848, nothing of the town remained but the old cemetery, which you can find a short drive from the Fort Morris State Historic Site; ask a park employee for directions.

The museum, church, and cemetery are 30 miles from Savannah and easy to find: take exit 76 from I-95 south, and take a right on U.S. 84 (Oglethorpe Hwy.). Turn right on U.S. 17, and they're just ahead on the right.

MAP 6: 491 N. Coastal Hwy., 912/884-5837, www.themidwaymuseum.org; Tues.-Sat. 10am-4pm; $3

Seabrook Village

West off Islands Highway is Seabrook Village, a unique living-history museum chronicling the everyday life of Liberty County's African Americans, with a direct link to Sherman's famous "40 acres and a mule" Field Order No. 15. There are eight restored vernacular buildings on the 100-acre site, including the simple but sublime one-room Seabrook School. From Savannah, take exit 76 off I-95, and then a left onto U.S. 84. After about two miles take a left onto Trade Hill Road.

MAP 6: 660 Trade Hill Rd., 912/884-7008; Tues.-Sat. 10am-4pm; $3

OSSABAW ISLAND

Ossabaw Island

Owned and operated by Georgia as a heritage and wildlife preserve, the island was a gift to the state in 1978 from Eleanor Torrey-West and family, who still retain some property on the island. All public use of the island is managed by the Ossabaw Island Foundation (www.ossabawisland.org).

The 12,000-acre island is much older than Wassaw Island to its north and so has traces of human habitation back to 2000 BC. The island's name comes from an old Muskogean word referring to yaupon holly, found in abundance on the island and used by Native Americans in purification rituals to induce vomiting. There are several tabby ruins on the island, along with many miles of walking trails. Unlike the much-younger Wassaw, Ossabaw Island was not only timbered extensively but hosted several rice and cotton plantations.

Descendants of the island's slaves moved to the Savannah area after the Civil War, founding the community of Pin Point. Similarly to Jekyll Island to the south, Ossabaw was a hunting preserve for wealthy families in the Roaring '20s. Even today, hunting is an important activity on the island, with lotteries choosing who gets a chance to pursue its overly large populations of deer and wild hogs, the latter of which are descended from pigs brought by the Spanish.

Now reserved exclusively for educational and scientific purposes, the island is accessible only by boat. Georgia law ensures public access to all beaches up to the high-tide mark—which simply means that the public can ride out to Ossabaw and go on the beach for day use, but any travel to the interior is restricted and you must have permission first. Contact the Ossabaw Island Foundation for information. Boat trips take about 1.5 hours and vary in price. Day trips can be arranged with charter operators at the marinas in Savannah.

MAP 6: Ossabaw Island, www.ossabawisland.org

WASSAW ISLAND
Wassaw Island National Wildlife Refuge

Unique in that it's the only Georgia barrier island never cleared for agriculture or development, the 10,000-acre Wassaw Island National Wildlife Refuge is accessible only by boat. There are striking driftwood-strewn beaches, and the interior of the island has some beautiful old-growth stands of longleaf pine and live oak. Wassaw is a veritable paradise for nature lovers and bird-watchers, with migratory activity in the spring and fall, waterfowl in abundance in the summer, and manatee and loggerhead turtle activity (about 10 percent of Georgia's transient loggerhead population makes use of Wassaw for nesting). There are also about 20 miles of trails and a decaying Spanish-American War-era battery, Fort Morgan, on the north end. National Wildlife Refuge Week is celebrated in October.

Because of its comparatively young status—it was formed only about 1,600 years ago—Wassaw Island also has some unique geographical features. You can still make out the parallel ridge features, vestiges of successive ancient shorelines. A central ridge forms the backbone of the island, reaching an amazing (for this area) elevation of 45 feet above sea level at the south end. Native Americans first settled the island, whose name comes from an ancient word for sassafras, which was found in abundance here. During the Civil War, both Confederate and Union troops occupied the island successively. In 1866 the wealthy New England businessman George

Parsons bought the island, which stayed in that family's hands until it was sold to the Nature Conservancy in 1969 for $1 million. The Conservancy in turn sold Wassaw to the U.S. government for $1 to be managed as a wildlife refuge.

It's easiest to get to Wassaw Island from Savannah. Boat rides take roughly 30 minutes and cost around $50 round-trip. Charters and scheduled trips are available from **Captain Walt's Charters** (Thunderbolt Marina, 3124 River Dr., 912/507-3811, www.waltsadventure.com/charters), the **Bull River Marina** (8005 E. U.S. 80, 912/897-7300), **Delegal Marina** (1 Marina Dr., 912/598-0023), **Captain Joe Dobbs** (Delegal Marina, 1 Marina Dr., 912/598-0090, www.captjdobbs.com), and **Isle of Hope Marina** (50 Bluff Dr., 912/354-8187, www.isleofhopemarina.com). Most docking is either at the beaches on the north and south ends or in Wassaw Creek, where the U.S. Fish and Wildlife Service dock is also located (temporary mooring only). There's no camping allowed on Wassaw Island; it's for day use only.

MAP 6: Wassaw Island, www.fws.gov/wassaw; daily dawn-dusk

WEST CHATHAM

Coastal Georgia Botanical Gardens at the Historic Bamboo Farm

A joint project of the University of Georgia and Chatham County, this farm is an education and demonstration center featuring a wide array of native species in addition to the garden's eponymous Asian "wonder weed," which has its roots in a private collection dating from the late 1800s. Many of the mature trees were planted in the 1930s. The garden also periodically holds you-pick-'em harvest days for berries. To get here, take exit 94 off of I-95 and take Highway 204 east toward Savannah. Turn right on East Gateway Boulevard, then left on Canebrake Road. Enter at the Canebrake gate.

MAP 6: 2 Canebrake Rd., 912/921-5460, www.coastalgeorgiabg.org; Mon.-Fri. 8am-5pm, Sat. 10am-5pm, Sun. noon-5pm; free

Mighty Eighth Air Force Museum

Military and aviation buffs mustn't miss the Mighty Eighth Air Force Museum in Pooler, Georgia, right off I-95. The 8th Air Force was born at Hunter Field in Savannah as the 8th Bomber Command in 1942, becoming the 8th Air Force in 1944; it is now based in Louisiana.

A moving testament to the men and machines who conducted those strategic bombing campaigns over Europe in World War II, the museum also features later 8th Air Force history such as the Korean War, the Linebacker II bombing campaigns over North Vietnam, and the Persian Gulf. Inside you'll find airplanes like the P-51 Mustang and the German ME-109, and there's also a restored B-17 bomber, the newest jewel of the collection. Outside are several more aircraft, including a MiG-17, an F-4 Phantom, and a B-47 Stratojet bomber like the one that dropped the fabled "Tybee Bomb" in 1958. The nearby Chapel of the Fallen Eagles is a fully

The Salzburgers of New Ebenezer

Perhaps the most unsung chapter in Europe's great spiritual diaspora of the 1700s, the Salzburgers of New Ebenezer—a thrifty, peaceful, and hard-working people—were Georgia's first religious refugees and perhaps the most progressive as well. The year after Oglethorpe's arrival, a contingent of devout Lutherans from Salzburg in present-day Austria arrived after being expelled from their home country for their beliefs. Oglethorpe, mindful of Georgia's mission to provide sanctuary for persecuted Protestants and also wishing for a military buffer to the west, eagerly welcomed them. Given land about 25 miles west of Savannah, the Salzburgers named their first settlement Ebenezer ("stone of help" in Hebrew). They later moved the site to better land nearer to the river and called it New Ebenezer, and so it remains to this day.

Because the settlers spoke German instead of English, the upriver colony maintained its isolation. Still, the Salzburgers were among Oglethorpe's most ardent and loyal supporters. Their pastor and de facto political leader, Johann Martin Boltzius, seeking to build an enlightened agrarian utopia, was an outspoken foe of slavery and the exploitative plantation system. The fragile silk industry thrived in New Ebenezer while it had failed miserably in Savannah, and the nation's first rice mill was built here.

The Trustees' turnover of Georgia to the crown in 1750 signaled the final victory of pro-slavery forces—even Pastor Boltzius acquired a couple of slaves as domestic servants. New Ebenezer's influence began a decline that accelerated when British forces pillaged much of the town in the Revolution. Fifty years later, nothing at all remained except the old Jerusalem Church, now the **Jerusalem Evangelical Lutheran Church.**

Although New Ebenezer is often called a "ghost town," this is a misnomer. Extensive archaeological work continues in the area, and the Georgia Salzburger Society works hard to maintain several historic buildings and keep the legacy alive through special events.

functioning sanctuary that honors the more than 26,000 members of the Mighty Eighth that died during World War II.

To get to the Mighty Eighth Museum from downtown, take I-16 west until it intersects I-95. Take I-95 north, take exit 102, and follow the signs. MAP 6: 175 Bourne Ave., Pooler, 912/748-8888, www.mightyeighth.org; daily 9am-5pm; $10 adults, $6 children and active-duty military

RICHMOND HILL AND BRYAN COUNTY

Known as the "town that Henry Ford built," Richmond Hill is a growing bedroom community of Savannah in adjacent Bryan County. Sherman's March to the Sea ended here with much destruction, so little history before that time is left. Most of what remains is due to Ford's philanthropic influence, still felt in many place-names around the area, including the main drag, Highway 144, known as Ford Avenue. After the auto magnate and his wife Clara made the area, then called Ways Station, a summer home, they were struck by the area's incredible poverty and determined to help improve living conditions, building hospitals, schools, churches, and homes. The Fords eventually acquired over 85,000 acres in Bryan County, including the former Richmond plantation. What is now known as Ford Plantation—currently a private luxury resort—was built in the 1930s and centered on the main house, once the central building of the famous Hermitage Plantation on the Savannah River, purchased and moved by Ford south to Bryan County.

Fort McAllister State Historic Site

Perhaps the main attraction in Richmond Hill, especially for Civil War buffs, is Fort McAllister State Historic Site. Unlike the masonry forts of Savannah, Fort McAllister is an all-earthwork fortification on the Ogeechee River, the site of a short but savage assault by Sherman's troops in December 1864 in which 5,000 Union soldiers quickly overwhelmed the skeleton garrison of 230 Confederate defenders. After the war, the site fell into disrepair until Henry Ford funded and spearheaded restoration in the 1930s, as he did with so many historic sites in Bryan County. The fort, which features many reenactments throughout the year, has a **Civil War Museum** (Mon.-Sat. 9am-5pm, Sun. 2pm-5pm, $5). An adjacent recreational site features a beautiful oak-lined picnic ground, a nature trail, and the nearby 65-site Savage Island Campground. Bryan County is just 15 minutes from Savannah. Take I-95 south and then exit 90. From there, head east about six miles on Highway 144/Ford Drive.

MAP 6: 3894 Ft. McAllister Rd., Richmond Hill, 912/727-2339, www.gastateparks.org/info/ftmcallister; daily 7am-10pm; $7.50 adults, $4.50 children

Richmond Hill Historical Society and Museum

The little Richmond Hill Historical Society and Museum is housed in a former kindergarten built by Henry Ford.

MAP 6: Ford Ave. and Timber Trail Rd., Richmond Hill, 912/756-3697; daily 10am-4pm; donations accepted

NEW EBENEZER
Jerusalem Evangelical Lutheran Church

Few people visit New Ebenezer today, west of Savannah in Effingham County. Truth is, there's not much there anymore except for one old church. But oh, what a church. The Jerusalem Evangelical Lutheran Church hosts the oldest continuous congregation in the United States. Built of local clay brick in 1769, its walls are 21 inches thick. Some original panes of glass remain, and its European bells are still rung before each service. Several surrounding structures are also heirs to New Ebenezer's Salzburg legacy.

MAP 6: 2966 Ebenezer Rd., Rincon, 912/754-3915, http://jerusalematebenezer.org; service Sun. 11am

Around the corner from the Jerusalem Evangelical Lutheran Church is a much newer spiritually themed site, the New Ebenezer Retreat and Conference Center. Built in 1977, the retreat provides acres of calm surroundings, lodging, and meals in an ecumenical Christian setting.

The New Ebenezer Retreat and Conference Center offers a range of very reasonably priced lodgings, most including meals, in a beautiful setting. The extremely fast-growing town of Rincon, through which you will most likely drive on your way to New Ebenezer, offers an assortment of the usual chain food and lodging establishments.

While most facilities are for guests of the retreat, you can tour the grounds on your own. It's scenic and peaceful, and the cottages are charming.

MAP 6: 2887 Ebenezer Rd., Rincon, 912/754-9242, www.newebenezer.org

SIGHTS
GREATER SAVANNAH

Restaurants and Nightlife

PRICE KEY

💲 Entrées less than $10

💲💲 Entrées $10–20

💲💲💲 Entrées more than $20

Savannah is a fun food town, with a selection of cuisine concocted by a cast of executive chefs who despite their many personal idiosyncrasies tend to go with what works rather than experimenting for the sake of experimentation. Here's a breakdown of the most notable offerings, by area and by type of cuisine.

You'll note there's rarely a separate *Seafood* section listed; that's because seafood is an intrinsic part of most restaurant fare in Savannah, whether through regular menu offerings or through specials. For the freshest seafood, consider a trip to Tybee Island or Thunderbolt (which is on the way to Tybee). As the downtown area continues to focus more and more on tourism, locals are tending to popularize more humble, often culturally diverse restaurants outside of the historic district that are well worth a stop.

Beyond its dining scene, Savannah is known for its copious watering holes hosting a diverse range of local residents and adventurous visitors. Savannah is a hard-drinking town, and not just on St. Patrick's Day. The ability to legally walk downtown streets with beer, wine, or a cocktail in hand definitely contributes to the overall *joie de vivre*.

Bars close in Savannah at 3am. A citywide indoor smoking ban is in effect and you may not smoke cigarettes in any bar in Savannah. Recent legislation finally allows Savannah bars that don't serve food to open on Sundays, but not all have made the switch; call ahead.

Previous: B. Matthew's Eatery; Vic's on the River.

Look for ★ to find
recommended restaurants and nightlife.

Highlights

★ **Best Breakfast Downtown:** Hands down, it's **B. Matthew's Eatery** on Bay Street, where you can't go wrong with the omelets or the pancakes (page 85).

★ **Closest Thing to a Charleston Restaurant in Savannah:** Find amazing takes on savory Southern classics at **Sapphire Grill,** where chef Chris Nason brings the expertise he acquired running world-class restaurants in nearby Charleston, South Carolina (page 88).

★ **Best Place to Get a Little Rowdy:** Sing karaoke with college students, have a Guinness with rugby players, do shots with roller derby girls, and more at **The Rail Pub** (page 89).

★ **Most Luscious Lunch:** The dishes at **Kayak Kafe** are light and adventurous and make for a perfect pit stop during a day of shopping on Broughton Street (page 90).

★ **Tastiest Brush with Hollywood:** Movie producer and Savannah native Stratton Leopold is often seen behind the counter at **Leopold's Ice Cream,** helping dish out scoops of his old family recipe ice cream flavors among Hollywood memorabilia (page 90).

★ **Most Historical Tavern:** Abraham Lincoln never set foot in Savannah and Lincoln Street isn't named for him, but **Abe's on Lincoln** is the oldest surviving bar in Savannah, with roots going back to colonial days (page 92).

★ **Most Authentic Irish Pub:** In a town with deep ties to Irish culture, tiny **O'Connell's** is without a doubt the closest thing here to an old school Emerald Isle pub (page 93).

★ **Most Authentic Southern Experience:** Eat around a communal table in a convivial atmosphere at **Mrs. Wilkes' Dining Room** and enjoy what many consider the finest fried chicken in the South, among other classic dishes (page 93).

★ **Best Celebrity Chef's Place:** Nope, it's not Paula Deen's—regional foodie guru Hugh Acheson brings unique takes on Northern Italian cuisine to **The Florence** (page 95).

★ **Most Romantic Date Night:** One of Savannah's original fine-dining restaurants, **Elizabeth on 37th** remains the local gold standard for a wonderful evening with wonderful food and service (page 96).

BREAKFAST

★ B. Matthew's Eatery $$

If you're downtown and need something more than your hotel breakfast—and you will!—go to B. Matthew's Eatery, widely considered the best breakfast in the entire Savannah Historic District. The omelets—most under $10—are uniformly wonderful, and the sausage and bacon are excellent and not greasy. There are more healthful selections as well, and you can actually get a decent bowl of oatmeal—but I suggest something more decadent. Sunday brunch is incredible. And they don't do just breakfast—lunch sandwiches and salads are of similarly high quality, and dinner entrées (from $17) include killer osso buco, lamb, and seafood.

MAP 1: 325 E. Bay St., 912/233-1319, www.bmatthewseatery.com; Mon.-Thurs. 8am-9pm, Fri.-Sat. 8am-10pm, Sun. 9am-3pm

CLASSIC SOUTHERN

Vic's on the River $$$

Very few restaurants on River Street rise above tourist schlock, but a standout is Vic's on the River. With dishes like wild Georgia shrimp, stone-ground grits, and blue crab cakes with a three-pepper relish, Vic's combines a romantic old Savannah atmosphere with an adventurous take on Lowcountry cuisine. Note the entrance to the dining room is not on River Street but on the Bay Street level on Upper Factor's Walk.

MAP 1: 16 E. River St., 912/721-1000, www.vicsontheriver.com; Sun.-Thurs. 11am-10pm, Fri.-Sat. 11am-11pm

GREEK

Olympia Café $$

Another worthwhile place to stop for a relaxing and tasty meal on River Street is Olympia Café, which serves a variety of Greek dishes such as dolmas, spanokopita, seafood, and lemon chicken in a friendly atmosphere. The standard menu items aren't particularly cheap, but the daily specials often offer a surprisingly good deal for your money.

MAP 1: 5 E. River St., 912/233-3131, www.olympiacafe.net; daily 11am-10pm

BARS AND PUBS

Kevin Barry's Irish Pub

The main landmark on the west end of River Street is the famous (or infamous, depending on which side of "The Troubles" you're on) Kevin Barry's Irish Pub, one of Savannah's most beloved establishments. KB's is open seven days a week, with evenings seeing performances by a number of Irish troubadours, all veterans of the East Coast trad circuit.

MAP 1: 117 W. River St., 912/233-9626, www.kevinbarrys.com; daily 11am-3am

Clockwise from top left: B. Matthew's Eatery; Chuck's Bar; Lulu's Chocolate Bar.

Uncharacteristically, Savannah now sports several good hotel bars, and one of the best is Rocks on the Roof, atop the Bohemian Hotel Savannah Riverfront on the waterfront. In good weather the exterior walls are opened up to reveal a large wraparound seating area with stunning views of downtown on one side and of the Savannah River on the other.

MAP 1: 102 W. Bay St., 912/721-3800; daily 11am-3pm

GAY AND LESBIAN
Chuck's Bar

A friendly, kitschy little tavern at the far west end of River Street near the Jefferson Street ramp, Chuck's Bar is a great place to relax and see some interesting local characters. Karaoke at Chuck's is especially a hoot, and they keep the Christmas lights up all year.

MAP 1: 301 W. River St., 912/232-1005; Mon.-Wed. 8pm-3am, Thurs.-Sat. 7pm-3am

Club One Jefferson

Any examination of gay and lesbian nightlife in Savannah must, of course, begin with Club One Jefferson of *Midnight in the Garden of Good and Evil* fame, with its famous drag shows, including the notorious Lady Chablis, upstairs in the cabaret and its rockin' 1,000-square-foot dance floor downstairs. Cabaret show times are Thursday-Saturday 10:30pm and 12:30am, Sunday 10:30pm, and Monday 11:30pm. Call for Lady Chablis's show times. As at all local gay nightclubs, straights are more than welcome.

MAP 1: 1 Jefferson St., 912/232-0200, www.clubone-online.com; Mon.-Sat. 5pm-3am, Sun. 5pm-2am

City Market   Map 1

CLASSIC SOUTHERN
The Lady & Sons ⑤⑤

Every year, thousands of visitors come to Savannah for the privilege of waiting for hours outside in all weather, the line stretching a full city block, for a chance to eat at The Lady & Sons and sample some of local celebrity Paula Deen's "home" cooking—actually a fairly typical Southern buffet with some decent fried chicken, collard greens, and mac-and-cheese. For the privilege, you must begin waiting in line as early as 9:30am for lunch and as early as 3:30pm for dinner in order to be assigned a dining time. You almost assuredly will never see Paula, who has precious little to do with the restaurant these days.

MAP 1: 102 W. Congress St., 912/233-2600, www.ladyandsons.com; Mon.-Sat. 11am-3pm and 5pm-close, Sun. 11am-5pm

COFFEE, TEA, AND SWEETS

Lulu's Chocolate Bar $

Combine a hip bar with outrageously tasty dessert items and you get Lulu's Chocolate Bar. While the whole family is welcome before 10pm to enjoy chocolate-chip cheesecake and the like, after that it's strictly 21-and-over. The late crowd is younger and trendier and comes mostly for the unique specialty martinis, including the pineapple upside-down martini.

MAP 1: 42 MLK Jr. Blvd., 912/238-2012, www.luluschocolatebar.net; Fri.-Sat. 2pm-2am, Sun.-Thurs. noon-midnight

ITALIAN

Vinnie VanGoGo's $

One would never call Savannah a great pizza town, but the best pizza here is Vinnie VanGoGo's at the west end of City Market on Franklin Square. Their pizza is a thin-crust Neapolitan style—although the menu claims it to be New York style—with a delightful tangy sauce and fresh cheese. Individual slices are huge, so don't feel obliged to order a whole pie. The waiting list for a table can get pretty long. It's cash only.

MAP 1: 317 W. Bryan St., 912/233-6394, www.vinnievangogos.com; Mon.-Thurs. 4pm-11:30pm, Fri. 4pm-1am, Sat. noon-1am, Sun. noon-11:30pm; cash only

NEW SOUTHERN

★ Sapphire Grill $$$

Accomplishing the difficult task of being achingly hip while also offering some of the best food in town, Sapphire Grill comes closer than any other Savannah restaurant to replicating a high-class trendy Manhattan eatery—at prices to match. With its bare stone walls, lean ambience, and romantically dark interior, you'd be tempted to think it's all sizzle and no steak. But executive chef Chris Nason, former exec at Charleston's Anson Restaurant, has a way with coastal cuisine, relying on the freshest local seafood. His classic meat dishes like lamb, filet mignon, and veal are equally skillful. The lobster bisque is a must-have.

MAP 1: 110 W. Congress St., 912/443-9962, www.sapphiregrill.com; Fri.-Sat. 5:30pm-11:30pm, Sun.-Thurs. 6pm-10:30pm

BARS AND PUBS

Moon River Brewing Company

The only brewpub in Savannah, Moon River Brewing Company is directly across from the Hyatt Regency Savannah and offers half a dozen handcrafted beers in a rambling old space, including a new deck area, that housed Savannah's premier hotel in antebellum days.

MAP 1: 21 W. Bay St., 912/447-0943, www.moonriverbrewing.com; Mon.-Thurs. 11am-11pm, Fri.-Sat. 11am-midnight, Sun. 11am-10pm

The To-Go Cup Tradition

Arguably the single most civilized trait of Savannah, and certainly one of the things that most sets it apart, is the glorious old tradition of the "to-go cup." True to its history of hard partying and general open-mindedness, Savannah, like New Orleans, legally allows you to walk the streets downtown with an open container of your favorite adult beverage. Of course, you have to be 21 or over, and the cup must be Styrofoam or plastic, never glass or metal, and no more than 16 ounces. While there are boundaries to where to-go cups are legal, in practice this includes almost all areas of the historic district frequented by visitors. The quick and easy rule of thumb is, keep your to-go cups north of Jones Street.

Every other election year, some local politician tries to get the church folk all riled up and proposes doing away with to-go cups in the interest of public safety, and he or she is inevitably shouted down by the outcry from the tourism-conscious chamber of commerce and from patriotic Savannahians defending their way of life. Every downtown watering hole has stacks of cups at the bar for patrons to use. You can either ask the bartender for a to-go cup—aka a "go cup"—or just reach out and grab one yourself. Don't be shy; it's the Savannah way.

★ The Rail Pub

In the City Market area, your best bet is The Rail Pub, one of Savannah's oldest and most beloved taverns and a great place to get a pint or a shot in a quite boisterous but still cozy and friendly environment. They give you roasted peanuts with your drink; just let the shells fall on the floor like everyone else does.

MAP 1: 405 W. Congress St., 912-238-1311, www.therailpub.com; Mon.-Sat. 3pm-3am

22 Square

In the modernist Andaz Savannah hotel overlooking bustling Ellis Square, 22 Square is a great place for an upscale cocktail and for meeting interesting people from all over. Try the refreshing Savannah Fizz or one of their mean Sazeracs.

MAP 1: 14 Barnard St., 912-233-2116, www.savannah.andaz.hyatt.com; Mon.-Thurs. 4pm-10pm, Fri.-Sat. 2pm-midnight, Sun. 4pm-10pm

LIVE MUSIC AND KARAOKE
The Jinx

Despite its high-volume offerings, The Jinx is a friendly watering hole and the closest thing Savannah has to a full-on Athens, Georgia, music club, with a very active calendar of rock and metal shows. Shows start *very* late here, never before 11pm and often later than that. If you're here for the music and have sensitive ears, bring earplugs.

MAP 1: 127 W. Congress St., 912-236-2281, www.thejinx.net; Mon.-Sat. 4pm-3am

CLASSIC SOUTHERN

★ Kayak Kafe $$

The best lunch on Broughton Street is at Kayak Kafe, where you can get a killer fresh salad or a fish taco to refresh your energy level during a busy day of shopping or sightseeing. Vegetarians, vegans, and those on a gluten-free diet will be especially pleased by the available options. As one of the very few Broughton Street places with outdoor sidewalk tables, this is also a great people-watching spot.

MAP 1: 1 E. Broughton St., 912/233-6044, www.eatkayak.com; Mon.-Thurs. 11am-10pm, Fri.-Sat. 11am-11pm, Sun. 11am-5pm

Olde Pink House $$

Once the home of General James Habersham and the first place the Declaration of Independence was read aloud in Savannah, the Olde Pink House is still a hub of activity in Savannah, as visitors and locals alike frequent the classic interior of the dining room and the downstairs Planter's Tavern. Olde Pink House is known for its savvy (and often sassy) service and the uniquely regional flair it adds to traditional dishes, with liberal doses of pecans, Vidalia onions, shrimp, and crab. The she-crab soup and lamb chops in particular are crowd-pleasers, and the scored crispy flounder stacks up to similar versions of this dish at several other spots in town. Reservations are recommended.

MAP 1: 23 Abercorn St., 912/232-4286; Sun.-Thurs. 5:30pm-10:30pm, Fri.-Sat. 5:30pm-11pm

COFFEE, TEA, AND SWEETS

The Coffee Fox $

There's a Starbucks on Broughton Street, but the best coffee on that busy thoroughfare is at The Coffee Fox, a locally owned joint that expertly treads the fine line between hipster hangout and accessible hot spot. The freshly baked goodies are nearly as good as the freshly brewed java, which includes cold-brew and pour-over offerings.

MAP 1: 102 W. Broughton St., 912/401-0399, www.thecoffeefox.com; Mon.-Sat. 7am-11pm, Sun. 8am-4pm

★ Leopold's Ice Cream $

He helped produce *Mission Impossible III* and other movies, but Savannah native Stratton Leopold's other claim to fame is running the 100-year-old family business at Leopold's Ice Cream. Now in a new location but with the same delicious family ice cream recipe, Leopold's also offers soup and sandwiches to go with its delicious sweet treats. Memorabilia from Stratton's various movies is all around the shop, which stays open after every evening

Clockwise from top left: sundae at Leopold's Ice Cream; The Rail Pub; Olde Pink House.

performance at the Lucas Theatre around the corner. You can occasionally find Stratton himself behind the counter doling out scoops.

MAP 1: 212 E. Broughton St., 912/234-4442, www.leopoldsicecream.com; Sun.-Thurs. 11am-10pm, Fri.-Sat. 11am-11pm

Wright Square Cafe $

For a more upscale take on sweets, check out the chocolate goodies at Wright Square Cafe. While they do offer tasty wraps and sandwiches, let's not kid ourselves; the draw here is the outrageous assortment of high-quality European-style brownies, cookies, cakes, and other sweet treats.

MAP 1: 21 W. York St., 912/238-1150, www.wrightsquarecafe.com; Mon.-Fri. 7:30am-5:30pm, Sat. 9am-5:30pm

MEXICAN
Tequila's Town $$

The best Mexican spot downtown is Tequila's Town, a relatively new spot that fills an oft-noted void in the Savannah foodie scene. Their menu is comprehensive and authentic, a clear step above the usual gringo-oriented fat-fest. Highlights include the chiles rellenos and the seafood, not to mention the guacamole prepared tableside!

MAP 1: 109 Whitaker St., 912/236-3222, www.tequilastown.com; Mon.-Thurs. 11am-10pm, Fri.-Sat. 11am-11pm, Sun. noon-10pm

SOUTH AFRICAN
Zunzi's $

Look for the long lunchtime line outside the tiny storefront that is Zunzi's. This takeout joint is one of Savannah's favorite lunch spots, the labor of love of South African expatriates Gabby and Johnny DeBeer, who've gotten a lot of national attention for their robust, rich dishes like the exquisite South African-style sausage.

MAP 1: 108 E. York St., 912/443-9555, http://zunzis.com; Mon.-Sat. 11am-6pm

BARS AND PUBS
★ Abe's on Lincoln

No, Lincoln Street in Savannah isn't named for Abraham Lincoln. But dark, fun little Abe's is on Lincoln Street and it's also the oldest bar in town, with a very eclectic clientele.

MAP 1: 17 Lincoln St., 912/349-0525, http://abesonlincoln.com; Mon.-Sat. 4pm-3am

Chive Sea Bar and Lounge

For swank partying on Broughton Street, head to Chive Sea Bar and Lounge, which backs up its tasty menu with a high-end bar in a wonderful, modernist space.

MAP 1: 4 W. Broughton St., 912/233-1748, www.chivelounge.com; Mon.-Fri. 11am-10pm, Sat. noon-midnight, Sun. 5pm-10pm

Circa 1875

On Whitaker Street is a hip hangout with an excellent menu, Circa 1875, where the burgers are as good as the martinis.

MAP 1: 48 Whitaker St., 912/443-1875, www.circa1875.com; Mon.-Thurs. 6pm-10pm, Fri.-Sat. 6pm-11pm

Hang Fire

A much less touristy, more college scene can be found at Hang Fire, a late-night hangout where the real action generally cranks up no earlier than 11 p.m. Their signature cocktail is the wicked, house-blended Scorpion Tea, five bucks and served in Mason jars, and it's highly recommended.

MAP 1: 37 Whitaker St., 912/443-9956; Mon.-Sat. 5pm-3am

★ O'Connell's

The place in town that comes closest to replicating an actual Irish pub environment is tiny, cozy O'Connell's, where they know how to pour a Guinness, feature Magner's cider on tap, and the house specialty is the "pickleback"—a shot of Jameson's followed by a shot of, yes, pickle brine.

MAP 1: 42 Drayton St., 912/231-2298; daily 3pm-3am

Historic District South
Map 2

BARBECUE

Angel's BBQ $

A great local barbecue joint tucked away in a lane is Angel's BBQ, which was featured on the Travel Channel's *Man v. Food*. Get there by finding Independent Presbyterian Church at the northwest corner of Chippewa Square and walking down the lane next to the church. Angel's offers a particularly Memphis-style take on barbecue, but you might try the unique house specialty, the barbecued bologna. Don't miss the peanuts-and-greens on the side. Vegetarians can opt for the Faux-Q, barbecue-flavored tofu.

MAP 2: 21 W. Oglethorpe Lane, 912/495-0902, www.angels-bbq.com; Tues. 11:30am-3pm, Wed.-Sat. 11:30am-6pm

CLASSIC SOUTHERN

★ Mrs. Wilkes' Dining Room $$

The rise of Paula Deen and her Lady & Sons restaurant has only made local epicures even more exuberant in their praise for Mrs. Wilkes' Dining Room, Savannah's original comfort food mecca. President Obama's impromptu lunchtime visit with the mayor in 2010 further raised the restaurant's already legendary profile. The delightful Sema Wilkes herself has passed on, but nothing has changed—not the communal dining room, the cheerful service, the care taken with takeout customers, nor, most of all, the food, a succulent mélange of the South's greatest hits, including the best fried chicken in town, snap beans, black-eyed peas, and collard greens. While each day boasts a different set menu, almost all of the classics are on the table at each meal.

MAP 2: 107 W. Jones St., 912/232-5997, www.mrswilkes.com; Mon.-Fri. 11am-2pm

BARS AND PUBS
The Distillery

The Distillery is located in, yes, a former distillery. As such, the atmosphere isn't exactly dark and romantic—it's sort of one big open room—but the excellent location at the corner of MLK Jr. Boulevard and Liberty Street, the long vintage bar, and the great selection of beers on tap combine to make this a happening spot. The fish 'n' chips are also great.

MAP 2: 416 W. Liberty St., 912/236-1772, www.distillerysavannah.com; Mon.-Sat. 11am-close, Sun. noon-close

Pinkie Masters

Savannah's old-school dive is Pinkie Masters. Named for a legendary local political kingmaker, Pinkie's is a favorite not only with students, artists, and professors but also with lawyers, journalists, and grizzled vets. This is where Jimmy Carter, ironically a teetotaler, stood on the bar in 1978 to drum up support for his presidential run.

MAP 2: 318 Drayton St., 912/238-0447; Mon.-Fri. 4pm-3am, Sat. 5pm-3am

LIVE MUSIC AND KARAOKE
McDonough's

Savannah's undisputed karaoke champion is McDonough's, an advantage compounded by the fact that a lot more goes on here than karaoke. The kitchen at McDonough's is quite capable, and many locals swear you can get the best burger in town here. Despite the sports bar atmosphere, the emphasis is on the karaoke, which ramps up every night at 9:30pm.

MAP 2: 21 E. McDonough St., 912/233-6136, www.mcdonoughsofsavannah.com; Mon.-Sat. 8pm-3am, Sun. 8pm-2am

SoFo District   Map 3

BURGERS
Green Truck Neighborhood Pub ⑤

Cozy Green Truck Neighborhood Pub earns its raves on the basis of delicious regionally sourced meat and produce offered at reasonable prices. (The large selection of craft beers on tap is a big draw too). The marquee item is the signature five-ounce grass-fed burger. A basic burger is $7, but several other, increasingly more dressed-up versions are offered, none over $12.50. Burgers are also offered with chicken or veggie patties. It's a small room that often has a big line, and they don't take reservations, so be prepared.

MAP 3: 2430 Habersham St., 912/234-5885, http://greentruckpub.com; Tues.-Sat. 11am-11pm

COFFEE, TEA, AND SWEETS

Back in the Day Bakery ⑤

Primarily known for its sublime sweet treats, Back in the Day Bakery also offers a small but delightfully tasty (and tasteful) range of lunch soups, salads, and sandwiches (11am-2pm). Lunch highlights include the baguette with camembert, roasted red peppers, and lettuce, as well as the caprese, the classic tomato, mozzarella, and basil trifecta on a perfect ciabatta. But whatever you do, save room for dessert, which runs the full sugar spectrum: red velvet cupcakes, lemon bars, macaroons, carrot cake, and many others.

MAP 3: 2403 Bull St., 912/495-9292, www.backinthedaybakery.com; Tues.-Fri. 9am-5pm, Sat. 8am-3pm

Foxy Loxy ⑤

Foxy Loxy is a classic coffeehouse set within a cozy, multistory Victorian on Bull Street. Added pluses include the authentic Tex-Mex menu, wine and beer offerings, and freshly baked sweet treats.

MAP 3: 1919 Bull St., 912/401-0543, www.foxyloxycafe.com; Mon.-Sat. 7am-11pm

The Sentient Bean ⑤

The coffee at The Sentient Bean is all fair trade and organic, and the all-vegetarian fare is a major upgrade above the usual coffeehouse offerings. But "The Bean" is more than a coffeehouse—it's a community. Probably the best indie film venue in town, the Bean regularly hosts screenings of cutting-edge left-of-center documentary and kitsch films, as well as rotating art exhibits.

MAP 3: 13 E. Park Ave., 912/232-4447, www.sentientbean.com; daily 7:30am-10pm

ITALIAN

★ The Florence ⑤⑤⑤

Regionally famous chef Hugh Acheson is known for several high-profile restaurants in Atlanta and Athens, but The Florence is his first effort in Savannah. Inspired by Italian cuisine but influenced by a more modern and subtle spice palate, the entrées at the Florence are served in cast-iron skillets, reflecting the generally rustic ambience in this tastefully restored former warehouse literally alongside railroad tracks. Try one of the meatball appetizers and the ricotta cavatelli—scrumptious ricotta cheese dumplings with pork shoulder.

MAP 3: 1 W. Victory Dr., 912/234-5522, www.theflorencesavannah.com; Tues.-Wed. and Sun. 5pm-10pm, Thurs.-Sat. 5pm-11pm

RESTAURANTS AND NIGHTLIFE
SOFO DISTRICT

NEW SOUTHERN
Butterhead Greens $

A down-to-earth experience is at the farm-to-table diner Butterhead Greens, a favorite student and hipster hangout known for its sandwiches and fresh vegetarian dishes. Service is on the slow side and the vibe is very casual, but the eats are delicious and worth the wait.

MAP 3: 1813 Bull St., 912/201-1808, www.butterheadgreens.com; Mon.-Thurs. 7am-8pm, Fri.-Sat. 8am-5pm

★ Elizabeth on 37th $$$

Before there was Paula Deen, there was Elizabeth Terry, Savannah's first high-profile chef and founder of this most elegant of all Savannah restaurants, Elizabeth on 37th. Terry has since sold the place to two of her former waiters, Greg and Gary Butch, but this restaurant has continued to maintain her high standards. Executive chef Kelly Yambor uses eclectic, seasonally shifting ingredients that blend the South with the south of France. Along with generally attentive service, it makes for a wonderfully old-school fine-dining experience. Reservations are recommended.

MAP 3: 105 E. 37th St., 912/236-5547; daily 6pm-10pm

BARS AND PUBS
American Legion Bar

The real hipsters hang out in ironic fashion drinking PBRs at the American Legion Bar, located in, yes, an actual American Legion post. While the Legionnaires themselves are a straitlaced patriotic bunch, the patrons of "the Legion," as the bar is colloquially known, tend toward the counterculture. Here is where you'll find Savannah's movers and shakers in the grassroots arts and cultural community.

Fun historical fact: The building housing the Legion was the birthplace of the U.S. 8th Air Force during World War II.

MAP 3: 1108 Bull St., 912/233-9277, http://alpost135.com; Mon.-Sat. 4pm-2am

Victorian District   Map 3

ITALIAN
Leoci's Trattoria $$

The hot Italian place in town is Leoci's Trattoria, named for its skillful and personable young executive chef, Roberto Leoci. His compact but diverse menu offers delights such as a crispy delicious pizza, excellent panini, and a wild-mushroom risotto. The room is small and intimate, and the restaurant is quite popular, so a wait is not unusual.

MAP 3: 606 Abercorn St., 912/335-7027, www.leocis.com; daily 11am-10pm

Top: The Coffee Fox. **Bottom:** Foxy Loxy.

To Market, To Market

Savannah's first and still premier health-food market, **Brighter Day Natural Foods** (1102 Bull St., 912/236-4703, www.brighterdayfoods. com, Mon.-Sat. 9am-7pm, Sun. noon-5:30pm) has been the labor of love of Janie and Peter Brodhead for 30 years, all of them in the same location at the southern tip of Forsyth Park. Boasting organic groceries, regional produce, a sandwich and smoothie bar with a takeout window, and an extensive vitamin, supplement, and herb section, Brighter Day is an oasis in Savannah's sea of chain supermarkets.

Just opened in 2013, **Whole Foods Market** (1815 E. Victory Dr., www.wholefoodsmarket.com, daily 8am-9pm) offers the chain's usual assortment of organic produce, with a very good fresh meat and seafood selection.

Fairly new but already thriving, the **Forsyth Park Farmers Market** (www.forsythfarmersmarket.org, Sat. 9am-1pm) happens in the south end of scenic and wooded Forsyth Park. You'll find very fresh fruit and produce from a variety of fun and friendly re-gional farmers. If you have access to a real kitchen while you're in town, you might be glad to know there's usually a very good selection of organic, sustainably grown meat and poultry products as well—not always a given at farmers markets.

If you need some good-quality groceries downtown—especially after hours—try **Parker's Market** (222 E. Drayton St., 912/231-1001, daily 24 hours). In addition to a pretty wide array of gourmet-style victuals inside, there are gas pumps outside to fuel your vehicle.

A local tradition for 20 years, **Keller's Flea Market** (5901 Ogeechee Rd., I-95 exit 94, 912/927-4848, www.ilovefleas.com, Sat.-Sun. 8am-6pm, free) packs in about 10,000 shoppers over the course of a typical weekend, offering a range of bargains in antiques, home goods, produce, and general kitsch. There are concessions on-site.

There's one 24-hour full-service supermarket in downtown Savannah: **Kroger** (311 E. Gwinnett St., 912/231-2260, daily 24 hours).

Eastside

Map 4

BARBECUE

Sandfly BBQ $

If you're out this way visiting Wormsloe or Skidaway Island State Park, definitely make a point to hit little Sandfly BBQ, unique in town for its dedication to real Memphis-style barbecue. Anything is great—this is the best brisket in the area—but for the best overall experience try the Hog Wild platter.

MAP 4: 8413 Ferguson Ave. 912/356-5463, www.sandflybbq.com; Mon.-Sat. 11am-8pm

CLASSIC SOUTHERN

Desposito's $$

Located just across the Wilmington River from the fishing village of Thunderbolt, Desposito's is a big hit with locals and visitors alike, although it's not in all the guidebooks. The focus here is on crab, shrimp, and oysters,

and lots of them, all caught wild in local waters and served humbly on tables
covered with newspapers.

MAP 4: 187 Old Tybee Rd., 912/897-9963, www.despositosseafood.com; Tues.-Fri.
5pm-10pm, Sat. noon-10pm

Tybee Island   Map 5

BREAKFAST AND BRUNCH
The Breakfast Club $

Considered the best breakfast in the Savannah area for 30 years and count-
ing, The Breakfast Club, with its brisk diner atmosphere and hearty Polish
sausage-filled omelets, is like a little bit of Chicago in the South. Lines start
early for a chance to enjoy such house specialties as Helen's Solidarity, the
Athena Omelet, and the Chicago Bear Burger, but don't worry—you'll inevitably strike up a conversation with someone interesting while you wait.

MAP 5: 1500 Butler Ave., 912/786-5984, http://tybeeisland.com/breakfast-club; daily
6:30am-1pm

CASUAL DINING
The Crab Shack $$

Set in a large former fishing camp overlooking Chimney Creek, The Crab
Shack is a favorite local seafood place and also something of an attrac-
tion in itself. Don't expect gourmet fare or quiet seaside dining; the em-
phasis is on mounds of fresh, tasty seafood, heavy on the raw-bar action.
Getting there is a little tricky: Take U.S. 80 to Tybee, cross the bridge over
Lazaretto Creek, and begin looking for Estill Hammock Road to Chimney
Creek on the right. Take Estill Hammock Road and veer right. After that,
it's hard to miss.

MAP 5: 40 Estill Hammock Rd., 912/786-9857, www.thecrabshack.com; Mon.-Thurs.
11:30am-10pm, Fri.-Sun. 11:30am-11pm

Huc-a-Poo's Bites & Booze $

Known far and wide for its sublime pizza is Huc-a-Poo's Bites & Booze.
Individual slices run about four bucks, can easily feed two, and are quite
delicious. Out of the tourist ruckus and tucked away within a small shopping center just as you arrive onto Tybee proper, Huc-a-Poo's also has a
lively bar scene.

MAP 5: 1213 E. Hwy. 80, 912/786-5900, http://hucapoos.com; daily 11am-11pm

North Beach Grill $$

One of Tybee's most cherished restaurants is on the north end in the shadow
of the Tybee Light Station. Like a little slice of Jamaica near the dunes, the
laid-back North Beach Grill deals in tasty Caribbean fare, such as its signature jerk chicken, fish sandwiches, and, of course, delicious fried plantains,

all overseen by chef-owner "Big George" Spriggs. Frequent live music adds to the island vibe.

MAP 5: 33 Meddin Ave., 912/786-4442; daily 11:30am-10pm

Tybee Island Social Club ⑤⑤

For a leisurely and tasty dinner, try Tybee Island Social Club. Their menu is somewhat unusual for this seafood-heavy island: It's primarily an assortment of gourmet-ish tacos, including fish, duck, and lime- and tequila-marinated steak, all under $10 each. The beer and wine list is accomplished, and the live entertainment is usually very good—which is fortunate, since the service here is on the slow side.

MAP 5: 1311 Butler Ave., 912/472-4044, http://tybeeislandsocialclub.com; Tues. 5pm-9:30pm, Wed.-Fri. noon-9:30pm, Sat.-Sun. 11:30am-10pm

Greater Savannah   Map 6

MIDWAY AND LIBERTY COUNTY
Holton's Seafood ⑤⑤

Many locals eat at least once a week at Holton's Seafood, an unpretentious and fairly typical family-run fried seafood place just off I-95 at the Midway exit.

MAP 6: 13711 E. Oglethorpe Hwy., Midway, 912/884-9151, daily lunch and dinner

Sunbury Crab Company ⑤⑤

A restaurant of note in Midway is the Sunbury Crab Company, providing, you guessed it, great crab cakes in a casual atmosphere on the Midway River. Get here by taking Highway 38 east of Midway and then a left onto Fort Morris Road.

MAP 6: 541 Brigantine Dunmore Rd., Midway, 912/884-8640; Wed.-Fri. dinner, Sat.-Sun. lunch and dinner

RICHMOND HILL
Steamers Restaurant & Raw Bar ⑤⑤

A popular place on U.S.-17 is Steamers Restaurant & Raw Bar, home of some good Lowcountry boil in a relaxed, homey atmosphere.

MAP 6: 4040 U.S. 17, Richmond Hill, 912/756-3979; daily 5pm-10pm

The Upper Crust Pizzeria ⑤

There's no end to the chain food offerings in Richmond Hill, but one of the better restaurants in town is The Upper Crust, a casual American place with great pizza in addition to soups, salads, and hot sandwiches.

MAP 6: 1702 U.S. 17, Richmond Hill, 912/756-6990; Mon.-Sat. lunch and dinner, Sun. dinner

Arts and Culture

Look for ★ to find
recommended arts and culture.

Highlights

★ **Classiest Night on the Town:** The ornate gold-leafed interior of the historic **Lucas Theatre for the Arts** is an echo of the golden age of classic American movie houses, now fully restored and offering a packed schedule of screenings and live performances (page 104).

★ **Most Engaging Concertos:** In a time where symphony orchestras are often in financial straits, the **Savannah Philharmonic** is going strong, offering a vibrant and challenging season of opera, classical music, and choral performances in various venues all around town (page 106).

★ **Sweetest Shopping:** Now a growing regional boutique chain, **Savannah Bee Company** offers an amazing and delicious array of locally sourced honey, honey-themed gifts, and cuisine complements (page 106).

★ **Uniquely Euro Style:** A great mix of hard-to-find genuine French vintage home goods and regional boutique cosmetics, bath items, and jewelry highlight **The Paris Market & Brocante,** which also sports a cool little coffee/tea café with a great window-front view of Broughton Street (page 107).

★ **Authentically Artistic:** A few blocks outside of the historic district in a restored train depot, the black box theater of **Muse Arts Warehouse** is where Savannah's theater and counterculture communities stage the most challenging and enriching performances available in town (page 107).

★ **Most Old School Old Stuff:** Savannah legend **Alex Raskin Antiques** on Monterey Square is the most authentic and delightful antiquing experience in town, in a historic building festooned with world-class wrought ironwork (page 109).

★ **Best Brush With Local Literati:** Savannah takes its literary tradition seriously. **The Book Lady** works overtime to highlight local and regional authors with frequent signings and literary events (page 109).

There are more art galleries per capita in Savannah than in New York City—one gallery for every 2,191 residents, to be exact. Savannah College of Art & Design (SCAD) galleries are in abundance all over town, displaying the handiwork of students, faculty, alumni, and important regional and national artists. Savannah's arts scene also shines a spotlight on theater, classical music, and cool movie houses.

Savannah has also perfected the fine art of shopping, with a focus on antiques and independent home goods stores, with some unique boutiques sprinkled throughout the city. Downtown Savannah's main shopping district is **Broughton Street.** The historic center of downtown shopping has recently seen a major renaissance and is once again home to the most vibrant shopping scene in Savannah, just like it was in the 1940s and 1950s. Several chain stores have made inroads onto the avenue, including Anthropologie, Banana Republic, Marc Jacobs, Urban Outfitters, Free People, and The Gap.

Focusing on upscale art and home goods, the small but chic and friendly **Downtown Design District** runs three blocks on Whitaker Street, a short walk from beautiful Forsyth Park.

Previous: Lucas Theatre for the Arts; 24e Design Co.

Amid the throng of nondescript T-shirt and tchotchke places, Savannah's waterfront area has a handful of quality shopping options.

SHOPS
Antiques
Jere's Antiques

One of the coolest antiques shops in town is Jere's Antiques. It's in a huge historic warehouse on Factor's Walk and has a concentration on fine European pieces.

MAP 1: 9 N. Jefferson St., 912/236-2815, www.jeresantiques.com; Mon.-Sat. 9:30am-5pm

Clothes
Harley-Davidson

You won't be buying a Softail Deluxe at this little retail merchandise store, but you can certainly clothe your inner biker here.

MAP 1: 503 E. River St., 912/231-8000, www.savannahhd.com; Mon.-Sat. 10am-6pm, Sun. noon-6pm

The Mad Hatter

Probably the closest thing to a unique shop on River Street proper is The Mad Hatter, which as the name suggests, offers a wide variety of headwear.

MAP 1: 123 E. River St., 912/232-7566

Gourmet Treats
River Street Sweets

Cater to your sweet tooth—and bring some goodies back with you—at River Street Sweets, where you can witness Southern delicacies like pralines being made as you shop. And of course there are free samples.

MAP 1: 13 E. River St., 912/234-4608, www.riverstreetsweets.com; daily 9am-11pm

Historic District North   Map 1

CINEMA
★ Lucas Theatre for the Arts

The ornate, beautifully restored historic Lucas Theatre for the Arts downtown is a classic Southern movie house. The Savannah Film Society and Savannah College of Art and Design host screenings there throughout the year. Check the website for scheduling.

MAP 1: 32 Abercorn St., 912/525-5040, www.lucastheatre.com; most screenings under $10

Clockwise from top left: The Paris Market & Brocante; Lucas Theatre for the Arts; the Savannah Philharmonic.

MUSIC

★ Savannah Philharmonic

The Savannah Philharmonic is a professional symphony orchestra that performs concertos and sonatas at various venues around town and is always worth checking out.

MAP 1: 216 E. Broughton St. (box office), 912/525-5050, www.savannahphilharmonic.org; Mon.-Fri 10am-5pm

SHOPS

Art Supply

Blick Art Materials

A great art town needs a great art supply store, and in Savannah that would be Blick Art Materials, which has all the equipment and tools for the serious artist—priced to be affordable for students. But casual shoppers will enjoy it as well for its collection of offbeat gift items.

MAP 1: 318 E. Broughton St., 912/234-0456, www.dickblick.com; Mon.-Fri. 8am-8pm, Sat. 10am-7pm, Sun. 11am-6pm

Clothes

Globe Shoe Co.

Perhaps Broughton Street's most beloved old shop is Globe Shoe Co., a Savannah institution and a real throwback to a time of personalized retail service. They have no website and no Facebook page—they're all about simple one-to-one service, like in the old days.

MAP 1: 17 E. Broughton St., 912/232-8161; Mon.-Sat. 10am-6pm

Gourmet Treats

Chocolat by Adam Turoni

Chocolate lovers need to head straight to Chocolat by Adam Turoni, a tiny space with a big taste. Adam's handcrafted, high-quality chocolates are miniature works of art—and delicious ones at that. Be prepared to be overwhelmed.

MAP 1: 323 W. Broughton St., 912/335-2914, www.chocolatat.com; daily 11am-6pm

★ Savannah Bee Company

One of the more unique Savannah retail shops is the Savannah Bee Company, which carries an extensive line of honey-based merchandise, from foot lotion to lip balm. All the honey comes from area hives owned by company founder and owner Ted Dennard. The flagship Broughton location provides plenty of sampling opportunities at the little café area and even boasts a small theater space for instructional films.

MAP 1: 104 W. Broughton St., 912/233-7873, www.savannahbee.com; Mon.-Sat. 10am-7pm, Sun. 11am-5pm

Home Goods

★ The Paris Market & Brocante

While Savannah is an Anglophile's dream, Francophiles will enjoy The Paris Market & Brocante on a beautifully restored corner of Broughton Street. Home and garden goods, bed and bath accoutrements, and a great selection of antique and vintage items combine for a rather opulent shopping experience. Plus there's an old-school Euro café inside where you can enjoy a coffee, tea, or hot chocolate.

MAP 1: 36 W. Broughton St., 912/232-1500, www.theparismarket.com; Mon.-Sat. 10am-6pm, Sun. 11am-4pm

24e Design Co.

Those looking for great home decorating ideas with inspiration from both global and Southern aesthetics, traditional as well as sleekly modern, should check out 24e Design Co., located in an excellently restored 1921 storefront. Be sure to check out the expansive second-floor showroom.

MAP 1: 24 E. Broughton St., 912/233-2274, www.24estyle.com; Mon.-Thurs. 10am-6pm, Fri.-Sat. 10am-7pm, Sun. noon-5pm

Outdoor Outfitters
Half Moon Outfitters

Outdoors lovers should make themselves acquainted with Half Moon Outfitters, a full-service camping, hiking, skiing, and kayaking store. Half Moon is part of a regional chain.

MAP 1: 15 E. Broughton St., 912/201-9313, www.halfmoonoutfitters.com; Mon.-Sat. 10am-7pm, Sun. noon-6pm

Historic District South

Map 2

PERFORMING ARTS
Historic Savannah Theatre

The semipro troupe at the Historic Savannah Theatre performs a busy rotating schedule of oldies revues (a typical title: *Return to the '50s*), but they make up for their lack of originality with the tightness and energy of their talented young cast of regulars.

MAP 2: 222 Bull St., 912/233-7764, www.savannahtheatre.com

★ Muse Arts Warehouse

The multiuse venue Muse Arts Warehouse hosts community-based plays and performances within a well-restored historic train depot, converted into a black box setting. Get there by taking Liberty Street west from downtown, where it turns into Louisville Road.

MAP 2: 703D Louisville Rd., 912/713-1137, www.musesavannah.org

Clockwise from top left: 24e Design Co.; Custard Boutique; Savannah Bee Company.

SHOPS

Antiques

★ Alex Raskin Antiques

Possibly the most beloved antiques store in town is Alex Raskin Antiques in Monterey Square, catty-corner from the Mercer-Williams House Museum, set in the historic Hardee Mansion. A visit is worth it just to explore the home. But the goods Alex lovingly curates are among the best and most tasteful in the region.

MAP 2: 441 Bull St., 912/232-8205, www.alexraskinantiques.com; Mon.-Sat. 10am-5pm

The Corner Door

For a European take on antiques and collectibles, try The Corner Door, set in a unique building and staffed by very friendly and knowledgeable antiques experts.

MAP 2: 417 Whitaker St., 912/238-5869; Tues.-Sat. 10am-5pm

Small Pleasures

Small Pleasures is one of Savannah's hidden gems. They deal in a tasteful range of vintage and estate jewelry, in a suitably small but delightfully appointed space.

MAP 2: 412 Whitaker St., 912/234-0277; Mon.-Sat. 10:30am-5pm

Books

★ The Book Lady

Specializing in "gently used" books in good condition, The Book Lady on Liberty Street features many rare first editions. Enjoy a gourmet coffee while you browse the stacks.

MAP 2: 6 E. Liberty St., 912/233-3628; Mon.-Sat. 10am-5:30pm

E. Shaver Bookseller

The fact that E. Shaver Bookseller is one of the few locally owned independent bookstores left in town should not diminish the fact that it is also one of the best bookstores in town. Esther Shaver and her friendly, well-read staff can help you around the rambling old interior of their ground-level store and its generous stock of regionally themed books. Don't miss the rare map room, with some gems from the 17th and 18th centuries.

MAP 2: 326 Bull St., 912/234-7257; Mon.-Sat. 9am-6pm

V&J Duncan

The beautiful Monterey Square location and a mention in *Midnight in the Garden of Good and Evil* combine to make V&J Duncan a Savannah "must-shop." Owner John Duncan and his wife Virginia ("Ginger" to friends) have collected an impressive array of prints, books, and maps over the past quarter century, and are themselves a treasure trove of information.

MAP 2: 12 E. Taylor St., 912/232-0338, www.vjduncan.com; Mon.-Sat. 10:30am-4:30pm

Clothes

Custard Boutique

Custard Boutique has a cute, cutting-edge selection of women's clothes in a range of styles, and is easily the match of any other women's clothing store in town.

MAP 2: 414 Whitaker St., 912/232-4733; Mon.-Sat. 10:30am-6pm, Sun. noon-5pm

Gifts and Souvenirs

Folklorico

Set in a stunningly restored multilevel Victorian within a block of Forsyth Park, the globally conscious Folklorico brings in a fascinating and diverse collection of sustainably made jewelry, gifts, and home goods from around the world, focusing on Central and South America and Asia.

MAP 2: 440 Bull St., 912/232-9300; Mon.-Sat. 10am-5pm, Sun. 1pm-5pm

Saints and Shamrocks

In this town so enamored of all things Irish, a great little locally owned shop is Saints and Shamrocks, across the intersection from The Book Lady. Pick up your St. Patrick's-themed gear and gifts to celebrate Savannah's highest holiday along with high-quality Irish imports.

MAP 2: 309 Bull St., 912/233-8858, www.saintsandshamrocks.org; Mon.-Sat. 9:30am-5:30pm, Sun. 11am-4pm

shopSCAD

Not only a valuable outlet for SCAD students and faculty to sell their artistic wares, shopSCAD is also one of Savannah's most unique boutiques. You never really know what you'll find, but whatever it is, it will be one-of-a-kind. The jewelry in particular is always cutting edge in design and high quality in craftsmanship. The designer T-shirts are a hoot too.

MAP 2: 340 Bull St., 912/525-5180, www.shopscadonline.com; Mon.-Wed. 9am-5:30pm, Thurs.-Fri. 9am-8pm, Sat. 10am-8pm, Sun. noon-5pm

Home Goods

Madame Chrysanthemum

Madame Chrysanthemum, set in a charming, cozy corner spot, deals in fun home items and gift ideas with a hip and enjoyable Savannah style.

MAP 2: 101 W. Taylor St., 912/238-3355; Mon.-Sat. 10am-5pm

One Fish Two Fish

An eclectic European-style home goods store is One Fish Two Fish. Owner Jennifer Beaufait Grayson, a St. Simons Island native, came to town a decade ago to set up shop in this delightfully restored old dairy building.

MAP 2: 401 Whitaker St., 912/484-4600; Mon.-Sat. 10am-5:30pm, Sun. noon-5pm

PERFORMING ARTS

Armstrong State University Masquers

There are few things to recommend Savannah's south side to the visitor, but one of them is the Armstrong State University Masquers, the second-oldest college theater group in the country (only Harvard's Hasty Pudding Theatricals is older). Now celebrating 75 years in existence, the Masquers boast a newly restored performance space at the Jenkins Theatre, and might surprise you with the high quality of their performances despite being a student program. Parking is never a problem.

MAP 4: 11935 Abercorn St., 912/927-5381, www.finearts.armstrong.edu

SHOPS

Malls

Oglethorpe Mall

The mall closest to downtown—though not that close, at about 10 miles south—is Oglethorpe Mall. Its anchor stores are Sears, Belk, J. C. Penney, and Macy's.

MAP 4: 7804 Abercorn St., 912/354-7038, www.oglethorpemall.com; Mon.-Sat. 10am-9pm, Sun. noon-6pm

A City of Art

For art lovers, the no-brainer package experience for the visitor is the combo of the **Telfair Academy of Arts and Sciences** (121 Barnard St., 912/790-8800, www.telfair.org) and the **Jepson Center for the Arts** (207 W. York St., 912/790-8800, www.telfair.org). These two arms of the Telfair Museums run the gamut of art, from old-school portraiture to cutting-edge contemporary art.

SCAD galleries (912/525-5225, www.scad.edu) are abundant. Outposts with consistently impressive exhibits are the **Gutstein Gallery** (201 E. Broughton St.) and **Pinnacle Gallery** (320 E. Liberty St.). The college also runs its own museum, the **SCAD Museum of Art** (227 MLK Jr. Blvd., 912/525-7191, www.scad.edu), which recently doubled in size to accommodate a new wing devoted to the Walter O. Evans Collection of African American Art.

The small and avant-garde **ArtRise Savannah** (2427 DeSoto Ave., 912/335-8204, www.artrisesavannah. org) helps coordinate "Art March" gallery crawls in the SoFo (South of Forsyth) district the first Friday of the month. **Non-Fiction Gallery** (1522 Bull St., 912/662-5152), also in SoFo, exhibits work by many of Savannah's up-and-coming talents. **Indigo Sky Community Gallery** (915 Waters Ave., 912/233-7659), a bit outside of downtown, hosts adventurous painting and sculpture shows, often with a performance element.

Sports and Activities

S avannah offers copious outdoor options that take full advantage of the city's temperate climate and the natural beauty of its marshy environment next to the Atlantic Ocean.

Savannah is a saltwater angler's paradise, rich in trout, flounder, and king and Spanish mackerel. Offshore there's a fair amount of deep-sea action, including large grouper, white and blue marlin, wahoo, snapper, sea bass, and big amberjack near some of the many offshore wrecks.

Diving is a challenge off the Georgia coast because of the silty nature of the water and its mercurial currents. Though not particularly friendly to the novice, plenty of great offshore opportunities abound around the many artificial reefs created by the Georgia Department of Natural Resources (www.coastalgadnr.org).

Other than some action around the pier, the surfing is poor on Tybee Island, with its broad shelf, tepid wave action, and lethal rip currents. But board surfers and kiteboarders have a lot of fun on the south end of Tybee beginning at about 17th Street. The craziest surf is past the rock jetty, but be advised that the rip currents are especially treacherous there.

Hiking in Savannah and the Lowcountry is largely a 2-D experience given the flatness of the terrain, but there are plenty of good nature trails from which to observe the area's rich flora and fauna up close, in beautiful settings.

The best guided water tour in the area is Capt. Rene Heidt's **Sundial Nature Tours** (912/786-9470, www.sundialcharters.com). Rene is an expert in local marine life and offers a variety of tours, including dolphin watches, fossil hunts, and trips to various barrier islands. Rates start at about $160 for two people.

Previous: surfer at Tybee Island Beach; Savannah Fly Fishing Charters.

Look for ★ to find
recommended activities.

Highlights

★ **Best Birding:** Sitting smack dab on the coastal migratory flyway, **Skidaway Island State Park** offers a wealth of bird-watching in its expansive, wooded trail area, in addition to its marshfront (page 119).

★ **Closest Brush with The Babe:** Historic Grayson Stadium, home ballpark of the minor league baseball team **Savannah Sand Gnats,** in its day hosted such greats as Babe Ruth, Mickey Mantle, Jackie Robinson, and Derek Jeter (page 122).

★ **Most Old-School Transportation:** For a brief period of time in the 1800s, the **Savannah-Ogeechee River Canal** did the job the railroad would later do, transporting goods inland to the Savannah River harbor. Today you can walk the old locks and enjoy scenic views of the Ogeechee River (page 128).

★ **Best Water that Looks Like Iced Tea:** Winding **Ebenezer Creek** outside of Savannah in Effingham County is a great place to take a scenic kayak or canoe run, its blackwater naturally stained dark from tree tannins (page 128).

★ **Most Expertly Repurposed Old Rice Plantation:** Now impounded for ecological purposes, old rice fields and paddies help form a thriving waterfowl and marsh habitat at the **Savannah National Wildlife Refuge,** a wonderful destination for kayakers (page 129).

Bicycling is fun all around the Savannah area. Plenty of folks ride their
bikes downtown, and it is particularly enriching and fun to pedal around
the squares. Legally, however, you're not allowed to ride through the
squares; you're supposed to stay on the street around them. And always
yield to traffic already within the square as you enter. Other good cycling
opportunities are at Fort Pulaski and Tybee Island.

Savannah was the first city in Georgia to unveil a public **bike-share
program** (http://catchacat.org, $2 per half hour, daily 5:30am-11pm),
and you can now be the beneficiary. Head to Ellis Square adjacent to City
Market; the rack is on the south side of the square.

Waterfront

Map 1

TOURS
Water Tours
Savannah Belles

If you've just *got* to get out on the river for a short time, by far the best bargain is to take one of the four little Savannah Belles water ferries, named
after famous women in Savannah history, which shuttle passengers from
River Street to Hutchinson Island and back every 15-20 minutes. Pick one
up on River Street in front of City Hall or at the Waving Girl landing a
few blocks east.

MAP 1: River St. at City Hall and Waving Girl Landing, www.catchacat.org; daily
7:30am-10:30pm; free

Savannah Riverboat Cruises

The heavy industrial buildup on the Savannah River means that the main
river tours, all departing from the docks in front of the Hyatt Regency
Savannah, tend to be disappointing in their unrelenting views of cranes,
docks, storage tanks, and smokestacks. Still, for those into that kind of
thing, narrated trips up and down the river on the *Georgia Queen* and the
Savannah River Queen are offered by Savannah Riverboat Cruises.

MAP 1: 9 E. River St., 800/786-6404, www.savannahriverboat.com; $21.95 adults, $12.95
ages 4-12

Horse and Carriage

Ah, yes—what could be more romantic and more traditional than enjoying downtown Savannah the way it was originally intended to be traveled, by horse-drawn carriage? Indeed, this is one of the most fun ways to see the city, for couples as well as for those with horse-enamored children. Yes, the horses sometimes look tired, but the tour operators generally take great care to keep the horses hydrated and out of the worst of the heat. There are three main purveyors of equine tourism in town: **Carriage Tours** **of Savannah** (912/236-6756, www.carriagetoursofsavannah.com), **Historic Savannah Carriage Tours** (888/837-1011, www.savannahcarriage.com), and **Plantation Carriage Company** (912/201-0001). The length of the basic tour and the price are about the same for all—45-60 minutes, about $20 adults and $10 children. All offer specialty tours as well, from ghost tours to evening romantic rides with champagne. Embarkation points vary; check company websites for pickup points. Some will pick you up at your hotel.

Historic District North   Map 1

BIKING

Savannah Bike Tours

To see downtown Savannah by bicycle—quite a refreshing experience—try Savannah Bike Tours for a two-hour trip through all 19 squares and Forsyth Park with your "rolling concierge." Pedaling around the squares and stopping to explore certain sights is a unique pleasure. Tours leave daily at 9:30am, 12:30pm, and 4pm. Rent bikes from them or ride your own.

MAP 1: 41 Habersham St., 912/704-4043, www.savannahbiketours.com; $15 adults, $10 under age 12

Historic District South   Map 2

SPECTATOR SPORTS

Savannah Derby Devils

For sports action that's a good bit more hard-hitting and comes with a certain hipster kitsch quotient, check out the bruising bouts of the women of the Savannah Derby Devils, who bring the roller derby thunder against other regional teams. They skate downtown at the Savannah Civic Center, and the matches are usually quite well attended.

MAP 2: Savannah Civic Center, 301 W. Oglethorpe Ave., 912/651-6556, www.savannahderby.com

Specialty Tours
Savannah Movie Tour

To learn about Savannah's history of filmmaking and to enjoy the best of local cuisine, try a Savannah Movie Tour, taking you to various film locations in town. The company also offers the Foody Tour ($48) featuring 6-9 local eateries.

MAP 2: Meeting point Savannah Visitors Center, 301 MLK Jr. Blvd., 912/234-3440, www. savannahmovietours.com; $25 adults, $15 children

Sightseeing in Savannah

Savannah's tourist boom has resulted in a similar explosion of well over 50 separate tour services, ranging from simple guided trolley journeys to horse-drawn carriage rides to specialty tours to ecotourism adventures. Fair warning: Although local tour guides technically must pass a competency test demonstrating their knowledge of Savannah history, in practice whatever they learned is often thrown out the window in favor of whatever sounds good to them at the time. I've heard the craziest, most untrue things said from passing trolleys and horse carriages. By all means go on a tour, but do so with the knowledge that some of what you're likely to hear won't be true at all.

Storyteller and author Ted Eldridge leads **A Walk Through Savannah Tours** (meeting point at various locations in the historic district, 912/921-4455, www.awalkthroughsavannah. bravehost.com; $15 adults, $5 6-12, free under age 6) and offers all kinds of specialty walking tours, such as a garden tour, a ghost tour, a historic churches tour, and of course, a *Midnight in the Garden of Good and Evil* tour.

For a unique tour experience, take a seat on the **Savannah Slow Ride** (various meeting points, 912/414-5634, www.savannahslowride.com, $25), a sort of combination bar, bicycle, and carriage ride. You get on with a group and everyone helps pedal around the squares on about a two-hour ride at five miles per hour or less. You can even bring your to-go cup with you. Pickup points depend on the tour; call for details.

The copious ghost tours, offered by all the companies, can be fun for the casual visitor who wants entertainment rather than actual history. Students of the paranormal are likely to be disappointed by the cartoonish, Halloween aspect of some of the tours. A standout in the ghost field is **Hearse Ghost Tours** (various pick-up locations, 912/695-1578, www.hearseghosttours.com, $15), a unique company that also operates tours in New Orleans and St. Augustine, Florida. Up to eight guests at a time ride around in the open top of a converted hearse, painted all black, of course, and get a 90-minute, suitably over-the-top narration from the driver-guide. It's still pretty cheesy, but a hip kind of cheesy.

SPORTS AND ACTIVITIES

HISTORIC DISTRICT SOUTH

Trolley Tours

The vehicle of choice for the bulk of the masses visiting Savannah, trolleys allow you to sit back and enjoy the views in reasonable comfort. As in other cities, the guides provide commentary while attempting, with various degrees of success, to navigate the cramped downtown traffic environment. The main trolley companies in town are **Old Savannah Tours** (912/234-8128, www.old-savannahtours.com, basic on-off tour $27 adults, $12 children), **Old Town Trolley Tours** (800/213-2474, www.trolleytours.com, basic on-off tour $27.99 adults, $10 children), and **Oglethorpe Trolley Tours** (912/233-8380, www.oglethorpe-tours.com, basic on-off tour $22.50 adults, $10 children). All embark from the Savannah Visitors Center on Martin Luther King Jr. Boulevard about every 20-30 minutes on the same schedule, daily 9am-4:30pm.

Frankly there's not much difference between them, as they all offer a very similar range of services for similar prices, with most offering pickup at your downtown hotel. While the common "on-off privileges" allow trolley riders to disembark for a while and pick up another of the same company's trolleys at marked stops, be aware there's no guarantee the next trolley—or the one after that—will have enough room to take you on board.

Savannah's Uncommon Walk

An offbeat tour option is Savannah's Uncommon Walk, a two-hour exploration of little-known Savannah attractions leaving at 9:30am and 1:30pm daily from Chippewa Square.

MAP 2: Chippewa Square, W. Perry St. and Bull St., 912/358-0700, www.sellersandhiggins.com; $20

Savannah Tours by Foot

Longtime tour guide and raconteur Greg Proffit and his staff offer fun walking "pub crawls," Savannah Tours by Foot, wherein the point is to meet your guide at some local tavern, ramble around, learn a little bit, and imbibe a lot, though not necessarily in that order. The adult tour is the "Creepy Crawl" ($18) whereas the tour suitable for kids and Girl Scouts is the "Creepy Stroll" ($10 adults, $5 Girl Scouts). You may not want to believe everything you hear, but you're sure to have a lot of fun. The tours book up early, so make arrangements in advance.

MAP 2: 527 E. Gordon St., 912/238-3843, www.savannahtours.com; $10-18 adults

Sixth Sense Savannah Ghost Tour

For those who take their paranormal activity *very* seriously, there's Shannon Scott's Sixth Sense Savannah Ghost Tour, an uncensored, straightforward look at Savannah's poltergeist population.

MAP 2: Meeting point Clary's Cafe, 404 Abercorn St., 866/666-3323, www.sixthsensesavannah.com; $20, midnight tour $38.50

TOURS
Ecotours
Wilderness Southeast

The 35-year-old nonprofit Wilderness Southeast offers guided trips, including paddles to historic Mulberry Grove, birding trips, and beach explorations. Regularly scheduled "Walks on the Wild Side" run the gamut from "Alligators to Anhingas" to the "Urban Forest" to "Explore the Night Sky" to the "Blackwater River Float." Custom tours are also available.

MAP 3: 3025 Bull St., 912/897-5108, www.naturesavannah.org; $10-35

Victorian District   Map 3

TENNIS
Forsyth Park

The closest public courts to the downtown area are at the south end of Forsyth Park, which features four free lighted courts. They are first-come, first-served and unstaffed, and as you might expect, they get serious use.

MAP 3: Bordered by Drayton St., Gaston St., Whitaker St., and Park Ave., 912/351-3850; daily 8am-dusk; free

Southside   Map 4

BIRD-WATCHING
★ Skidaway Island State Park

Skidaway Island State Park is part of the **Colonial Coast Birding Trail** (http://georgiawildlife.dnr.state.ga.us). Spring and fall bring a lot of the usual warbler action, while spring and summer feature nesting ospreys and painted buntings, always a delight.

MAP 4: 52 Diamond Causeway, 912/598-2300, www.gastateparks.org; daily 7am-10pm; parking $5 per vehicle per day

FISHING
Miss Judy Charters

Perhaps the best-known local angler is Captain Judy Helmey, aka "Miss Judy." In addition to her frequent and entertaining newspaper columns, she runs a variety of well-regarded charters out of Miss Judy Charters. Four-hour trips start at $500. To get there, go west on U.S. 80, take a right onto Bryan Woods Road, a left onto Johnny Mercer Boulevard, a right onto Wilmington Island Way, and a right down the dirt lane at her sign.

MAP 4: 124 Palmetto Dr., 912/897-2478, www.missjudycharters.com; from $500

SPORTS AND ACTIVITIES

SOUTHSIDE

A great inshore charter service is offered by Telecaster Charters, with 4-, 6-, and 8-hour inshore trips priced from $300 for two anglers.

MAP 4: 2812 River Dr., Thunderbolt, 912/308-4622, www.telecastercharters.com; from $300

GOLF
Wilmington Island Club
The Wilmington Island Club has arguably the quickest greens in town and is unarguably the most beautiful local course, set close by the Wilmington River amid lots of mature pines and live oaks.

MAP 4: 501 Wilmington Island Rd., 912/897-1612; greens fees about $70

HIKING
Skidaway Island State Park
My favorite trails are at Skidaway Island State Park. The three-mile Big Ferry Trail is the best overall experience, taking you out to a wooden viewing tower from which you can see the vast expanse of the Skidaway Narrows. A detour takes you past a Native American shell midden, Confederate earthworks, and even a rusty old still—a nod to Skidaway Island's former notoriety as a bootlegger's sanctuary. The shorter but still fun Sandpiper Trail is wheelchair-accessible.

MAP 4: 52 Diamond Causeway, 912/598-2300, www.gastateparks.org; daily 7am-10pm; parking $5 per vehicle per day

KAYAKING AND CANOEING
Moon River Kayak Tours
Run by Captain Mike Neal, an experienced local boatman and conservationist, Moon River Kayak Tours focuses on 2.5-hour tours of the Skidaway Narrows and scenic Moon River, departing from the public boat ramp at the foot of the bridge to Skidaway Island. No kayaking experience is required.

MAP 4: 45 Diamond Causeway, 912/898-1800, www.moonriverkayak.com; $50

Skidaway Narrows
A pleasant kayaking route is the Skidaway Narrows. Begin this paddle at the public boat ramp, which you find by taking Waters Avenue all the way until it turns to Whitefield Avenue and then Diamond Causeway. Continue all the way over the Moon River to a drawbridge; park at the foot of the bridge. Once in the water, paddle northeast. Look for the osprey nests on top of the navigational markers in the narrows as you approach Skidaway Island State Park. Continuing on, you'll find scenic Isle of Hope high on a bluff to your left, with nearly guaranteed dolphin sightings around marker 62.

MAP 4: Intersection of Moon River and Diamond Causeway

Clockwise from top left: carriage horses on Market Street; ferry between downtown and Hutchinson Island; Telecaster Charters boat.

TENNIS
Bacon Park

On the south side, Bacon Park has 16 lighted hard courts. It's the city's best tennis facility, but it's the farthest from downtown. It's the most heavily trafficked of the city's courts, and a destination for local expert players.

MAP 4: 6262 Skidaway Rd., 912/351-3850; daily 8am-dusk; $3

Eastside

Map 4

FISHING
Savannah Fly Fishing Charters

Shallow-water fly-fishers might want to contact Savannah Fly Fishing Charters. Captain Scott Wagner takes half- and full-day charters both day and night from Savannah all the way down to St. Simons Island. Half-day rate starts at $300. Book early.

MAP 4: 56 Sassafras Trail, 912/308-3700, www.savannahfly.com; from $300

KAYAKING AND CANOEING
Savannah Canoe & Kayak

. The most highly regarded local canoe and kayak tour operator and rental house is Savannah Canoe & Kayak, run by the husband-wife team of Nigel and Kristin Law. They offer several kayak trips, including a short jaunt to Little Tybee Island.

MAP 4: 414 Bonaventure Rd., 912/341-9502, www.savannahcanoeandkayak.com; half-day tour $55

SPECTATOR SPORTS
★ Savannah Sand Gnats

Topping the list of local spectator sports is the Savannah Sand Gnats baseball franchise, currently a Single-A affiliate of the New York Mets. The attraction here is not the level of play but the venue itself: Historic Grayson Stadium in Daffin Park in the city's midtown area, which has hosted such greats as Babe Ruth, Jackie Robinson, and Mickey Mantle over the years. There's not a bad seat in the house, so your best bet by far is to just buy a general admission ticket. The games never sell out, so there's no need to stress. Entertainment runs the usual gamut of minor league shenanigans, including frequent fireworks displays after the games.

MAP 4: Historic Grayson Stadium, 1401 E. Victory Dr., 912/351-9150, www.sandgnats.com; Apr.-Sept.; $8 general admission

Baseball Greats

Long before gaining notoriety for his role on the infamous Chicago "Black Sox" team that threw the 1919 World Series, baseball legend Shoeless Joe Jackson was a stalwart on the South Atlantic or "Sally" League circuit. Playing for the Savannah Indians in 1909, Joe played predominantly at Bolton Street Park, off what's now Henry Street.

Curt Flood, who played for the Savannah Redlegs in 1957, refused to report to the Phillies after the Cardinals traded him in 1969. Flood sued Major League Baseball the next year, saying the so-called "reserve clause" allowing the trade violated antitrust laws. While Flood would lose the lawsuit in the U.S. Supreme Court, the narrowly worded decision left the way open for collective bargaining and today's massive free agent salaries.

The Savannah Braves, a double-A team, began a successful run in 1971, including a 12-game-winning season by pitcher and controversial *Ball Four* writer Jim Bouton, followed in 1984 by the Savannah Cardinals.

The current single-A team, the Savannah Sand Gnats, rarely conjures mental images of Shoeless Joe or the Babe, but the Sand Gnats' most famous face so far has been Cy Young Award-winning pitcher Éric Gagné, who pitched his very first professional game with the local club.

TENNIS
Daffin Park
South of Highway 80 is Daffin Park, where there are six clay courts and three lighted hard courts. This is mostly a locals-frequented spot, but the park is nice to visit.

MAP 4: 1001 E. Victory Dr., 912/351-3850; daily 8am-dusk; $3

Tybee Island
Map 5

BIKING
Fort Pulaski National Monument
Many locals like to load up their bikes and go to Fort Pulaski. From the grounds you can ride all over scenic and historic Cockspur Island.

MAP 5: 912/786-5787, www.nps.gov; fort daily 8:30am-5:15pm, visitors center daily 9am-5pm; $2 pp, free under age 16

McQueen's Island Trail
Outside of town, much biking activity centers on Tybee Island, with the six-mile McQueen's Island Trail being a popular and simple ride. The trail started as a rail route for Central of Georgia Railway and was converted to a multiuse trail in the 1990s. Over half of the trail was closed in late 2013 for safety reasons; water has eroded portions of the trail over the years. In 2014, erosion repair work began.

MAP 5: U.S. 80 near Fort Pulaski National Monument

Clockwise from top left: golf course in Savannah; sunset on a Savannah beach; Savannah Fly Fishing Charters guide.

BIRD-WATCHING

North Beach

An excellent birding spot on the **Colonial Coast Birding Trail** (http://georgiawildlife.dnr.state.ga.us) is Tybee Island's North Beach area. You'll see a wide variety of shorebirds and gulls, as well as piping plover, northern gannets, and purple sandpipers (winter).

MAP 5: Savannah River to 1st St., Tybee Island; parking $5 per day, meters available

FISHING

Amick's Deep Sea Fishing

A highly regarded local fishing charter is Tybee-based Amick's Deep Sea Fishing. Captain Steve Amick and crew run offshore charters daily starting at $120 per person. Go east on U.S. 80 and turn right just past the Lazaretto Creek Bridge.

MAP 5: 1 Old Hwy. 80, Tybee Island, 912/897-6759, www.amicksdeepseafishing.com; from $120 pp

KAYAKING AND CANOEING

Lazaretto Creek

Lazaretto Creek, on the western edge of the island, is a great place to explore Tybee and environs. From here you can meander several miles through the marsh, or go the other way and actually head into a channel of the Savannah River. If you're into ocean kayaking, you can even head into the Atlantic from here. Put in at the Lazaretto Creek landing, at the foot of the Lazaretto Creek bridge on the south side of U.S. 80 on the way to Tybee Island. This is a peaceful, pretty paddle for novice and experienced kayakers alike. You can also put in at the nearby **Tybee Marina** (4 Old Tybee Rd., 912/786-5554, www.tybeeislandmarina.com), also on Lazaretto Creek.

MAP 5: Intersection of U.S. 80 and Tybee Island

Little Tybee Island

Maybe the single best kayak or canoe adventure in Savannah is the run across the Back River from Tybee to Little Tybee Island, an undeveloped state heritage site that despite its name is actually twice as big as Tybee, albeit mostly marsh. Many kayakers opt to camp on the island. You can even follow the shoreline out into the Atlantic, but be aware that wave action can get intense offshore. Begin the paddle at the public boat ramp on the Back River. To get here, take Butler Avenue all the way to 18th Street and take a right, then another quick right onto Chatham Avenue. The parking lot for the landing is a short way up Chatham Avenue on your left. Warning: Do not attempt to swim to Little Tybee, no matter how strong a swimmer you think you are—the currents are exceptionally vicious. Also, do not be tempted to walk far out onto the Back River beach at low tide. The tide comes in very quickly and often strands people on the sandbar.

MAP 5: South of Tybee Island

North Island Surf and Kayak

To rent an ocean-worthy kayak on Lazaretto Creek, stop by North Island Surf and Kayak, located at Tybee Marina. Reservations are recommended.

MAP 5: 1C Old Hwy. 80, 912/786-4000, www.northislandkayak.com; Mon.-Fri. 10am-5pm, Sat.-Sun. 9am-6pm; $45

Sea Kayak Georgia

On U.S. 80 just as you get on Tybee is a quality tour service, Sea Kayak Georgia. Run by locals Marsha Henson and Ronnie Kemp, Sea Kayak offers many different types of kayak tours.

MAP 5: 1102 U.S. 80, 888/529-2542, www.seakayakgeorgia.com; half-day tour $55

SURFING AND BOARDING
High Tides Surf Shop

The best—and pretty much only—surf shop in town is High Tides Surf Shop. You can get a good local surf report and forecasts at their website.

MAP 5: 405 U.S. 80, 912/786-6556, www.hightidesurfshop.com

TENNIS
Tybee Island Memorial Park

If you get the tennis jones on Tybee, there are two free hard courts at Tybee Island Memorial Park that are lighted.

MAP 5: Butler Ave. and 4th St., 912/786-4573, www.cityoftybee.org; daily 8am-dusk; free

Greater Savannah Map 6

BIRD-WATCHING
Laurel Hill Wildlife Drive

Wading birds in particular are in wide abundance at the **Savannah National Wildlife Refuge.** The views are excellent all along the Laurel Hill Wildlife Drive, which takes you through the heart of the old paddy fields that once crisscrossed the entire area. To get here, take U.S. 17 north over the big Talmadge Bridge, over the Savannah River into South Carolina. Turn left on Highway 170 south and look for the entrance to Laurel Hill Wildlife Drive on the left.

MAP 6: Two miles east of Port Wentworth, 843/784-2468, www.fws.gov/savannah; daily dawn-dusk; free

LeConte-Woodmanston Botanical Garden

LeConte-Woodmanston Botanical Garden is a bit hard to find. Part of William Bartram's historic nature trail, this was the home of Dr. Louis LeConte, renowned 19th-century botanist, and his sons John LeConte, first president of the University of California, Berkeley, and Joseph LeConte, who founded the Sierra Club with John Muir. The highlight here is the rare tidally influenced freshwater wetland, featuring the blackwater Bulltown Swamp. This visit is best done in a four-wheel-drive vehicle. The garden is about 40 minutes from Savannah. Take I-95 south to exit 76. Turn right on U.S. 84, then left on U.S. 17. Turn right on Barrington Ferry Road until the pavement ends at Sandy Run Road. Continue until you see the historical markers. Turn left onto the dirt road, then drive another mile.

MAP 6: 4918 Barrington Ferry Rd., Riceboro, 912/884-6500, www.leconte-woodmanston.org; daily 9am-5pm; $5

Youmans Pond

Youmans Pond is a prime stop for migratory fowl. Its main claim to fame is that it was visited in 1773 by the great naturalist William Bartram on one of his treks across the Southeast. Youmans Pond has changed little since then, with its tree-studded pond and oodles of owls, ospreys, herons, egrets, wood storks, and many more. Youmans Pond is about 40 minutes from Savannah. To get here, take I-95 south to exit 76. Take a left onto Highway 38 (Islands Hwy.) and then a left onto Camp Viking Road. About one mile ahead, take a right onto Lake Pamona Drive. About 0.75 mile ahead, look for the pond on the right. It's unmarked, but there's a wooden boardwalk.

MAP 6: Lake Pamona Dr., Midway; daily; free

DIVING

Gray's Reef National Marine Sanctuary

Certainly no underwater adventure in the area would be complete without a dive at Gray's Reef National Marine Sanctuary. Administered by the National Oceanic and Atmospheric Administration, this fully protected marine sanctuary 17 miles offshore is in deep enough water to provide divers good visibility of its live-bottom habitat. Not a classic living coral reef but rather one built by sedimentary deposits, Gray's Reef provides a look at a truly unique ecosystem. Some key dive charter operators that can take you to Gray's Reef are Captain Walter Rhame's **Mako Dive Charter** (600 Priest Landing Dr., 912/604-6256), which leaves from the Landings Harbor Marina; **Georgia Offshore** (1191 Lake Dr., Midway, 912/658-3884); and **Fantasia Scuba** (3 E. Montgomery Cross Rd., 912/921-8933).

The best all-around dive shop in town is **Diving Locker and Ski Chalet** (74 W. Montgomery Cross Rd., 912/927-6603, www.divinglockerskichalet. com, Mon.-Fri. 10am-6pm, Sat. 10am-5pm) on the south side.

MAP 6: 16 miles east of Sapelo Island, 912/598-2345, www.graysreef.noaa.gov

GOLF

Club at Savannah Harbor

A relatively new course but not one you'd call a bargain is the Club at Savannah Harbor, across the Savannah River on Hutchinson Island, adjacent to the Westin Savannah Harbor Resort. Home to the Liberty Mutual Legends of Golf Tournament each spring, the club's tee times are 7:30am-3pm.

MAP 6: 2 Resort Dr., 912/201-2007, www.theclubatsavannahharbor.com; greens fees $135, $70 for twilight

There are a couple of strong public courses in Savannah that are also very good bargains. Chief among these has to be the Henderson Golf Club, an excellent municipal course with very reasonable greens fees that include a half cart.

MAP 6: 1 Al Henderson Blvd., 912/920-4653, www.hendersongolfclub.com; greens fees Mon.-Fri. $28, Sat.-Sun. $33

HIKING

★ Savannah-Ogeechee River Canal

A relic of the pre-railroad days, the Savannah-Ogeechee River Canal is a 17-mile barge route joining the two rivers. Finished in 1830, it saw three decades of prosperous trade in cotton, rice, bricks, guano, naval stores, and food crops before the coming of the railroads finished it off. You can walk some of its length today near the Ogeechee River terminus, admiring the impressive engineering of its multiple locks used to stabilize the water level. Back in the day, the canal would continue through four lift locks as it traversed 16 miles before reaching the Savannah River. Naturalists will enjoy the built-in nature trail that walking along the canal provides. Be sure to check out the unique sand hills on a nearby trail, a vestige of a bygone geological era when this area was an offshore sandbar. Kids will enjoy the impromptu menagerie of gopher turtles near the site's entrance. Do bring mosquito repellent, although often there's a community spray can at the front door of the little visitors center/museum where you pay your fee.

To get here, get on I-95 south, take exit 94, and go west on Fort Argyle Road (Hwy. 204). The canal is a little over two miles from the exit.

MAP 6: 681 Ft. Argyle Rd., 912/748-8068, www.savannahogeecheecanal.com; daily 9am-5pm; $2 adults, $1 students

KAYAKING AND CANOEING

★ Ebenezer Creek

About 18 miles north of town, but worth the trip for any kayaker, is the beautiful blackwater Ebenezer Creek, near the tiny township of New Ebenezer in Effingham County. Cypress trees lining this nationally designated Wild and Scenic River hang overhead, and wildlife abounds on this peaceful paddle. Look for old wooden sluice gates, vestiges of the area's rice plantation past. To get here, take exit 109 off I-95. Go north on Highway 21 to Rincon, Georgia, then east on Highway 275 (Ebenezer Rd.). Put in at the private Ebenezer Landing.

MAP 6: Intersection of Ebenezer Rd. and Savannah River, New Ebenezer; $5 put-in fee

★ Savannah National Wildlife Refuge

One of the great overall natural experiences in the area is the massive Savannah National Wildlife Refuge. This 30,000-acre reserve—half in Georgia, half in South Carolina—is on the Atlantic Flyway, so you'll be able to see birdlife in abundance, in addition to alligators and manatees. Earthen dikes crisscrossing the refuge are vestigial remnants of paddy fields from plantation days.

You can kayak on your own, but many opt to take guided tours offered by **Wilderness Southeast** (912/897-5108, www.wilderness-southeast.org, two-hour trips from $37.50 for two people), **Sea Kayak Georgia** (888/529-2542, www.seakayakgeorgia.com, $55 pp), and **Swamp Girls Kayak Tours** (843/784-2249, www.swampgirls.com, $45). To get here, take U.S. 17 north over the big Talmadge Bridge, over the Savannah River into South Carolina. Turn left on Highway 170 south and look for the entrance to Laurel Hill Wildlife Drive on the left.

MAP 6: 694 Beech Hill Lane, Hardeeville, SC (visitors center), 843/784-2468, www.fws.gov/refuge/savannah; daily dawn-dusk; free

Hotels

PRICE KEY

$ Less than $100 per night

$$ $100–200 per night

$$$ More than $200 per night

The hotel scene in Savannah, once notorious for its absurdly high price-to-service ratio, has improved a great deal. Perhaps ironically, several stylish new downtown hotels opened concurrently with the recent economic downturn. Their appearance means increased competition, and therefore marginally lower prices, across the board.

The other good news for visitors is that there are now many comparatively new hotels of note directly in the downtown area within walking distance of most sites. Some of them are the more widely recognized chains, and others represent more boutique companies and provide a commensurately higher level of service. The less-good news, especially for locals, is that the ominously rising skyline the newer, bigger hotels represent is a change from the friendly, small-scale historical footprint Savannah is known for in the first place.

Savannah's many historic bed-and-breakfasts are competitive with the hotels on price, and often outperform them on service and ambience. If you don't need a swimming pool and don't mind climbing some stairs every now and then, a B&B is usually your best bet. And the breakfasts, of course, are great too.

The best campground in town is at the well-managed and rarely crowded **Skidaway Island State Park** (52 Diamond Causeway, 912/598-2300, www.gastateparks.org; parking $5 per vehicle per day, tent and RV sites $26-40). There are 88 sites with 30-amp electric hookups. A two-night minimum

---

Previous: Andaz Savannah; The Gastonian.

Look for ★ to find
recommended hotels.

Highlights

★ **Best Rooftop Bar:** The boutique **Bohemian Hotel Savannah Riverfront** isn't only a swank stay on the waterfront: Its Rocks on the Roof bar offers stunning wraparound alfresco views of the river and surrounding downtown area (page 133).

★ **Expertly Repurposed Coca-Cola Bottling Plant:** The historic building housing **The Brice** hasn't bottled soft drinks for decades, but it now hosts this tastefully modernist boutique hotel, complete with an upscale in-house Italian restaurant, Pacci. The Brice is in a comparatively quiet corner of downtown but still well within walking distance of most downtown attractions (page 133).

★ **Most Excellent View of Ellis Square:** A major part of the dramatic reclamation of Ellis Square was the building of the modernist **Andaz Savannah.** From its windows you get a great view of downtown, and the bar/restaurant combo is top-notch (page 134).

★ **Closest B&B to the Squares:** Probably the friendliest downtown B&B, **Foley House Inn** is also among the closest in walking distance to most of the downtown action (page 136).

★ **Classiest B&B near Forsyth Park:** It's not as close to the downtown squares as other places, but **The Gastonian** inn is a world-class stay just steps away from vast, green Forsyth Park and its iconic fountain (page 138).

★ **Best Stay on The Beach:** The lodging scene on Tybee Island is hit or miss. If you can get a room at the delightful and charming **Georgianne Inn,** circa 1910, you'll enjoy a peaceful stay that's still close to the entertainment on the south end of the island (page 139).

stay is required on weekends, and there's a three-night minimum for Memorial Day, Labor Day, Independence Day, and Thanksgiving. Despite these restrictions and the comparatively high rates, the natural beauty of the park and its easy access to some great nature trails make it worth the price.

There's one campground on Tybee Island, the **River's End Campground and RV Park** (915 Polk St., 912/786-5518, www.cityoftybee.org; water-and-electric sites $34, 50-amp full-hookup sites $45) on the north side. Owned by the city of Tybee Island, River's End offers 100 full-service sites plus some primitive tent sites. During Tybee's sometimes-chilly off-season (Nov.-Mar.), you can relax and get warm inside the common River Room. River's End also offers a swimming pool and laundry facilities.

Totally wilderness camping can be done on state-owned Little Tybee, accessible across the Back River by boat only; there are no facilities. The best camping and wilderness resource locally is **Half Moon Outfitters** (15 E. Broughton St., 912/201-9393, www.halfmoonoutfitters.com).

Waterfront

Map 1

★ Bohemian Hotel Savannah Riverfront ⑤⑤⑤

The Bohemian Hotel Savannah Riverfront is gaining a reputation as one of Savannah's premier hotels, both for the casual visitor as well as visiting celebrities. Located between busy River Street and bustling City Market, this isn't the place for peace and quiet, but its combination of boutique-style retro-hip decor and happening rooftop bar scene makes it a great place to go for a fun stay that's as much Manhattan as Savannah. Valet parking is available, which you will come to appreciate.

MAP 1: 102 W. Bay St., 912/721-3800, www.bohemianhotelsavannah.com

★ The Brice ⑤⑤⑤

It's not exactly brand-new—it occupies the space formerly occupied by the well-regarded Mulberry Inn—but The Brice features a complete boutique-style upgrade to this historic building, which formerly housed Savannah's first Coca-Cola bottling plant, on the eastern edge of the historic district. With great service and 145 rooms, most complete with a modernized four-poster bed, The Brice also features **Pacci Italian Kitchen + Bar** (breakfast daily 7am-10am, lunch daily 11am-3pm, brunch 10am-3pm Sat.-Sun., dinner 5pm-10pm Mon.-Thurs. and Sun., 5pm-10:30pm Sat., $15-25), one of the better hotel restaurant/bar combos in town. Executive chef Roberto Leoci also runs the popular Italian restaurant Leoci's Trattoria, also in the historic district.

MAP 1: 601 E. Bay St., 912/238-1200, www.thebricehotel.com

Hyatt Regency Savannah $$$

For years critics have called it an insult to architecture and to history. The modernist Hyatt Regency Savannah is more than three decades old, but a competent renovation means that the Hyatt—a sort of exercise in cubism straddling an entire block of River Street—has avoided the neglect of many older chain properties downtown. Three sides of the hotel offer views of the bustling Savannah waterfront, with its massive ships coming in from all over the world.

MAP 1: 2 E. Bay St., 912/238-1234, www.savannah.hyatt.com

Westin Savannah Harbor Golf Resort and Spa $$

If you require a swank pool, look no further than the Westin Savannah Harbor Golf Resort and Spa, which has a beautiful resort-style pool across the Savannah River from downtown and overlooking the old city. Accessing the hotel—located on a cross-channel island—is a bit of a process, but one made easier by charming river ferries that run regularly and free of charge. The attached golf course is a good one, and packages are available.

MAP 1: 1 Resort Dr., 912/201-2000, www.westinsavannah.com

City Market
Map 1

★ Andaz Savannah $$$

Providing a suitably modernist decor to go with its somewhat atypical architecture for Savannah, the Andaz Savannah overlooks restored Ellis Square and abuts City Market with its shopping, restaurants, and nightlife. A boutique offering from Hyatt, the Andaz's guest rooms and suites feature top-of-the-line linens, extra-large and well-equipped baths, in-room snack bars, and technological features such as MP3 docking stations, free Wi-Fi, and, of course, the ubiquitous flat-screen TV. Customer service is a particular strong suit. Just off the lobby is a very hip lounge-wine bar that attracts locals as well as hotel guests. Keep in mind things can get a little noisy in this area at night on weekends.

MAP 1: 14 Barnard St., 912/233-2116, www.savannah.andaz.hyatt.com

Inn at Ellis Square $$

A Days Inn property, the Inn at Ellis Square is smack-dab between City Market and Bay Street—in other words, the heart of the tourist action. Set in the renovated 1851 Guckenheimer Building, the inn is one of the better-appointed chain hotels in town.

MAP 1: 201 W. Bay St., 912/236-4440, www.innatellissquare.com

Clockwise from top left: Bohemian Hotel Savannah Riverfront; the Inn at Ellis Square; Westin Savannah Harbor Golf Resort and Spa.

Ballastone Inn $$$

Once a bordello, the 1838 mansion that is home to the 16-room Ballastone Inn is one of Savannah's favorite inns. Highlights include an afternoon tea service and one of the better full breakfasts in town. Note that some guest rooms are at what Savannah calls the "garden level," meaning sunken basement-level rooms with what amounts to a worm's-eye view.

MAP 1: 14 E. Oglethorpe Ave., 912/236-1484, www.ballastone.com

The Green Palm Inn $$

Easily the best bed-and-breakfast for the price in Savannah is The Green Palm Inn, a folksy and romantic little Victorian number with some neat gingerbread exterior stylings and four cute guest rooms, each named after a species of palm tree. It's situated on the very easternmost edge of the Savannah Historic District—hence its reasonable rates. Delightful inn-keeper Diane McCray provides a very good and generous breakfast plus a pretty much constant dessert bar.

MAP 1: 546 E. President St., 912/447-8901, www.greenpalminn.com

The Kehoe House $$

One of Savannah's favorite bed-and-breakfasts, The Kehoe House is a great choice for its charm and attention to guests. Its historic location, on quiet little Columbia Square catty-corner to the Isaiah Davenport House, is within walking distance to all the downtown action, but far enough from the bustle to get some peace out on one of the rocking chairs on the veranda.

MAP 1: 123 Habersham St., 912/232-1020, www.kehoehouse.com

Historic District South Map 2

Eliza Thompson House $$

One of Savannah's original historic B&Bs, the Eliza Thompson House is a bit out of the bustle on serene, beautiful Jones Street but still close enough to get involved whenever you feel the urge. You can enjoy the various culinary offerings—breakfast, wine and cheese, nighttime munchies—either in the parlor or on the patio overlooking the house's classic Savannah garden.

MAP 2: 5 W. Jones St., 912/236-3620, www.elizathompsonhouse.com

★ Foley House Inn $$

The circa-1896 Foley House Inn is a four-diamond B&B with some rooms available at a three-diamond price. Its 19 individualized, Victorian-decor guest rooms, in two town houses, range from the smaller Newport over-looking the "grotto courtyard" to the four-poster, bay-windowed Essex room, complete with a fireplace and a whirlpool bath. The location on Chippewa Square is pretty much perfect: well off the busy east-west

Clockwise from top left: The Green Palm Inn; The Kehoe House; The Gastonian.

thoroughfares but in the heart of Savannah's active theater district and within walking distance of anywhere.

MAP 2: 14 W. Hull St., 912/232-6622, www.foleyinn.com

Victorian District

Map 3

Dresser-Palmer House $$

A short walk from Forsyth Park, the Dresser-Palmer House features 15 guest rooms in two wings but still manages to make things feel pretty cozy. Garden-level rooms go for a song (under $200).

MAP 3: 211 E. Gaston St., 912/238-3294, www.dresserpalmerhouse.com

★ The Gastonian $$$

The 1868 Gastonian inn got a major renovation in 2005 and remains a favorite choice for travelers to Savannah, mostly for its 17 sumptuously decorated guest rooms and suites, all with working fireplaces, and the always outstanding full breakfast. They pile on the epicurean delights with teatime, evening nightcaps, and complimentary wine. This is one of the six properties owned by the local firm HLC, which seems to have consistently higher standards than most out-of-town chains.

MAP 3: 220 E. Gaston St., 912/232-2869, www.gastonian.com

Mansion on Forsyth Park $$$

How ironic that a hotel built in a former mortuary would be one of the few Savannah hotels not to have a resident ghost story. But that's the case with Mansion on Forsyth Park, which dominates an entire block alongside Forsyth Park, including partially within the high-Victorian former Fox & Weeks Mortuary building. Its sumptuous guest rooms, equipped with big beds, big baths, and big-screen TVs, scream "boutique hotel," as does the swank little bar and the alfresco patio area.

MAP 3: 700 Drayton St., 912/238-5158, www.mansiononforsythpark.com

Tybee Island

Map 5

Most of the hotels on Tybee Island are what we describe in the South as "rode hard and put away wet," meaning that they see a lot of wear and tear from eager vacationers. They aren't particularly recommended. Also be aware that places on Butler Avenue, even the substandard ones, charge a premium during the high season (Mar.-Oct.).

Stay the Week

For long-term stays on Tybee Island, weekly rentals are the name of the game. Though not cheap—expect to pay roughly $1,000 per week in the summer—they provide a higher level of accommodations than some hotels on the island. For weekly rentals, try **Oceanfront Cottage Rentals** (800/786-5889, www.oceanfrontcottage.com), **Tybee Island Rentals** (912/786-4034, www.tybeeislandrentals.com), or **Tybee Vacation Rentals** (866/359-0297, www.tybeevacationrentals.com).

Atlantis Inn ⑤

For those looking for the offbeat, try the Atlantis Inn. Its reasonably priced, whimsically themed rooms are a hoot, and you're a short walk from the ocean and a very easy jaunt around the corner from busy Tybrisa Street. The downside is no dedicated parking, however.

MAP 5: 20 Silver Ave., 912/786-8558, www.atlantisinntybee.com

★ The Georgianne Inn ⑤⑤

The best B&B-style experience on Tybee can be found at The Georgianne Inn, a short walk off the beach and close to most of the island's action, yet not so close that you can't get away when you want to. The complimentary bikes to use while you're there are a nice plus.

MAP 5: 1312 Butler Ave., 912/786-8710, www.georgianneinn.com

Greater Savannah   Map 6

MIDWAY AND LIBERTY COUNTY
Dunham Farms ⑤⑤

While industry is coming quickly to Liberty County, it's still a small self-contained community with not much in the way of tourist amenities (many would say that is part of its charm). A great choice for a stay is Dunham Farms. The B&B ($165-205) is in the converted 1940s Palmyra Barn, and the self-catered circa-1840 Palmyra Cottage ($300) nearby is right on the river, with plenty of kayaking and hiking opportunities. Your hosts, Laura and Meredith Devendorf, couldn't be more charming or informed about the area, and the breakfasts are absurdly rich and filling in that hearty and deeply comforting Southern tradition.

MAP 6: 5836 Islands Hwy., Midway, 912/880-4500, www.dunhamfarms.com

Hilton Head and the Golden Isles

The Georgia coast just outside Savannah retains a timeless mystique evocative of an era before the coming of Europeans, even before humankind itself. Often called the Golden Isles because of the play of the afternoon sun on the vistas of marsh grass, its other nickname, "the Debatable Land," is a nod to its centuries-long role as a constantly shifting battleground of European powers.

On the map it looks relatively short, but Georgia's coastline is the longest contiguous salt marsh environment in the world—a third of the country's remaining salt marsh. Abundant with wildlife, vibrant with exotic, earthy aromas, constantly refreshed by a steady, salty sea breeze, it's a place with no real match anywhere else. Filled with rich sediments from rivers upstream and replenished with nutrients from the twice-daily ocean tide, Georgia's marshes from the mainland to the barrier islands are an amazing engine of natural production. Generating more food energy than any estuary on the East Coast, each acre of marsh produces about 20 tons of biomass—making it four times more productive than an acre of corn.

Literally the prototype of the modern planned resort community, Hilton Head Island on South Carolina's coast is also a case study in how a landscape can change when money is introduced. From Reconstruction until the post-World War II era, the island consisted almost entirely of African Americans with deep roots in the area. In the mid-1950s Hilton Head began its transformation into an almost all-white, upscale golf, tennis, and shopping mecca populated largely by Northern transplants and retirees. As

---

Previous: shrimping fleet on the Darien riverfront; wild horse on Cumberland Island.

Look for ★ to find
recommended sights and activities.

Highlights

★ **Pinckney Island National Wildlife Refuge:** This well-maintained sanctuary is a major birding location and a great getaway from nearby Hilton Head (page 145).

★ **Coastal Discovery Museum at Honey Horn:** This beautifully repurposed plantation house with spacious grounds near the island's entrance is a great place to learn about Hilton Head history, both human and natural (page 147).

★ **Jekyll Island Historic District:** Relax and soak in the salty breeze at this onetime playground of the country's richest people (page 178).

★ **The Village:** The center of social life on St. Simons Island has shops, restaurants, a pier, and a beachside playground (page 189).

★ **Fort Frederica National Monument:** This excellently preserved tabby fortress dates from the first days of English settlement in Georgia (page 190).

★ **Harris Neck National Wildlife Refuge:** This former wartime airfield is now one of the East Coast's best birding locations (page 200).

★ **Cumberland Island National Seashore:** Wild horses—such as the ones that live here—might not be able to drag you off this evocative, undeveloped island paradise (page 211).

★ **Okefenokee National Wildlife Refuge:** More than just a swamp, the Okefenokee is a natural wonderland that takes you back into the mists of prehistory (page 218).

you can imagine, the flavor here is now quite different from surrounding areas of the Lowcountry, to say the least, with an emphasis on material excellence, top prices, get-it-done-yesterday punctuality, and the attendant aggressive traffic.

One of the unsung positive aspects of modern Hilton Head is its dedication to sustainable living. With the support of voters, the town routinely buys large tracts of land to preserve as open space. Hilton Head was the first municipality in the country to mandate the burying of all power lines, and one of the first to regularly use covenants and deed restrictions. All new development must conform to rigid guidelines on setbacks and tree canopy. It has one of the most comprehensive signage ordinances in the country as well, which means no garish commercial displays will disrupt your views of the night sky. If those are "elite" values, then certainly we might do well in making them more mainstream.

Ancient Native Americans held the area in special regard, intoxicated not only by the easy sustenance it offered but also by its spiritual solace. Their shell middens, many still in existence, are a sign of well-fed people thankful for nature's bounty. Avaricious for gold as they were, the Spanish also admired the almost monastic enchantment of Georgia's coast, choosing it as the site of their first colony in North America. Their subsequent chain of Roman Catholic missions are now long gone but certainly testified to their own quest here. While the American tycoons who used these barrier islands as personal playgrounds had avarice of their own, we must give credit where it's due: Their self-interest kept these places largely untouched by the kind of development that has plagued many of South Carolina's barrier islands to the north. Though isolated even today, the Golden Isles played an irreplaceable role in the defense of the young United States. It was here that massive live oaks were forested and used in the construction of the bulked-up superfast frigates of the fledgling U.S. Navy. The USS *Constitution* got its nickname, "Old Ironsides," from the strength of these pieces of Georgia oak, so resilient as to literally repel British cannonballs during the War of 1812. Although the South Carolina Sea Islands are generally seen as the center of Gullah culture, the African American communities of the Golden Isles, Georgia's Sea Islands, also boast a long and fascinating history of survival, resourcefulness, and proud cultural integrity that carries on to this day.

PLANNING YOUR TIME

Generally speaking, the peak season in this area is March-Labor Day. With the exception of some resort accommodations on St. Simons Island, Little St. Simons Island, and Sea Island, lodging is generally far more affordable than up the coast in Savannah.

Many travelers take I-95 south from Savannah to the Golden Isles, but U.S. 17 roughly parallels the interstate—in some cases so closely that drivers on the two roads can see each other—and is a far more scenic and enriching drive for those with a little extra time to spend. Indeed, U.S. 17 is an intrinsic part of the life and lore of the region, and you are likely to spend a fair amount of time on it regardless.

While the New York accents fly fast and furious on Hilton Head Island, that's no reason for you to rush. Certainly a casual visitor can do Hilton Head in a day, but its natural attractions beg for a more considered sort of enjoyment. Plan on at least half a day just to enjoy the fine, broad beaches. I recommend another half day to tour the island itself.

Geographically, Brunswick lies on a peninsula laid out roughly north-south. It's separated from the Atlantic by the barrier islands St. Simons and Jekyll. The city of Brunswick has a lot in common with Savannah due to its Oglethorpe-designed grid layout, although Brunswick itself can easily be fully experienced in a single afternoon. But really—as its nickname "Gateway to the Golden Isles" indicates—Brunswick's main role is as an economic and governmental center for Glynn County, to which Jekyll Island and St. Simons Island, the real attractions in this area, belong.

Both Jekyll Island and St. Simons Island are well worth visiting and have their own separate pleasures—Jekyll more contemplative, St. Simons more upscale. Give an entire day to Jekyll so you can take full advantage of its relaxing, open feel. A half day can suffice for St. Simons because most of its attractions are clustered in the Village area near the pier, and there's little beach recreation to speak of.

Getting to the undeveloped barrier islands, Sapelo and Cumberland, takes planning in advance because there is no bridge to either. Both require a ferry booking and hence a more substantial commitment of time. There are no real stores and few facilities on these islands, so pack along whatever you think you'll need, including food, water, medicine, suntan lotion, insect repellent, and so on. Sapelo Island is limited to day use unless you have prior reservations, with the town of Darien in McIntosh County as the gateway. The same is true for Cumberland Island National Seashore, with the town of St. Marys in Camden County as the gateway.

Hilton Head Island

The second-largest barrier island on the East Coast was named in 1663 by adventurer Sir William Hilton, who thoughtfully named the island—with its notable headland or "head"—after himself. Later it gained fame as the first growing location of the legendary "Sea Island cotton," a long-grain variety that, following its introduction in 1790 by William Elliott II of the Myrtle Bank Plantation, would soon be the dominant version of the cash crop.

Nearby Bluffton was settled by planters from Hilton Head Island and the surrounding area in the early 1800s as a summer retreat. Though Charleston likes to claim the label today, Bluffton was actually the genuine "cradle of secession." Indeed, locals still joke that the town motto is "Divided We Stand."

Though it seems unlikely given the island's modern demographics, Hilton Head was almost entirely African American through much of the 20th century. When Union troops occupied the island at the outbreak of the Civil War, freed and escaped slaves flocked to the island, and most of the dwindling number of African Americans on the island today are descendants of this original Gullah population.

In the 1950s the Fraser family bought 19,000 of the island's 25,000 acres with the intent to continue forestry on them. But in 1956—not at all coincidentally the same year the first bridge to the island was built—Charles Fraser convinced his father to sell him the southern tip. Fraser's brainchild and decades-long labor of love—some said his obsession—Sea Pines Plantation became the prototype for the golf-oriented resort communities so common today on both U.S. coasts. Fraser himself was killed in a boating accident in 2002 and is buried under the famous Liberty Oak in Harbour Town.

SIGHTS

Contrary to what many think, there are things to do on Hilton Head that don't involve swinging a club at a little white ball or shopping for designer labels, but instead celebrate the area's history and natural setting. The following are some of those attractions, arranged in geographical order from where you first access the island.

★ Pinckney Island National Wildlife Refuge

Actually consisting of many islands and hammocks, **Pinckney Island National Wildlife Refuge** (912/652-4415, daily dawn-dusk, free) is the only part of this small but very well-managed 4,000-acre refuge that's open to the public. Almost 70 percent of the former rice plantation is salt marsh and tidal creeks, making it a perfect microcosm for the Lowcountry as a whole, as well as a great place to kayak or canoe. Native Americans liked the area as well, with a 10,000-year presence and over 100 archaeological sites being identified to date. Like many coastal refuges, it was a private game preserve for much of the 20th century. Some of the state's richest birding opportunities abound here, with observers able to spot gorgeous white ibis and rare wood storks, along with herons, egrets, eagles, and ospreys, with little trouble from the refuge's miles of trails. Getting here is easy: On U.S. 278 east to Hilton Head, the refuge entrance is right between the two bridges onto the island.

Green's Shell Enclosure

Less known than the larger Native American shell ring farther south at Sea Pines, **Green's Shell Enclosure** (803/734-3886, daily dawn-dusk) is certainly easier to find, and you don't have to pay $5 to enter the area, as with Sea Pines. This three-acre heritage preserve dates back to at least the 1300s. The heart of the site comprises a low embankment, part of the original fortified village. To get here, take a left at the intersection of U.S. 278

Hilton Head Island

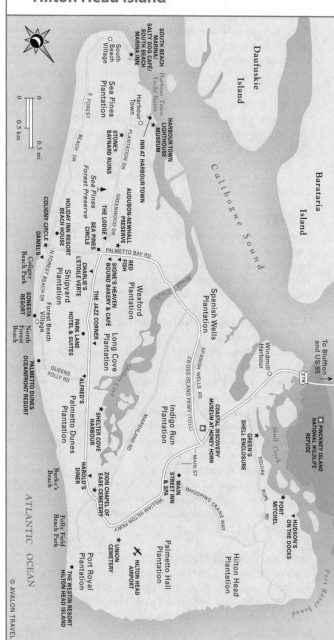

and Squire Pope Road. Turn left into Green's Park, pass the office on the left, and park. The entrance to the shell enclosure is on the left behind a fence. You'll see a small community cemetery that has nothing to do with the shell ring; veer to your right to get to the short trail entrance.

★ Coastal Discovery Museum at Honey Horn

With the acquisition of Honey Horn's 70-acre spread of historic plantation land, Hilton Head finally has a full-fledged museum worthy of the name, and the magnificent **Coastal Discovery Museum** (70 Honey Horn Dr., 843/689-6767, www.coastaldiscovery.org, Mon.-Sat. 9am-4:30pm, Sun. 11am-3pm, free) is a must-see, even for those who came to the island mostly to golf and soak up sun.

The facility centers on the expertly restored Discovery House, the only antebellum house still existing on Hilton Head, with exhibits and displays devoted to the history of the island. The museum is also a great one-stop place to sign up for a variety of specialty on-site and off-site guided tours, such as birding and Gullah history tours. The cost for most on-site tours is a reasonable $10 adults and $5 children.

But the real draw is the 0.5-mile trail through the Honey Horn grounds, including several boardwalk viewpoints over the marsh, a neat little butterfly habitat, a few gardens, and a stable and pasture that host Honey Horn May and Tadpole, the museum's two marsh tackies—short, tough little ponies descended from Spanish horses and used to great effect by Francis "Swamp Fox" Marion and his freedom fighters in the American Revolution. The trail even features a replica of an ancient Native American shell ring of oyster shells, but do be aware that it is not a genuine shell ring (you can find the real thing at Green's Shell Enclosure a bit farther west on U.S. 278 and in Sea Pines at the south end of the island).

While a glance at a map and area signage might convince you that you must pay the $1.25 toll on the Cross Island Parkway to get to Honey Horn, that isn't so. The exit to Honey Horn on the parkway is actually before you get to the toll plaza, therefore access is free.

Union Cemetery

A modest but key aspect of African American history on Hilton Head is at **Union Cemetery** (Union Cemetery Rd.), a small burial ground featuring several graves of black Union Army troops (you can tell by the designation "USCI" on the tombstone, for "United States Colored Infantry"). Also of interest are the charming, hand-carved cement tombstones of nonveterans. To get here, turn north off of William Hilton Parkway onto Union Cemetery Road. The cemetery is a short way ahead on the left. There is no signage or site interpretation.

Zion Chapel of Ease Cemetery

More like one of the gloriously desolate scenes common to the rest of the Lowcountry, this little cemetery in full view of the William Hilton Parkway at Folly Field Road is all that remains of one of the "Chapels of Ease," a string of chapels set up in the 1700s. The **Zion Chapel of Ease Cemetery** (daily dawn-dusk, free) is said to be haunted by the ghost of William Baynard, whose final resting place is in a mausoleum on the site (the remains of his ancestral home are farther south at Sea Pines Plantation).

Audubon-Newhall Preserve

Plant lovers shouldn't miss this small but very well-maintained 50-acre wooded tract in the south-central part of the island on Palmetto Bay Road between the Cross Island Parkway and the Sea Pines Circle. Almost all plant life, even that in the water, is helpfully marked and identified. The **Audubon-Newhall Preserve** (year-round dawn-dusk, free) is open to the public, but you can't camp here. For more information, call the **Hilton Head Audubon Society** (843/842-9246).

Sea Pines Plantation

This private residential resort development at the extreme west end of the island—the first on Hilton Head and the prototype for every other such development in the country—hosts several attractions that collectively are well worth the $5 per vehicle "road use" fee, which you pay at the main entrance gate.

Harbour Town

It's not particularly historic and not all that natural, but **Harbour Town** is still pretty cool. The dominant element is the squat, colorful **Harbour Town Lighthouse Museum** (149 Lighthouse Rd., 843/671-2810, www.harbourtownlighthouse.com, daily 10am-dusk, $3), which has never really helped a ship navigate its way near the island. The 90-foot structure was built in 1970 purely to give visitors a little atmosphere, and that it does, as kids especially love climbing the stairs to the top ($2 pp) and looking out over the island's expanse.

Stoney-Baynard Ruins

The **Stoney-Baynard ruins** (Plantation Dr., dawn-dusk, free), tabby ruins in a residential neighborhood, are what remains of the circa-1790 central building of the old Braddock's Point Plantation, first owned by patriot and raconteur Captain "Saucy Jack" Stoney and later by the Baynard family. Active during the island's heyday as a cotton center, the plantation was destroyed after the Civil War. Two other foundations are nearby, one for slave quarters and one whose use is still unknown.

Sea Pines Forest Preserve

The **Sea Pines Forest Preserve** (175 Greenwood Dr., 843/363-4530, free) is set amid the Sea Pines Plantation golf resort development, but you don't need a bag of clubs to enjoy this 600-acre preserve, which is built on the site of an old rice plantation (dikes and logging trails are still visible). Here

Clockwise from top left: lighthouse on Hilton Head Island; heron in the trees of Pinckney Island; shops in Harbour Town.

you can ride a horse, fish, or just take a walk on the eight miles of trails (dawn-dusk) and enjoy the natural beauty around you. No bike riding is allowed on the trails, however.

In addition to the Native American shell ring farther north off Squire Pope Road, the Sea Pines Forest Preserve also boasts a shell ring set within a canopy of tall pines. Scientists date the ring itself to about 1450 BC, although human habitation on the island goes as far back as 8000 BC.

Tours and Cruises

Most guided tours on Hilton Head focus on the water. **Harbour Town Cruises** (843/363-9023, www.vagabondcruise.com, $30-60) offers several sightseeing tours as well as excursions to Daufuskie and Savannah. They also offer a tour on a former America's Cup racing yacht.

Dolphin tours are extremely popular on Hilton Head, and there is no shortage of operators. **Dolphin Watch Nature Cruises** (843/785-4558, $25 adults, $10 children) departs from Shelter Cove, as does **Lowcountry Nature Tours** (843/683-0187, www.lowcountrynaturetours.com, $40 adults, $35 children, free under age 3). The *Gypsy* (843/363-2900, www.bitemybait.com, $15 adults, $7 children) sails out of South Beach Marina, taking you all around peaceful Calibogue Sound. Two dolphin tours are based on Broad Creek, the large body of water that almost bisects the island through the middle: "Captain Jim" runs **Island Explorer Tours** (843/785-2100, www.dolphintourshiltonhead.com, two-hour tour $45 pp) from a dock behind the old Oyster Factory on Marshland Road. Not to be outdone, "Captain Dave" leads tours at **Dolphin Discoveries** (843/681-1911, two-hour tour $40 adults, $30 under age 13), leaving out of Simmons Landing next to the Broad Creek Marina on Marshland Road. **Outside Hilton Head** (843/686-6996, www.outsidehiltonhead.com) runs a variety of water eco-tours and dolphin tours as well as a guided day-trip excursion to Daufuskie, complete with golf cart rental.

There is a notable land-based tour by **Gullah Heritage Trail Tours** (leaves from the Coastal Discovery Museum at Honey Horn, 843/681-7066, www.gullahheritage.com, $32 adults, $15 children) delving into the island's rich, if poorly preserved, African American history, from slavery through the time of the freedmen.

ENTERTAINMENT AND EVENTS
Nightlife

The most high-quality live entertainment on the island is at **The Jazz Corner** (1000 William Hilton Pkwy., 843/842-8620, www.thejazzcorner.com, dinner daily 6pm-9pm, late-night menu after 9pm, dinner $15-20, cover varies), which brings in the best names in the country—and outstanding regulars like Bob Masteller and Howard Paul—to perform in this space in the unlikely setting of a boutique mall, the Village at Wexford. The dinners are actually quite good, but the attraction is definitely the music. Reservations are recommended. Live music starts around 7pm.

For years islanders have jokingly referred to the "Barmuda Triangle," an area named for the preponderance of bars within walking distance of Sea Pines Circle. While some of the names have changed over the years, the longtime anchor of the Barmuda Triangle is the **Tiki Hut** (1 S. Forest Beach Dr., 843/785-5126, Sun.-Thurs. 11am-8pm, Fri.-Sat. 11am-10pm, bar until 2am), actually part of the Holiday Inn Resort Beach House at the entrance to Sea Pines. This popular watering hole is the only beachfront bar on the island, which technically makes it the only place you can legally drink alcohol on a Hilton Head beach. Another Barmuda Triangle staple is **Hilton Head Brewing Company** (7 Greenwood Dr., 843/785-3900, daily 11am-2am), the only brewpub on the island and indeed South Carolina's first microbrewery since Prohibition. They offer a wide range of hand-crafted brews, from a Blueberry Wheat to a Mocha Porter. Another long-time Triangle fave is **The Lodge** (7 Greenwood Dr., 843/842-8966, www.hiltonheadlodge.com, daily 11:30am-midnight). After the martini and cigar craze waned, this popular spot successfully remade itself into a beer-centric place with 36 rotating taps. They still mix a mean martini, though.

Despite its location in the upscale strip mall of the Village at Wexford, the **British Open Pub** (1000 William Hilton Pkwy./U.S. 278, 843/686-6736, daily 11am-10pm) offers a fairly convincing English vibe with, as the name suggests, a heavy golf theme. The fish-and-chips and shepherd's pie are both magnificent.

Inside Sea Pines is the **Quarterdeck Lounge and Patio** (843/842-1999, www.seapines.com, Sun.-Thurs. 5:30pm-10pm, Fri.-Sat. 5:30pm-midnight) at the base of the Harbour Town Lighthouse. This is where the party's at after a long day on the fairways during the RBC Heritage golf tournament. Within Sea Pines at the South Beach Marina is also where you'll find **The Salty Dog Cafe** (232 S. Sea Pines Dr., 843/671-2233, www.saltydog.com, lunch daily 11am-3pm, dinner daily 5pm-10pm, bar daily until 2am), one of the area's most popular institutions (some might even call it a tourist trap) and something akin to an island empire, with popular T-shirts, a gift shop, books, and an ice cream shop, all overlooking the marina. My suggestion, however, is to make the short walk to the affiliated **Wreck of the Salty Dog** (232 S. Sea Pines Dr., 843/671-7327, daily until 2am), where the marsh views are better and the atmosphere not quite so tacky.

There's only one bona fide gay club on Hilton Head: **Vibe** (32 Palmetto Bay Rd., 843/341-6933, www.vibehhi.com, Mon.-Fri. 8pm-3am, Sat. 8pm-2am). Wednesday is karaoke night, and Thursdays bring an amateur drag revue.

Performing Arts

Because so many residents migrated here from art-savvy metropolitan areas in the Northeast, Hilton Head maintains a very high standard of top-quality entertainment. Much of the activity centers on the multimillion-dollar **Arts Center of Coastal Carolina** (14 Shelter Cove Ln., 843/842-2787,

www.artshhi.com), which hosts touring shows, resident companies, musical concerts, dance performances, and visual arts exhibits.

Now over a quarter-century old and under the direction of maestro John
Morris Russell, the **Hilton Head Symphony Orchestra** (843/842-2055,
www.hhso.org) performs a year-round season of masterworks and pops
programs at various venues, primarily the First Presbyterian Church (540
William Hilton Pkwy./U.S. 278). They also take their show on the road
with several concerts in Bluffton and even perform several "Symphony
Under the Stars" programs at Shelter Cove. **Chamber Music Hilton Head**
(www.cmhh.org) performs throughout the year with selections ranging
from Brahms to Smetana at All Saints Episcopal Church (3001 Meeting St.).

Cinema

There's an art house on Hilton Head, the charming **Coligny Theatre**
(843/686-3500, www.colignytheatre.com) in the Coligny Plaza shopping
center before you get to Sea Pines. For years this was the only movie theater
for miles around, but it has reincarnated as a primarily indie film venue.
Look for the entertaining murals by local artist Ralph Sutton. Show times
are Monday 11:30am and 4pm, Tuesday and Friday 11:30am, 4pm, and 7pm,
Wednesday-Thursday and Saturday-Sunday 4pm and 7pm.

Festivals and Events

Late February-early March brings the **Hilton Head Wine and Food
Festival** (www.hiltonheadhospitality.org), culminating in what they call
"The East Coast's Largest Outdoor Public Tasting and Auction," which is
generally held at the Coastal Discovery Museum at Honey Horn. Some
events charge admission.

Hilton Head's premier event is the **RBC Heritage golf tournament**
(843/671-2248, http://theheritagegolfsc.com), held each April (usually
the week after the Masters) at the Harbour Town Golf Links on Sea Pines
Plantation. Formerly known as the Verizon Heritage Classic, the event is
South Carolina's only PGA Tour event and brings thousands of visitors
to town.

A fun and fondly anticipated yearly event is the **Kiwanis Club Chili
Cookoff** (www.hiltonheadkiwanis.org), held each October at Honey Horn
on the south end. A low admission price gets you all the chili you can eat
plus free antacids. All funds go to charity, and all excess chili goes to a
local food bank.

Every November brings Hilton Head's second-largest event, the **Hilton
Head Concours d'Elegance & Motoring Festival** (www.hhiconcours.
com), a multiday event bringing together vintage car clubs from throughout the nation and culminating in a prestigious "Best of Show" competition. It started as a fund-raiser for the Hilton Head Symphony, but now
people come from all over the country to see these fine vintage cars in a
beautiful setting.

SHOPPING

As you'd expect, Hilton Head is a shopper's delight, with an emphasis on upscale stores and prices to match. Keep in mind that hours may be shortened in the off-season (Nov.-Mar.). Here's a rundown of the main island shopping areas in the order you'll encounter them as you enter the island.

Shelter Cove

Shelter Cove Towne Centre (40 Shelter Cove Ln., www.sheltercovetownecentre.com), a repurposed former mall, centers around a **Belk** anchor store and a Kroger. New retail shops have been steadily popping up since the 2013 opening. The nearby **Plaza at Shelter Cove** (50 Shelter Cove Ln., www.theplazaatsheltercove.com) features a Whole Foods and the flagship location of **Outside Hilton Head** (843/686-6996, www.outsidehiltonhead.com, Mon.-Sat. 10am-5:30pm, Sun. 11am-5:30pm), a complete outdoor outfitter with a knowledgeable staff.

Village at Wexford

Easily my favorite place to shop on Hilton Head, this well-shaded shopping center on William Hilton Parkway (U.S. 278) hosts plenty of well-tended shops, including the foodie equipment store **Le Cookery** (843/785-7171, Mon.-Sat. 10am-6pm), the Lily Pulitzer signature women's store **S. M. Bradford Co.** (843/686-6161, Mon.-Sat. 10am-6pm), and the aromatic **Scents of Hilton Head** (843/842-7866, Mon.-Fri. 10am-6pm, Sat. 10am-5pm).

My favorite shop on all Hilton Head is at Wexford. **The Oilerie** (843/681-2722, www.oilerie.com, Mon.-Sat. 10am-7pm, Sun. noon-5pm) provides free samples of all its high-quality Italian olive oils and vinegars. After you taste around awhile, you pick what you want and the friendly staff bottles it for you in souvenir-quality glassware. They also have a selection of spices, soaps, and other goodies.

Coligny Circle

This is the closest Hilton Head comes to funkier beach towns like Tybee Island, although it doesn't really come that close. You'll find dozens of delightful and somewhat quirky stores here, many keeping long hours in the summer, like the self-explanatory **Coligny Kite & Flag Co.** (843/785-5483, Mon.-Sat. 10am-9pm, Sun. 11am-6pm), the comprehensive and stylish **Quiet Storm Surf Shop** (843/671-2551) and **Fresh Produce** (843/842-3410, www.freshproduceclothes.com), actually a very fun women's clothing store. Kids will love both **The Shell Shop** (843/785-4900, Mon.-Sat. 10am-9pm, Sun. noon-9pm) and **Black Market Minerals** (843/785-7090, Mon.-Sat. 10am-10pm, Sun. 11am-8pm).

Harbour Town

Shoppes at Harbour Town (www.seapines.com) is a collection of about 20 mostly boutique stores along Lighthouse Road in Sea Pines Plantation.

At **Planet Hilton Head** (843/363-5177, www.planethiltonhead.com, daily 10am-9pm) you'll find some cute, eclectic gifts and home goods. Other clothing highlights include **Knickers Men's Store** (843/671-2291, daily 10am-9pm) and **Radiance** (843/363-5176, Mon.-Tues. 10am-5pm, Wed.-Sat. 10am.-9pm, Sun. 11am-9pm), a very cute and fashion-forward women's store.

The **Top of the Lighthouse Shoppe** (843/671-2810, www.harbourtown-lighthouse.com, daily 10am-9pm) is where many a climbing visitor has been coaxed to part with some of their disposable income. And, of course, as you'd expect being near the legendary Harbour Town links, there's the **Harbour Town Pro Shop** (843/671-4485), routinely voted one of the best pro shops in the nation.

South Beach Marina

On South Sea Pines Drive at the marina you'll find several worthwhile shops, including a good ship's store and all-around grocery dealer **South Beach General Store** (843/671-6784, daily 8am-10pm). I like to stop in **Blue Water Bait and Tackle** (843/671-3060, daily 7am-8pm) and check out the cool nautical stuff. They can also hook you up with a variety of kayak trips and fishing charters. And, of course, right on the water there's the ever-popular **Salty Dog Cafe** (843/671-2233, www.saltydog.com, lunch daily 11am-3pm, dinner daily 5pm-10pm), whose ubiquitous T-shirts seem to adorn every other person on the island.

Art Galleries

Despite the abundant wealth apparent in some quarters here, there's no freestanding art museum in the area, that role being filled by independent galleries. A good representative example is **Morris & Whiteside Galleries** (220 Cordillo Pkwy., 843/842-4433, www.morris-whiteside.com, Mon.-Fri. 9am-5pm, Sat. 10am-4pm), located in the historic Red Piano Art Gallery building, which features a variety of paintings and sculpture, heavy on landscapes but also showing some fine figurative work. The nonprofit **Art League of Hilton Head** (14 Shelter Cove Ln., 843/681-5060, Mon.-Sat. 10am-6pm) is located in the Walter Greer Art Gallery within the Arts Center of Coastal Carolina and displays work by member artists in all media. The **Nash Gallery** (13 Harbourside Ln., 843/785-6424, Mon.-Fri. 10am-9pm, Sat. 10am-8pm, Sun. 11am-5pm) in Shelter Cove Harbour deals more in North American craft styles. Hilton Head art isn't exactly known for its avant-garde nature, but you can find some whimsical stuff at **Picture This** (78D Arrow Rd., 843/842-5299, Mon.-Fri. 9:30am-5:30pm, Sat. 9:30am-12:30pm), including a selection of Gullah craft items. Regional painters, sculptors, and glass artists are featured at **Endangered Arts** (841 William Hilton Pkwy., 843/785-5075, www.endangeredarts.com).

Beaches

First, the good news: Hilton Head Island has 12 miles of some of the most beautiful, safe beaches you'll find anywhere. The bad news is that there are only a few ways to gain access, generally at locations referred to as "beach parks." Don't just drive into a residential neighborhood and think you'll be able to park and find your way to the beach; for better or worse, Hilton Head is not set up for that kind of casual access.

Driessen Beach Park has 207 long-term parking spaces, costing $0.25 for 30 minutes. There's free parking but fewer spaces at the **Coligny Beach Park** entrance and at **Fish Haul Creek Park**. Also, there are 22 metered spaces at **Alder Lane Beach Access**, 51 at **Folly Field Beach Park**, and 13 at **Burkes Beach Road**. Most other beach parks have permit parking only. Clean, well-maintained public restrooms are available at all the beach parks. You can find beach information at 843/342-4580 and www.hilton-headislandsc.gov. Beach park hours vary: Coligny Beach Park is open daily 24 hours; all other beach parks are open March-September daily 6am-8pm and October-February daily 6am-5pm.

Alcohol is strictly prohibited on Hilton Head's beaches. There are lifeguards on all the beaches during the summer, but be aware that the worst undertow is on the northern stretches. Also remember to leave the sand dollars where they are; their population is dwindling due to souvenir hunting.

Kayaking

Kayakers will enjoy Hilton Head Island, which offers several gorgeous routes, including Calibogue Sound to the south and west and Port Royal Sound to the north. For particularly good views of life on the salt marsh, try Broad Creek, which nearly bisects Hilton Head Island, and Skull Creek, which separates Hilton Head from the natural beauty of Pinckney Island. Broad Creek Marina is a good place to put in. There are also two public landings, Haigh Landing and Buckingham Landing, on Mackay Creek at the entrance to the island, one on either side of the bridge.

If you want a guided tour, there are plenty of great kayak tour outfits to choose from in the area. Chief among them is **Outside Hilton Head** (32 Shelter Cove Ln., 800/686-6996, www.outsidehiltonhead.com). They offer a wide range of guided trips, including "The Outback," in which you're first boated to a private island and then taken on a tour of tidal creeks, and five- or seven-hour "Ultimate Lowcountry Day" trips to Daufuskie, Bluffton, or Bull Creek. Other good places to book a tour or just rent a kayak are **Water-Dog Outfitters** (Broad Creek Marina, 843/686-3554) and **Kayak Hilton Head** (Broad Creek Marina, 843/684-1910). Leaving out of the Harbour Town Yacht Basin is **H2O Sports** (843/671-4386, www.h2o-sportsonline.com), which offers 90-minute guided kayak tours ($30) and rents kayaks for about $20 per hour. Within **Palmetto Dunes Oceanfront Resort** (4 Queens Folly Rd., 800/827-3006, www.palmettodunes.com) is

Palmetto Dunes Outfitters (843/785-2449, www.pdoutfitters.com, daily 9am-5pm), which rents kayaks and canoes and offers lessons on the resort's 11-mile-long lagoon.

Fishing and Boating

As you'd expect, anglers and boaters love the Hilton Head/Bluffton area, which offers all kinds of saltwater, freshwater, and fly-fishing opportunities. Captain Brian Vaughn runs **Off the Hook Charters** (68 Helmsman Way, 843/298-4376, www.offthehookcharters.com), which offers fully licensed half-day trips ($400). **Miss Carolina Sportfishing** (168 Palmetto Bay Rd., 843/298-2628, www.misscarolinafishing.com) offers deep-sea action at a little over $100 per hour. Captain Dave Fleming of **Mighty Mako Sport Fishing Charters** (164 Palmetto Bay Rd., 843/785-6028, www.mightymako.com) can take you saltwater fishing, both backwater and near-shore, on the 25-foot *Mighty Mako* for about $400 for a half day. If you're at the South Beach Marina area of Sea Pines Plantation, head into **Blue Water Bait and Tackle** (843/671-3060) and see if they can hook you up with a trip.

Public landings in the Hilton Head area include the Marshland Road Boat Landing and the Broad Creek Boat Ramp under the Charles Fraser Bridge, and the Haigh Landing on Mackay Creek.

Hiking and Biking

Although the very flat terrain is not challenging, Hilton Head provides some scenic and relaxing cycling opportunities. Thanks to wise planning and foresight, the island has an extensive and award-winning 50-mile network of biking trails that does a great job of keeping cyclists out of traffic. A big plus is the long bike path paralleling the William Hilton Parkway, enabling cyclists to use that key artery without braving its traffic. There is even an underground bike path beneath the parkway to facilitate crossing that busy road. There are also routes along Pope Avenue and North and South Forest Beach Drives. Go to www.hiltonheadisland.org/biking to download a map of the island's entire bike path network.

Palmetto Dunes Oceanfront Resort (4 Queens Folly Rd., 800/827-3006, www.palmettodunes.com) has a particularly nice 25-mile network of bike paths that all link up to the island's larger framework. Within the resort is **Palmetto Dunes Outfitters** (843/785-2449, www.pdoutfitters.com, daily 9am-5pm), which will rent you any type of bike you might need. Sea Pines Plantation also has an extensive 17-mile network of bike trails; you can pick up a map at most information kiosks within the plantation.

But the best bike path on Hilton Head is the simplest of all, and where no one will ask you where you're staying that night: the beach. For a few hours before and after low tide, the beach effectively becomes a 12-mile bike path around most of the island, and a pleasant morning or afternoon ride may well prove to be the highlight of your trip.

There's a plethora of bike rental facilities on Hilton Head with competitive rates. Be sure to ask if they offer free pickup and delivery. Try **Hilton**

Hikers will particularly enjoy Pinckney Island National Wildlife Refuge, which takes you through several key Lowcountry ecosystems, from maritime forest to salt marsh. Other peaceful, if nonchallenging, trails are at the Audubon-Newhall Preserve.

Horseback Riding

Within the Sea Pines Forest Preserve is **Lawton Stables** (190 Greenwood Dr., 843/671-2586, www.lawtonstableshhi.com), which features pony rides, a small-animal farm, and guided horseback rides through the preserve. You don't need any riding experience, but you do need reservations.

Bird-Watching

The premier birding locale in the area is the **Pinckney Island National Wildlife Refuge** (U.S. 278 east, just before Hilton Head, 912/652-4415, www.fws.gov, free). You can see bald eagles, ibis, wood storks, painted buntings, and many more species. Birding is best in spring and fall. The refuge has several freshwater ponds that serve as wading bird rookeries. During migration season, so many beautiful birds make such a ruckus that you'll think you've wandered onto an *Animal Planet* shoot.

Golf

Hilton Head is one of the world's great golf centers, with no fewer than 23 courses, and one could easily write a book about nothing but that. This, however, is not that book. Perhaps contrary to what you might expect, most courses on the island are public, and some are downright affordable. All courses are 18 holes unless otherwise described; greens fees are averages and vary with season and tee time.

The best-regarded course, with prices to match, is **Harbour Town Golf Links** (Sea Pines Plantation, 843/363-4485, www.seapines.com, $239). It's on the island's south end at Sea Pines and is the home of the annual RBC Heritage golf tournament, far and away the island's number-one tourist draw.

There are two Arthur Hills-designed courses on the island, **Arthur Hills at Palmetto Dunes Resort** (843/785-1140, www.palmettodunes.com, $125) and **Arthur Hills at Palmetto Hall** (Palmetto Hall Plantation, 843/689-4100, www.palmettohallgolf.com, $130), both of which now offer the use of Segway vehicles on the fairways. The reasonably priced **Barony Course** at Port Royal Plantation (843/686-8801, www.portroyalgolfclub.com, $98) also boasts some of the toughest greens on the island. Another challenging and affordable course is the **George Fazio** at Palmetto Dunes Resort (843/785-1130, www.palmettodunes.com, $105).

Hilton Head National Golf Club (60 Hilton Head National Dr., 843/842-5900, www.golfhiltonheadnational.com), which is actually on the mainland just before you cross the bridge to Hilton Head, is still highly rated for both condition and service, despite recently losing nine holes to a road widening project. *Golf Week* has named it one of the country's best golf courses. The 18-hole course is public, and green fees are below $100.

It's a good idea to book tee times through the **Golf Island Call Center** (888/465-3475, www.golfisland.com), which can also hook you up with good packages.

Tennis

One of the top tennis destinations in the country, Hilton Head has over 20 tennis clubs, some of which offer court time to the public (walk-on rates vary; call for information). They are: **Palmetto Dunes Tennis Center** (Palmetto Dunes Resort, 843/785-1152, www.palmettodunes.com, $30 per hour), **Port Royal Racquet Club** (Port Royal Plantation, 843/686-8803, www.portroyalgolfclub.com, $25 per hour), **Sea Pines Racquet Club** (Sea Pines Plantation, 843/363-4495, www.seapines.com, $25 per hour), **South Beach Racquet Club** (Sea Pines Plantation, 843/671-2215, www.seapines.com, $25 per hour), and **Shipyard Racquet Club** (Shipyard Plantation, 843/686-8804, $25 per hour).

Free, first-come, first-served play is available at the following public courts, maintained by the Island Recreation Association (www.island-reccenter.org): **Chaplin Community Park** (Singleton Beach Rd., four courts, lighted), **Cordillo Courts** (Cordillo Pkwy., four courts, lighted), **Fairfield Square** (Adrianna Lane, two courts), **Hilton Head High School** (School Rd., six courts), and **Hilton Head Middle School** (Wilborn Rd., four courts).

Zip Line

Billing itself as the only zip-line experience within 250 miles, the **Zip Line Hilton Head** (33 Broad Creek Marina Way, 843/682-6000, www.zipline-hiltonhead.com) offers an extensive canopy tour making great use of the area's natural scenery and features. You generally "fly" in groups of about eight. Reservations are strongly encouraged. The "Aerial Adventure" is a challenging two-hour trip ($50) with about 50 obstacles.

ACCOMMODATIONS

Generally speaking, accommodations on Hilton Head are often surprisingly affordable given their overall high quality and the breadth of their amenities.

Under $150

You can't beat the price at **Park Lane Hotel and Suites** (12 Park Ln., 843/686-5700, www.hiltonheadparklanehotel.com, $130). This is your basic suite-type hotel (formerly a Residence Inn) with kitchens, laundry, a pool, and a tennis court. The allure here is the price, hard to find anywhere these days at a resort location. For a nonrefundable fee, you can bring your pet. The one drawback is that the beach is a good distance away. The hotel does offer a free shuttle, however, so it would be wise to take advantage of that and avoid the usual beach-parking hassles. As you'd expect given the price, rooms here tend to go quickly; reserve early.

$150-300

By Hilton Head standards, the ★ **Main Street Inn & Spa** (2200 Main St., 800/471-3001, www.mainstreetinn.com, $160-210) can be considered a bargain stay, and with high quality to boot. With its Old World touches, sumptuous appointments, charming atmosphere, and attentive service, this 33-room inn and attached spa on the grounds of Hilton Head Plantation seems like it would be more at home in Savannah than Hilton Head. The inn serves a great full breakfast—not continental—daily 7:30am-10:30am.

Another good place for the price is the **South Beach Marina Inn** (232 S. Sea Pines Dr., 843/671-6498, www.sbinn.com, $186) in Sea Pines. Located near the famous Salty Dog Cafe and outfitted in a similar nautical theme, the inn not only has some pretty large guest rooms for the price, it offers a great view of the marina and has a very friendly feel. As with all Sea Pines accommodations, staying on the plantation means you don't have to wait in line with other visitors to pay the $5-per-day "road fee." Sea Pines also offers a free trolley to get around the plantation.

One of Hilton Head's favorite hotels for beach lovers is the **Holiday Inn Resort Beach House** (1 S. Forest Beach Dr., 855/474-2882, www.beach-househhi.com, $200), home of the famed Tiki Hut bar on the beach. Staff turnover is less frequent here than at other local accommodations, and while it's no Ritz-Carlton and occasionally shows signs of wear, it's a good value in a bustling area of the island.

One of the better resort-type places for those who prefer the putter and the racquet to the Frisbee and the surfboard is the **Inn at Harbour Town** (7 Lighthouse Ln., 843/363-8100, www.seapines.com, $199) in Sea Pines. The big draw here is the impeccable service, delivered by a staff of "butlers" in kilts, mostly Europeans who take the venerable trade quite seriously. While it's not on the beach, you can take advantage of the free Sea Pines Trolley every 20 minutes.

Recently rated the number-one family resort in the United States by *Travel + Leisure,* the well-run ★ **Palmetto Dunes Oceanfront Resort** (4 Queens Folly Rd., 800/827-3006, www.palmettodunes.com, $150-300) offers something for everybody in terms of lodging. There are small, cozy condos by the beach or larger villas overlooking the golf course and pretty much everything in between. The prices are perhaps disarmingly afford-able considering the relative luxury and copious recreational amenities, which include 25 miles of very well-done bike trails, 11 miles of kayak and canoe trails, and, of course, three signature links. As with most de-velopments of this type on Hilton Head, most of the condos are privately owned, and therefore each has its own particular set of guidelines and cleaning schedule.

A little farther down the island you'll find the **Sonesta Resort** (130

Shipyard Dr., 843/842-2400, www.sonesta.com/hiltonheadisland, $160-200), which styles itself as Hilton Head's only green-certified accommodation. The guest rooms are indeed state-of-the-art, and the expansive, shaded grounds near the beach are great for relaxation. No on-site golf here, but immediately adjacent is a well-regarded tennis facility with 20 courts.

Another good resort-style experience heavy on the golf is on the grounds of the Port Royal Plantation on the island's north side, **The Westin Resort Hilton Head Island** (2 Grasslawn Ave., 843/681-4000, www.westin.com/hiltonhead, from $200), which hosts three PGA-caliber links. The beach is also but a short walk away. This AAA four diamond-winning Westin offers a mix of suites and larger villas.

Vacation Rentals

Many visitors to Hilton Head choose to rent a home or villa for an extended stay, and there is no scarcity of availability. Try **Resort Rentals of Hilton Head** (www.hhivacations.com) or **Destination Vacation** (www.destinationvacationhhi.com).

FOOD

Because of the cosmopolitan nature of the population, with so many transplants from the northeastern United States and Europe, there is uniformly high quality in Hilton Head restaurants. And because of another demographic quirk of the area, its large percentage of senior citizens, you can also find some great deals by looking for some of the common "early bird" dinner specials, usually starting around 5pm.

Breakfast and Brunch

There are a couple of great diner-style places on the island. Though known more for its hamburgers and Philly cheesesteaks, **Harold's Diner** (641 William Hilton Pkwy., 843/842-9292, Mon.-Sat. 7am-3pm, $4-6) has great pancakes as well as its trademark brand of sarcastic service. Unpretentious and authentic in a place where those two adjectives are rarely used, it has been said of Harold's that "the lack of atmosphere *is* the atmosphere." The place is small, popular, and does not take reservations.

If you need a bite in the Coligny Plaza area, go to **Skillets** (1 N. Forest Beach Dr., 843/785-3131, www.skilletscafe.com, breakfast daily 7am-5pm, dinner daily 5pm-9pm, $5-23) in Coligny Plaza. Their eponymous stock-in-trade is a layered breakfast dish of sautéed ingredients served in a porcelain skillet, like the Kitchen Sink (pancakes ringed with potatoes, sausage, and bacon, topped with two poached eggs).

A great all-day breakfast place with a twist is ★ **Signe's Heaven Bound Bakery & Café** (93 Arrow Rd., 843/785-9118, www.signesbakery.com, Mon.-Fri. 8am-4pm, Sat. 9am-2pm, $5-10). Breakfast is tasty dishes like frittatas and breakfast polenta, while the twist is the extensive artisanal bakery, with delicious specialties like the signature key lime pound cake.

German

I'm pretty sure you didn't come all the way to South Carolina to eat traditional German food, but while you're here . . . check out ★ **Alfred's** (807 William Hilton Pkwy./U.S. 278, 843/341-3117, www.alfredsofhiltonhead. com, $20-30), one of the more unique spots on Hilton Head and a big favorite with the locals. Expect a wait. Bratwurst, veal cordon bleu, and of course Wiener schnitzel are all standouts. I recommend the German Mix Platter ($25), which features a brat, some sauerbraten, and a schnitzel.

Mediterranean

For upscale Italian, try **Bistro Mezzaluna** (55 New Orleans Rd., 843/842-5011, daily 5-9:30pm, $18-25), known far and wide for its osso buco as well as its impeccable service. There's also a great little bar for cocktails before or after dinner.

Middle Eastern

Hard to describe but well worth the visit, ★ **Daniel's Restaurant and Lounge** (2 N. Forest Beach Dr., 843/341-9379, http://danielshhi.com, daily 4pm-2am, tapas $10-12) combines elements of a traditional Middle Eastern eatery, an upscale tapas place, a beach spot, and a swank bar scene to create one of the more memorable food-and-beverage experiences on the island. Add in the fact that the prices are actually quite accessible and you've got a must-visit. Their "big small plates," meaning larger-portion tapas, run about $10-12 per plate. While they market their Middle Eastern flavor with plates like the cinnamon lamb kebab, their tapas have a cosmopolitan feel; they range from a Caribbean salmon steak to chicken pesto sliders.

Seafood

Not to be confused with Charley's Crab House next door to Hudson's, seafood lovers will enjoy the experience down near Sea Pines at ★ **Charlie's L'Etoile Verte** (8 New Orleans Rd., 843/785-9277, http://charliesgreenstar. com, lunch Tues.-Sat. 11:30am-2pm, dinner Mon.-Sat. 5:30pm-10pm, $25-40), which is considered by many connoisseurs to be Hilton Head's single best restaurant. The emphasis here is on "French country kitchen" cuisine—think Provence, not Paris. In keeping with that theme, each day's menu is concocted from scratch and handwritten. Listen to these recent entrées and feel your mouth water: flounder sautéed meunière, grilled wild coho salmon with basil pesto, and breast of duck in a raspberry demiglace. Get the picture? Of course, you'll want to start with the escargot and leeks vol-au-vent, the house pâté, or even some pan-roasted Bluffton oysters. Reservations are essential.

A longtime Hilton Head favorite is **Red Fish** (8 Archer Rd., 843/686-3388, www.redfishofhiltonhead.com, lunch Mon.-Sat. 11:30am-2pm, dinner daily beginning with early-bird specials at 5pm, $20-37). Strongly Caribbean in decor as well as menu, with romanticism and panache to match, this is a great place for couples. The creative but accessible menu by executive chef Sean Walsh incorporates unique spices, fruits, and vegetables for a fresh, zesty palate. Reservations are essential.

Fresh seafood lovers will enjoy one of Hilton Head's staples, the huge **Hudson's on the Docks** (1 Hudson Rd., 843/681-2772, www.hudsonsonthedocks.com, lunch daily 11am-4pm, dinner daily from 5pm, $14-23) on Skull Creek just off Squire Pope Road on the less-developed north side. Much of the catch—though not all of it, by any means—comes directly off the boats you'll see dockside. Try the stuffed shrimp filled with crabmeat. Leave room for one of the homemade desserts crafted by Ms. Bessie, a 30-year veteran employee of Hudson's.

INFORMATION AND SERVICES

The best place to get information on Hilton Head, book a room, or secure a tee time is just as you come onto the island at the **Hilton Head Island Chamber of Commerce Welcome Center** (100 William Hilton Pkwy., 843/785-3673, www.hiltonheadisland.org, daily 9am-6pm).

GETTING THERE AND AROUND

A few years back, the **Savannah/Hilton Head International Airport** (SAV, 400 Airways Ave., Savannah, 912/964-0514, www.savannahairport.com) added Hilton Head to its name specifically to identify itself with that lucrative market. The move has been a success, and this facility remains the closest large airport to Hilton Head Island and Bluffton. However, it's not actually *that* close: Keep in mind that when your plane touches down in Savannah, you're still about a 45-minute drive to Hilton Head proper. From the airport, go north on I-95 into South Carolina and take exit 8 onto U.S. 278 east.

There is a local regional airport as well, the **Hilton Head Island Airport** (HXD, 120 Beach City Rd., 843/689-5400, www.bcgov.net). While it's attractive and convenient, keep in mind that it hosts only propeller-driven commuter planes because of the runway length and concerns about noise.

Hilton Head is about 30 minutes from I-95. If you're entering the area by car, the best route is exit 8 off I-95 onto U.S. 278, which takes you by Bluffton and right into Hilton Head. Near Bluffton, U.S. 278 is called Fording Island Road, and on Hilton Head proper it becomes the William Hilton Parkway business route.

Hilton Head Islanders have long referred to their island as the "shoe" and speak of driving to the toe or going to the heel. If you take a look at a map, you'll see why: Hilton Head bears an uncanny resemblance to a running shoe pointed toward the southwest, with the aptly named Broad Creek forming a near facsimile of the Nike "swoosh" symbol.

Running the length and circumference of the shoe is the main drag, U.S. 278 Business (William Hilton Parkway), which crosses onto Hilton

Head right at the "tongue" of the shoe, a relatively undeveloped area. The Cross Island Parkway toll route (U.S. 278), beginning up toward the ankle as you first get on the island, is a quicker route straight to the toe near Sea Pines.

While it is technically the business spur, when locals say "278" they're talking about the William Hilton Parkway. It takes you along the entire sole of the shoe, including the beaches, and on down to the toe, where you'll find a confusing, crazy British-style roundabout called Sea Pines Circle. It's also the site of the Harbour Town Marina and the island's oldest planned development, Sea Pines Plantation.

While making your way around the island, always keep in mind that the bulk of it consists of private developments, and local law enforcement frowns on people who aimlessly wander among the condos and villas.

Other than taxi services, there is no public transportation to speak of in Hilton Head, unless you want to count the free shuttle around Sea Pines Plantation. Taxi services include **Yellow Cab** (843/686-6666), **Island Taxi** (843/683-6363), and **Ferguson Transportation** (843/842-8088).

The Golden Isles

HISTORY

For over 5,000 years, the Golden Isles of what would become Georgia were an abundant food and game source for Native Americans. In those days, long before erosion and channel dredging had taken their toll, each barrier island was an easy canoe ride away from the next one—a sort of early Intracoastal Waterway—and there was bounty for everyone. But all that changed in 1526 when the Golden Isles became the site of the first European settlement in what is now the continental United States, the fabled San Miguel de Gualdape, founded nearly a century before the first English settlements in Virginia. Historians remain unsure where expedition leader Lucas de Ayllón actually set up camp with his 600 colonists and slaves, but recent research breakthroughs have put it somewhere around St. Catherine's Sound. San Miguel disintegrated within a couple of months, but it set the stage for a lengthy Spanish presence on the Georgia coast that culminated in the mission period (1580-1684). With cooperation from the coastal chiefdoms of Guale and Mocama, almost all of Georgia's barrier islands and many interior spots hosted Catholic missions, each with an accompanying contingent of Spanish regulars. The missions began retreating with the English incursion into the American Southeast in the 1600s, and the coast was largely free of European presence until an early English outpost, Fort King George near modern-day Darien, Georgia, was established decades later in 1721. Isolated and hard to provision, the small fort was abandoned seven years later.

The next English project was Fort Frederica on St. Simons Island,

The Golden Isles

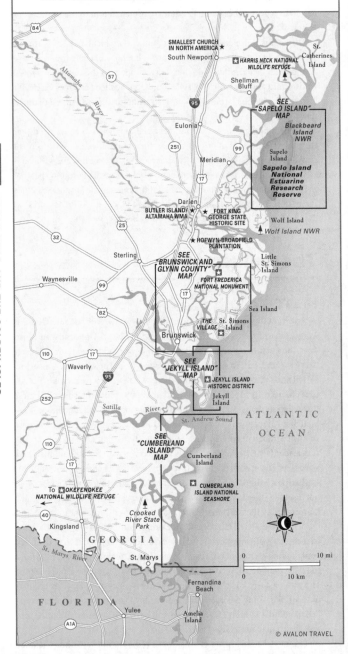

SMALLEST CHURCH IN NORTH AMERICA ★
South Newport
★ HARRIS NECK NATIONAL WILDLIFE REFUGE
St. Catherines Island
Shellman Bluff
SEE "SAPELO ISLAND" MAP
Eulonia
Blackbeard Island NWR
Meridian
Sapelo Island
Sapelo Island National Estuarine Research Reserve
Darien
BUTLER ISLAND/ ★ ALTAMAHA WMA
★ FORT KING GEORGE STATE HISTORIC SITE
Wolf Island
Wolf Island NWR
Sterling
★ HOFWYN-BROADFIELD PLANTATION
Little St. Simons Island
SEE "BRUNSWICK AND GLYNN COUNTY" MAP
Waynesville
FORT FREDERICA NATIONAL MONUMENT
Sea Island
THE VILLAGE
St. Simons Island
Brunswick
SEE "JEKYLL ISLAND" MAP
Waverly
JEKYLL ISLAND HISTORIC DISTRICT
Jekyll Island
ATLANTIC OCEAN
Satilla River
St. Andrew Sound
SEE "CUMBERLAND ISLAND" MAP
Cumberland Island
To OKEFENOKEE NATIONAL WILDLIFE REFUGE
CUMBERLAND ISLAND NATIONAL SEASHORE
Crooked River State Park
Kingsland
GEORGIA
St. Marys
Altamaha River
St. Marys River
Fernandina Beach
FLORIDA
Yulee
Amelia Island

0   10 mi
0   10 km

© AVALON TRAVEL

commissioned by General James Edward Oglethorpe following his establishment of Savannah to the north. Oglethorpe's settlement of Brunswick and Jekyll Island came soon afterward. With the final vanquishing of the Spanish at the Battle of Bloody Marsh near Fort Frederica, the Georgia coast quickly emulated the profitable rice-based plantation culture of the South Carolina Lowcountry, and indeed many notable Carolina planters expanded their holdings with marshland on the Georgia coast.

During the Civil War the southern reaches of Sherman's March to the Sea came down as far as Darien, a once-vital trading port that was burned to the ground by Union troops. With slavery gone and the plantation system in disarray, the coast's African American population was largely left to its own devices. Although the famous "40 acres and a mule" land and wealth redistribution plan for freed slaves would not fruition, the black population of Georgia's Sea Islands, like that of South Carolina's, developed an inward-looking culture that persists to this day. The generic term for this culture is Gullah, but in Georgia you'll also hear it referred to as Geechee, local dialect for the nearby Ogeechee River.

As with much of the South after the Civil War, business carried on, with the area becoming a center for lumber, the turpentine trade, and an increasing emphasis on fishing and shrimping. But by the start of the 20th century, the Golden Isles had become firmly established as a playground for the rich, who hunted and dined on the sumptuous grounds of exclusive retreats such as the Jekyll Island Club.

As it did elsewhere, World War II brought new economic growth in the form of military bases, even as German U-boats ranged off the coast. Today the federal presence is most obvious in the massive Trident submarine base at Kings Bay toward the Florida border.

BRUNSWICK AND GLYNN COUNTY

Consider Brunswick sort of a junior Savannah, sharing with that larger city to the north a heavily English flavor, great manners, a city plan with squares courtesy of General James Oglethorpe, a thriving but environmentally intrusive seaport, and a busy shrimping fleet. While Brunswick never became the dominant commercial center, à la Savannah, that it was envisioned to be, it has followed the Savannah model in modern times, both in terms of downtown revitalization and an increasing emphasis on port activity. Sadly, unlike Savannah, Brunswick has not seen fit to preserve the integrity of its six existing squares; all but one (Hanover Square) have been bisected by streets or built on.

The first real English-speaking settler in the area, Mark Carr, began cultivating land near Brunswick in 1738, but the city wasn't laid out until 1771, in a grid design similar to Savannah's. Originally comprising nearly 400 acres, Brunswick was named for Braunschweig, the seat of the House of Hanover in Germany, and also for the Duke of Brunswick, a brother of King George III. The Brunswick area hosted profitable plantations and a burgeoning lumber industry, but a series of financial panics in the late

Brunswick and Glynn County

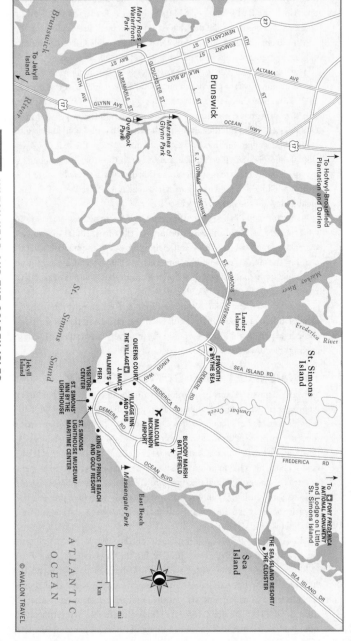

© AVALON TRAVEL

1830s hit particularly hard. When the Civil War started, most white citizens fled to nearby Waynesville, Georgia, and wharves and key buildings were burned to keep them out of Union hands. Brunswick saw a boom in population during World War II as a home of wartime industry such as the J. A. Jones Construction Company, which in a two-year span built 99 massive Liberty ships and at its peak employed 16,000 workers (they managed to build seven ships in a single month in 1944).

Since the war, the shrimping industry has played a big role in Brunswick's economy, so much so that the city calls itself the "Shrimp Capital of the World." But lately the local shrimping industry has been in steep decline, from both depleted coastal stocks and increased competition from Asian shrimp farms. Hit hard by the recent economic downturn, Brunswick has seen better days. Despite an admirable effort at downtown revitalization centering on Newcastle Street, most visitors to the area seem content to employ Brunswick, as its nickname implies, as a "Gateway to the Golden Isles" rather than as a destination in itself.

Sights

Brunswick Historic District

Technically, Brunswick has an "Old Town" district on the National Register of Historic Places as well as an adjacent district called "Historic Brunswick" centering on the storefronts of Newcastle Street. Since it's all pretty close together, we'll consider it all one nice package. Unlike Savannah, which renamed many of its streets in a fit of patriotism after the American Revolution, Brunswick's streets bear their original Anglophilic names, like Gloucester, Albemarle, and Norwich. You'd be forgiven for thinking that Brunswick's Union Street is a post-Civil War statement of national unity, but the name actually commemorates the union of Scotland and England in 1707. Most of the visitor-friendly activity centers on **Newcastle Street**, where you'll find the bulk of the galleries, shops, and restored buildings. Adjacent in the more historic areas are some nice residential homes.

The new pride of downtown is **Old City Hall** (1212 Newcastle St., 912/265-4032, www.brunswickgeorgia.net/och2.html), an amazing circa-1889 Richardsonian Romanesque edifice designed by noted regional architect Alfred Eichberg, who also planned many similarly imposing buildings in Savannah. Today it doubles as a rental event facility as well as a part-time courthouse; call ahead to take a gander inside.

Another active restored building is the charming **Ritz Theatre** (1530 Newcastle St., 912/262-6934, www.goldenislearts.org), built in 1898 to house the Grand Opera House and the offices of the Brunswick and Birmingham Railroad. This ornate three-story Victorian transitioned with the times, becoming a vaudeville venue, then a movie house. Under the management of the Golden Isles Arts and Humanities Association since 1989, the Ritz now hosts performances, studios, an art gallery, and classes.

Brunswick

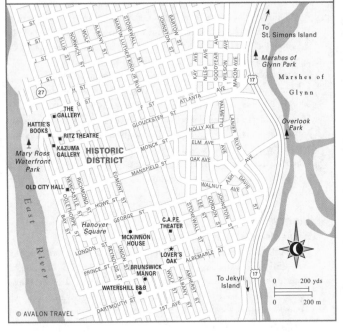

Mary Ross Waterfront Park

Mary Ross Waterfront Park, a downtown gathering place at Bay and Gloucester Streets, also has economic importance as a center of local industry—it's here where Brunswick's shrimp fleet is moored and the town's large port facilities begin. Unfortunately, nearby is a huge factory, dispensing its unpleasant odor over the waterfront 24/7. In 1989 the park was dedicated to Mary Ross, member of a longtime Brunswick shrimping family and author of the popular Georgia history book *The Debatable Land.* While the book is still a great read, sadly Ms. Ross was wrong when she wrote that the tabby ruins in the area were of Spanish origin. Devastated by the discovery that they actually dated from later and were of English construction, she vowed never to publish another word again.

At the entrance to the park is a well-done model of a Liberty ship, similar to the thousands that were built in Brunswick during World War II.

Lover's Oak

At the intersection of Prince and Albany Streets, you'll find the **Lover's Oak,** a nearly 1,000-year-old tree. Local lore tells us that it has been a secret meeting place for young lovers for centuries (though one does wonder how much of a secret it actually could have been). It's about 13 feet in diameter and has 10 sprawling limbs.

Amid the light industrial sprawl of this area of the Golden Isles Parkway is the interesting little **Overlook Park,** just south of the visitors center on U.S. 17—a good, if loud, place for a picnic. From the park's picnic grounds or overlook you can see the fabled Marshes of Glynn, which inspired Georgia poet Sidney Lanier to write his famous poem of the same title under the **Lanier Oak,** located a little farther up the road in the median.

Hofwyl-Broadfield Plantation

A well-preserved old rice plantation, the **Hofwyl-Broadfield Plantation** (5556 U.S. 17, 912/264-7333, www.gastateparks.org, Thurs.-Sat. 9am-5pm, last main house tour 4:45pm, $7 adults, $4 children) is a short drive north of Brunswick. With its old paddy fields along the gorgeous and relatively undeveloped Altamaha River estuary, the plantation's main home is an antebellum wonder, with an expansive porch and a nice house museum that includes silver, a model of a rice plantation, and a slide show. There's also a pleasant nature trail.

William Brailsford of Charleston finished the plantation in 1807, and it soon passed into the hands of the Troup family, who expanded the holdings to over 7,000 acres. Rice finally became financially unfeasible in the early 20th century, and the plantation turned to dairy farming, a pursuit that lasted until World War II. Ophelia Troup Dent would ultimately will the site to the state of Georgia in 1973.

The best way to get here is by taking U.S. 17 north of Brunswick for about 10 miles until you see the signs; the plantation entrance is on the east side of the road.

Entertainment and Events

The **Golden Isles Arts and Humanities Association** (1530 Newcastle St., 912/262-6934, www.goldenislesarts.org) is an umbrella organization for many arts activities in the Brunswick, Jekyll, and St. Simons area. They also manage the historic **Ritz Theatre** (1530 Newcastle St., 912/262-6934) in downtown Brunswick, which offers a yearly performance season that's worth checking out if you have a free weekend night.

Nightlife

Brunswick is a conservative place with little bar scene to speak of. But a few miles offshore is quite a different story when the **Emerald Princess Casino** (Gisco Point, 912/265-3558, www.emeraldprincesscasino.com, Mon.-Thurs. 7pm-midnight, Fri.-Sat. 11am-4pm and 7pm-1am, Sun. 1pm-6pm, $10) is operating. This is the classic gambling and party boat experience, with the action starting when the *Emerald Princess* slips into international waters and out of domestic gambling regulations. Ten bucks for the cruise gets you a light dinner. Drinks and casino chips, of course, are on you. No one under age 21 is allowed, and minimum and maximum bets vary by table. Reservations are required. To get to the dock, take U.S. 17 over the massive

In the Footsteps of Bartram

In March 1773, the 33-year-old William Bartram—son of royal botanist John Bartram—arrived in Savannah to begin what would become a four-year journey through eight colonies. Bartram not only exhaustively documented his encounters with nature and with Native Americans, he made discoveries whose impact has stayed with us to this day.

Young "Willie," born near Philadelphia in 1739, had a talent for drawing and for plants. A failure at business, Bartram was happy to settle on a traveling lifestyle that mixed both his loves. After accompanying his father on several early trips, Bartram set out on his own at the request of an old friend of his father's in England, Dr. John Fothergill, who paid Bartram 50 pounds per year plus expenses to send back specimens and drawings.

Though Bartram's quest would eventually move farther inland and encompass much of the modern American South, most of its first year was spent in coastal Georgia. After arriving in Savannah he moved southward, roughly paralleling modern U.S. 17, to Sunbury, through Midway, and on to Darien, where he stayed at the plantation of Lachlan McIntosh on the great Altamaha River, which inspired Bartram to pen some of his most beautiful writing. Bartram also journeyed to Sapelo Island, Brunswick, St. Marys, and even into the great Okefenokee Swamp. Using Savannah and Charleston as bases, Bartram mostly traveled alone, either by horse, by boat, or on foot. Word of his trip preceded him, and he was usually greeted warmly by local traders and Indian chiefs. In many places, he was the first European seen since De Soto and the Spanish. His epic journey ended in late 1776, when Bartram gazed on his beloved Altamaha for the last time. Heading north and crossing the Savannah River south of Ebenezer, he proceeded to Charleston and from there to his hometown of Philadelphia—where he would remain for the rest of his days.

At its publication, his 1791 chronicle, *Travels Through North and South Carolina, Georgia, East and West Florida,* was hailed as "the most astounding verbal artifact of the early republic." In that unassuming yet timeless work, Bartram cemented his reputation as the country's first native-born naturalist and practically invented the modern travelogue. Thanks to the establishment of the William Bartram Trail in 1976, you can walk in his footsteps. The trail uses a rather liberal interpretation, including memorials, trails, and gardens, but many specific "heritage sites" in coastal Georgia have their own markers:

- River and Barnard Streets in Savannah to mark the beginning of Bartram's trek

- LeConte-Woodmanston Plantation in Liberty County (Barrington Ferry Rd. south of Sandy Run Rd. near Riceboro)

- Off U.S. 17, 1.5 miles south of the South Newport River

- St. Simon's Island on Frederica Road near the Fort Frederica entrance

- Off U.S. 275 at Old Ebenezer Cemetery in Effingham County

Sidney Lanier Bridge. Take a left onto the Jekyll Island Causeway and then an immediate left onto Gisco Point Drive. Follow signs into the parking lot.

Performing Arts

Based in St. Simons Island, the **Coastal Symphony of Georgia** (912/634-2006, www.coastalsymphonyofgeorgia.org), under the baton of Vernon Humbert, plays concerts in Brunswick during its season at different venues. Check the website for details. **Art Downtown** (209 Gloucester St., 912/262-0628, www.artdowntowngallery209.com) hosts locally written shows performed by the Brunswick Actors Theatre in its black box space and showcases local visual artists in its attached **Gallery 209**. The **Brunswick Community Concert Association** (912/638-5616, www.brunswickcommunityconcert.org, $25 adults, $10 students) brings an eclectic variety of high-quality national and regional vocal acts to various venues. The **C.A.P.E. Theater** (916 Albany St., 912/996-7740, www.capetheater.org), short for Craft, Appreciation, Performance, and Education, is a community group that performs a mix of classics and musicals at various venues. No reservations are necessary unless you're attending a dinner theater show, which is about $30 adults, $15 students. The town's main dance group is **Invisions Dance Company**, which performs out of **Studio South** (1307 Grant St., 912/265-3255, www.studiosouthga.com).

Festivals and Events

Each Mother's Day at noon, parishioners of the local St. Francis Xavier Church hold the **Our Lady of Fatima Processional and Blessing of the Fleet** (www.brunswick.net), begun in 1938 by the local Portuguese fishing community. After the procession, at about 3pm at Mary Ross Waterfront Park, comes the actual blessing of the shrimping fleet.

Foodies will enjoy the **Brunswick Stewbilee** ($9 adults, $4 children), held on the second Saturday in October 11:30am-3pm. Pro and amateur chefs showcase their skills in creating the local signature dish and vying for the title of "Brunswick Stewmaster." There are also car shows, contests, displays, and much live music.

Shopping

Right in the heart of the bustle on Newcastle is a good indie bookstore, **Hattie's Books** (1531 Newcastle St., 912/554-8677, www.hattiesbooks.net, Mon.-Fri. 10am-5:30pm, Sat. 10am-4pm). Not only do they have a good selection of local and regional authors, but you can also get a good cup of coffee.

Brunswick has made the art gallery a central component of its downtown revitalization, with nearly all of them on Newcastle Street. Near Hattie's you'll find the eclectic **Kazuma Gallery** (1523 Newcastle St., 912/279-0023, Mon.-Fri. 10am-5:30pm, Sat. 10am-2pm) as well as the **Ritz Theatre** (1530 Newcastle St., 912/262-6934, Tues.-Fri. 9am-5pm, Sat. 10am-2pm), which has its own art gallery inside. Farther down is **The Gallery on Newcastle**

Clockwise from top left: Hofwyl-Broadfield Plantation; Blythe Island Regional Park; Newcastle Street in Brunswick.

Street (1626 Newcastle St., 912/554-0056, Thurs.-Sat. 11am-5pm), show-casing the original oils of owner Janet Powers.

Sports and Recreation
Hiking, Biking, and Bird-Watching

As one of the **Colonial Coast Birding Trail** sites, **Hofwyl-Broadfield Plantation** (5556 U.S. 17, 912/264-7333, www.gastateparks.org, Tues.-Sat. 9am-5pm) offers a great nature trail along the marsh. Clapper rails, marsh wrens, and a wide variety of warblers come through the site regularly.

Birders and hikers will also enjoy the **Earth Day Nature Trail** (1 Conservation Way, 912/264-7218), a self-guided, fully accessible walk where you can see such comparative rarities as the magnificent wood stork and other indigenous and migratory waterfowl. The trail includes observation towers. Binoculars available for checkout. To get here, take U.S. 17 south through Brunswick. Just north of the big Sidney Lanier Bridge, turn left on Conservation Way (you'll see signage) to reach the parking lot.

Just across the Brunswick River from town is **Blythe Island Regional Park** (6616 Blythe Island Hwy., 912/261-3805), a 1,100-acre public park with a campground, picnic area, and boat landing. The views are great, and it's big enough to do some decent biking and hiking. The best way to get here is to get back on I-95 and head south. Take exit 29, head north for 0.5 mile on U.S. 82, then take a right onto Highway 303.

Another scenic park with a campground is **Altamaha Park of Glynn County** (1605 Altamaha Park Rd., 912/264-2342), northwest of Brunswick off U.S. 341, with 30 campsites and a boat ramp.

Kayaking and Boating

Most recreational adventurers in the area prefer to launch from St. Simons Island. The key public landing in Brunswick, however, is **Brunswick Landing Marina** (2429 Newcastle St., 912/262-9264). You can also put in at the public boat ramps at **Blythe Island Regional Park** (6616 Blythe Island Hwy., 912/261-3805), which is on the Brunswick River, or the **Altamaha Park of Glynn County** (1605 Altamaha Park Rd., 912/264-2342), on the Altamaha River slightly north.

For expert guided tours at a reasonable price, check out **SouthEast Adventure Outfitters** (1200 Glynn Ave./U.S. 17, 912/265-5292, www.southeastadventure.com), which has a dock right on the fabled "Marshes of Glynn."

Accommodations

In addition to the usual variety of chain hotels—most of which you should stay far away from—there are some nice places to stay in Brunswick at very reasonable prices if you want to make the city a base of operations. In the heart of Old Town in a gorgeous Victorian is the ★ **McKinnon House** (1001 Egmont St., 912/261-9100, www.mckinnonhousebandb.com, $125), which had a cameo role in the 1974 film *Conrack*. Today, this bed-and-breakfast

Brunswick Stew

Virginians insist that the distinctive Southern dish known as Brunswick stew was named for Brunswick County, Virginia, in 1828, where a political rally featured stew made from squirrel meat. But Southern foodies know the dish is named for Brunswick, Georgia. There's a plaque to prove it in downtown Brunswick—although it says the first pot was cooked on July 2, 1898, on St. Simons Island, not in Brunswick at all.

What we now know as Brunswick stew is based on an old colonial recipe, adapted from Native Americans, that relied on the meat of small game—originally squirrel or rabbit but nowadays mostly chicken or pork—along with vegetables like corn, onions, and okra simmered over an open fire. Today, this tangy, thick, tomato-based delight is a typical accompaniment to barbecue throughout the Lowcountry and the Georgia coast, as well as a freestanding entrée on its own. Done traditionally, a proper pot of Brunswick stew is an involved kitchen project taking most of a day, but it's worth it. Here's a typical recipe from Glynn County, home of the famous Brunswick Stewbilee festival held the second Saturday of October:

Sauce

Melt ¼ cup butter over low heat, then add:
1¾ cups ketchup
¼ cup yellow mustard
¼ cup white vinegar

Blend until smooth, then add:
½ tablespoon chopped garlic
1 teaspoon ground black pepper
½ teaspoon crushed red pepper
½ ounce Liquid Smoke

Legend says the first Brunswick Stew was made in this pot.

1 ounce Worcestershire sauce
1 ounce hot sauce
½ tablespoon fresh lemon juice

Blend until smooth, then add:
¼ cup dark brown sugar
Stir constantly and simmer for 10 minutes, being careful not to boil. Set aside.

Stew

Melt ¼ pound butter in a two-gallon pot, then add:
3 cups diced small potatoes
1 cup diced small onion
2 14½-ounce cans chicken broth
1 pound baked chicken, cubed
8-10 ounces smoked pork, cubed

Bring to a boil, stirring until potatoes are nearly done, then add:
1 8½-ounce can early peas
2 14½-ounce cans stewed tomatoes
1 16-ounce can baby lima beans
¼ cup Liquid Smoke
1 14½-ounce can creamed corn

Stir in sauce. Simmer slowly for two hours. Makes one gallon of Brunswick stew.

is Jo Miller's labor of love, a three-suite affair with some plush interiors and an exterior that is one of Brunswick's most photographed spots.

Surprisingly affordable for its elegance, the **WatersHill Bed & Breakfast** (728 Union St., 912/264-4262, www.watershill.com, $100) serves a full breakfast and offers a choice of five themed suites, such as the French country Elliot Wynell Room or the large Mariana Mahlaney Room way up in the restored attic. Another good B&B is the **Brunswick Manor** (825 Egmont St., 912/265-6889, www.brunswickmanor.com, $130), offering four suites in a classic Victorian and a tasty meal each day.

The most unique lodging in the area is the ★ **Hostel in the Forest** (Hwy. 82, 912/264-9738, www.foresthostel.com, $25, cash only), essentially a group of geodesic domes and whimsical tree houses a little way off the highway. Formed more than 30 years ago as an International Youth Hostel, the place initially gives off a hippie vibe, with an evening communal meal (included in the rates) and a near-total ban on cell phones. But don't expect a wild time: No pets are allowed, the hostel discourages young children, and quiet time is strictly enforced beginning at 11pm. It's an adventurous, peaceful, and very inexpensive place to stay, but be warned that there is no heating or cooling. To reach the hostel, take I-95 exit 29 and go west for two miles. Make a U-turn at the intersection at mile marker 11. Continue east on Highway 82 for 0.5 mile. Look for a dirt road on the right with a gate and signage.

Food

Brunswick isn't known for its breadth of cuisine options, and, frankly, most discriminating diners make the short drive over the causeway to St. Simons Island. One exception in Brunswick that really stands out, however, is **Indigo Coastal Shanty** (1402 Reynolds St., 912/265-2007, www.indigocoastalshanty.com, Tues.-Fri. 11am-3pm, Fri.-Sat. also open 5pm-10pm, $12). This friendly, smallish place specializes in creative coastal themes, with dishes like the Charleston Sauté (shrimp and ham with peppers), Fisherman's Bowl (shrimp and fish in a nice broth), and even that old Southern favorite, a pimento cheeseburger.

Information and Services

The **Brunswick-Golden Isles Visitor Center** (2000 Glynn Ave., 912/264-5337, daily 9am-5pm) is at the intersection of U.S. 17 and the Torras Causeway to St. Simons Island. It features the famous pot in which the first batch of Brunswick stew was cooked across the bridge on St. Simons. A downtown **information station** is in the Ritz Theatre (1530 Newcastle St., 912/262-6934, Tues.-Fri. 9am-5pm, Sat. 10am-2pm).

The newspaper of record in town is the *Brunswick News* (www.thebrunswicknews.com). The main **post office** (805 Gloucester St., 912/280-1250) is downtown.

Jekyll Island

Driftwood Beach

CLAM CREEK PICNIC AREA

JEKYLL ISLAND

HORTON HOUSE TABBY RUINS

MAJOR HORTON RD

N RIVERVIEW DR

Brunswick River

CAPTAIN WYLLY RD

To Brunswick

JEKYLL ISLAND GOLF RESORT

GEORGIA SEA TURTLE CENTER

STABLE RD

PIER RD

WELCOME CENTER

LATITUDE 31

JEKYLL ISLAND MINI GOLF

JEKYLL ISLAND CLUB/ COURTYARD AT CRANE

SHELL RD

JEKYLL ISLAND CAUSEWAY

JEKYLL ISLAND HISTORIC DISTRICT

TOLL STATION

TIDELANDS 4-H NATURE CENTER

SUMMER WAVES

Jekyll Sound

HAMPTON INN & SUITES JEKYLL ISLAND

St. Andrews Park

S RIVERVIEW DR

Intracoastal Waterway

S BEACHVIEW DR

South Dunes

ATLANTIC OCEAN

0   1 mi

0   1 km

© AVALON TRAVEL

Getting There and Around

Brunswick is directly off I-95. Take exit 38 to the Golden Isles Parkway, and take a right on U.S. 17. The quickest way to the historic district is to make a right onto Gloucester Street. Plans and funding for a city-wide public transit system are pending, but currently Brunswick has no public transportation.

JEKYLL ISLAND

Few places in the United States have as paradoxical a story as Jekyll Island. Once the playground of the world's richest people—whose indulgence allowed it to escape the overdevelopment that plagues nearby St. Simons—Jekyll then became a dedicated vacation area for Georgians of modest means, by order of the state legislature. Today, it's somewhere in the middle—a great place for a relaxing nature-oriented vacation that retains some of the perks of luxury of its Gilded Age pedigree.

History

In prehistoric times, Jekyll was mainly a seasonal getaway for Native Americans. Indigenous people visited the area during the winter to enjoy its temperate weather and abundant shellfish. The Spanish also knew it well, calling it Isla de Las Ballenas (Island of the Whales) for the annual gathering of calving right whale families directly off the coast every winter—a mystical event that happens to this day. After securing safe access to the island from the Creeks in 1733, Georgia's founder, General James Oglethorpe, gave the island its modern name, after his friend Sir Joseph

Jekyll. The first English settler was Major William Horton in 1735, recipient of a land grant from the general, and the tabby ruins of one of Horton's homes remain today. A Frenchman, Christophe Poulain DuBignon, purchased the island in 1800 and remained a leading figure. A mysterious event happened in 1858, when Jekyll Island was the final port of entry for the infamous voyage of *The Wanderer,* the last American slave ship. After intercepting the ship and its contraband manifest of 409 African slaves—the importation of slaves having been banned in 1808—its owners and crew were put on trial in Savannah.

As a home away from home for the country's richest industrialists—including J. P. Morgan, William Rockefeller, and William Vanderbilt—in the late 1800s and early 1900s, Jekyll Island was the unlikely seat of some of the most crucial events in modern American history. It was at the Jekyll Island Club in 1910 that the Federal Reserve banking system was set up, the result of a secret convocation of investors and tycoons. Five years later on the grounds of the club, AT&T president Theodore Vail would listen in on the first transcontinental phone call.

Jekyll's unspoiled beauty prompted the state legislature in 1947 to purchase the island and—ironically, considering the island's former history—declare it a totally accessible "playground" for Georgians of low to middle income (a causeway wasn't completed until the mid-1950s). This stated public mission is why prices on the island—currently administered on behalf of the state by the Jekyll Island Authority—have stayed so low and development has been so well managed. Every so often a controversial redevelopment plan is proposed, with the potential to introduce high-dollar resort-style development to parts of Jekyll for the first time since the days of J. P. Morgan and company. Residents and conservationists alike continue to work together to protect this magical barrier island known as "Georgia's Jewel."

Orientation

You'll have to stop at the entrance gate and pay a $6 "parking fee" to gain access to this state-owned island. A friendly attendant will give you a map and a newsletter, and from there you're free to enjoy the whole island at your leisure.

As you dead-end into Beachview Drive, you're faced with a decision to turn either left or right. Most scenic and social activity is to the north, a left turn. For more peaceful beach-oriented activity with few services, turn right and head south. One historical reason for the lesser development at the south end is due to the fact that segregation laws were still in effect after the state's purchase of Jekyll in 1947. African American facilities were centered on the south end, while white activities were in the north.

★ Jekyll Island Historic District

A living link to one of the most glamorous eras of American history, the Jekyll Island Historic District is also one of the largest ongoing restoration projects in the southeastern United States. A visit to this 240-acre riverfront area is like stepping back in time to the Gilded Age, with croquet grounds, manicured gardens, and even ferry boats with names like the *Rockefeller* and the *J. P. Morgan*. The historic district essentially comprises the buildings and grounds of the old Jekyll Island Club, not only a full-service resort complex—consisting of the main building and several amazing "cottages" that are mansions themselves—but a sort of living history exhibit chronicling that time when Jekyll was a gathering place for the world's richest and most influential people.

The Queen Anne-style main clubhouse, with its iconic turret, dates from 1886. Within a couple of years the club had already outgrown it, and the millionaires began building the ornate cottages on the grounds surrounding it. The Chicora Cottage is gone, demolished after the supposedly accidental gunfire death of Edwin Gould in 1917, with only a hole in the ground remaining. But most of the others have been fully restored as lodgings. In 2000 renovations were done on the most magnificent outbuilding, the 24-bedroom Crane Cottage, a Mediterranean villa that also hosts a fine restaurant. In 2010, the Indian Mound Cottage, once William Rockefeller's vacation getaway, reopened to tours after renovation.

The Jekyll Island Museum (100 Stable Rd., 912/635-4036, www.jekyllisland.com, daily 9am-5pm, free), in the historic district at the old club stables, houses some good history exhibits. The museum also provides guided themed tours from $10 per person focusing on the historic district, including the popular "Passport to the Century" (which includes entrance to two restored cottages) and "In the Service of Others" (focusing on the support staff of the golden age of the Jekyll Island Club). You can also purchase a guidebook for self-guided tours of the historic district.

Georgia Sea Turtle Center

Within the grounds of the historic district in a whimsically renovated historic 1903 building is the Georgia Sea Turtle Center (214 Stable Rd., 912/635-4444, www.georgiaseaturtlecenter.org, Mon. 10am-2pm, Tues.-Sun. 9am-5pm, $7 adults, $5 children), which features interactive exhibits on these important marine creatures, for whom Jekyll Island is a major nesting ground. Don't miss the attached rehabilitation building, where you can see the center's turtles in various states of treatment and rehabilitation before they are released into the wild. Children and adults alike will enjoy this unique opportunity to see these creatures up close and learn about the latest efforts to protect them.

In an effort to raise awareness about the need to protect the nesting areas of the big loggerheads that lay eggs on Jekyll each summer, the Sea Turtle Center also guides nighttime tours (early June-Aug. daily 8:30pm

Clockwise from top left: Jekyll's Driftwood Beach; the tabby ruins of Horton House; legendary Jekyll Island Club.

and 9:30pm) on the beach in order to explain about the animals and their habitat and hopefully to see some loggerheads in action. These tours fill up fast, so make reservations in advance.

Driftwood Beach

Barrier islands like Jekyll are in a constant state of southward flux as currents erode the north end and push sand down the beach to the south end. This phenomenon has created **Driftwood Beach,** as the soil has eroded from under the large trees, causing them to fall and settle into the sand. In addition to being a naturalist's wonderland, it's also a starkly beautiful and strangely romantic spot. The newsletter you get as you enter the island has a map with Driftwood Beach on it, but here's a tip: Drive north on Beachview Drive until you see a pullover on your right immediately after the Villas by the Sea (there's no signage). Park and take the short trail through the maritime forest, and you'll find yourself right there among the fallen trees and sand.

Horton House Tabby Ruins

Round the curve and go south on Riverview Drive, and you'll see the large frame of a two-story house on the left (east) side of the road, the ruins of the old **Horton House,** built by Jekyll's original English-speaking settler, William Horton. Horton's house has survived two wars, a couple hurricanes, and a clumsy restoration in 1898. Its current state of preservation is thanks to the hands of the Jekyll Island Authority and various federal, state, and local partners. Horton's first house, also made of tabby, was burned by the Spanish during their retreat after losing the Battle of Bloody Marsh on nearby St. Simons Island. But the intrepid major rebuilt on the same spot in 1742, continuing to farm barley and indigo plants on the surrounding grounds as well as hosting Georgia's first brewery, the ruins of which are nearby.

Frenchman Christophe Poulain DuBignon would live in the Horton House for a while after purchasing the island in the 1790s. Across the street from the house is the poignant little **DuBignon Cemetery,** around which winds a nicely done pedestrian and bike path overlooking one of the most beautiful areas of marsh you'll see in all the Golden Isles.

Entertainment and Events

There's no real nightlife to speak of on Jekyll, it being intended for quiet, affordable daytime relaxation. The focus instead is on several annual events held at the **Jekyll Island Convention Center** (1 N. Beachview Dr., 912/635-3400), which has undergone a massive restoration to bring it in line with modern convention standards.

At the beginning of the new year comes one of the area's most beloved

Jekyll Island's Millionaires Club

As the Industrial Revolution gathered momentum seemingly everywhere but Georgia's Golden Isles, a couple of men decided to do something to break the foggy miasma of Reconstruction. In the late 1870s, John Eugene DuBignon and his brother-in-law Newton Finney came up with a plan to turn Jekyll into an exclusive winter hunting club. Their targeted clientele was a no-brainer: the newly minted American mega-tycoons of the Industrial Age. Finney found 53 such elite millionaires willing to pony up to become charter members of the Jekyll Island Club. Among them were William Vanderbilt, J. P. Morgan, and Joseph Pulitzer. In 1886 Finney purchased the island from DuBignon for $125,000.

With the formal opening in 1888 began Jekyll Island's half century as a playground for the country's richest citizens, centered on the Victorian "cottages" built by each member and preserved today in the historic district. In the 1920s, the focus shifted to golf, and you can still play a portion of the historic course at the club today. By 1900 the club's membership represented one-sixth of the world's wealth. Nonmembers were not allowed to enjoy the facilities, regardless of social stature. Winston Churchill and President William McKinley were refused admission.

These influential men often mixed business with pleasure. In 1910, secret meetings of the so-called "First Name Club" led to the development of the Aldrich Plan, which laid the groundwork for the modern Federal Reserve system. Under assumed names, Senator Nelson Aldrich, Assistant Treasury Secretary A. Piatt Andrew, Banker's Trust vice president Benjamin Strong, National City Bank president Frank Vanderlip, investment banker Paul Warburg, and J. P. Morgan partner Henry P. Davison visited the club with the cover story of participating in a duck hunt. When they arrived by train at Brunswick, reporters had already gathered. Davison took the station-master aside, saying, "Come out, old man, I will tell you a story." Returning a few minutes later, Davison told his colleagues, "That's all right. They won't give us away." What Davison's "story" was remains a mystery.

A few years later, AT&T president Theodore Vail, nursing a broken leg at his cottage on Jekyll, participated in the first transcontinental telephone call on January 25, 1915, involving New York City, San Francisco, and the special line strung down the coast from New York and across Jekyll Sound to the club grounds. Also on the line were the telephone's inventor, Alexander Graham Bell, his assistant Thomas Watson, the mayors of New York and San Francisco, and President Woodrow Wilson.

The millionaires continued to frolic on Jekyll through the Great Depression, but worsening international economic conditions reduced membership, even though the cost of membership was lowered in 1933. The outbreak of World War II and the resulting drain of labor into the armed forces put a further cramp in the club's workings, and it closed for good in 1942. By the time German U-boats began appearing off the Georgia coast, prompting island-wide blackouts, the Jekyll Island Club already seemed like ancient history. The state would acquire the island after the war in 1947, turning the once-exclusive playground of millionaires into a playground for all the people.

and well-attended events, the **Jekyll Island Bluegrass Festival** (www. aandabluegrass.com). Many of the genre's biggest traditional names come to play at this casual multiday gathering. The focus here is on the music, not the trappings, so come prepared to enjoy wall-to-wall bluegrass played by the best in the business. Keep in mind that during this weekend the island is awash in RVs from all over the country, so if you're camping, you'd better make reservations.

In September as the harvest comes in off the boats, the **Wild Georgia Shrimp and Grits Festival** (www.jekyllisland.com, free admission) seeks to promote the value of the Georgia shrimping industry by focusing on how good the little critters taste in various regional recipes.

Sports and Recreation
Hiking and Biking

Quite simply, Jekyll Island is a paradise for bicyclists and walkers, with a very well-developed and very safe system of paths totaling about 20 miles and running the entire circumference of the island. The paths go by all major sights, including the Jekyll Island Club in the historic district. In addition, walkers and bicyclists can enjoy much of the seven miles of beachfront at low tide.

Rent your bikes at **Jekyll Island Miniature Golf** (100 James Rd., 912/635-2648, daily 9am-8pm, $5.25 per hour, $11.50 per day). Take a left when you dead-end after the entrance gate, then another left.

Bird-Watching

The **Clam Creek Picnic Area** on the island's north end is on the **Colonial Coast Birding Trail**, and without even trying you will see a wide variety of wading birds and shorebirds. Shell collectors will also have a blast, as will those with a horticultural bent, who will marvel at the variety of species presented in the various ecosystems on the island, from beach to marsh hammock to maritime forest.

Golf and Tennis

True to Jekyll Island's intended role as a playground for Georgians of low to medium income, its golf and tennis facilities—all centrally located at the middle of the island—are quite reasonably priced. The **Jekyll Island Golf Resort** (322 Captain Wylly Rd., 912/635-2368, www.jekyllisland.com, greens fees $40-60) comprises the largest public golf resort in Georgia. A total of 63 holes on four courses—Pine Lakes, Indian Mound, Oleander, and Ocean Dunes (nine holes)—await. Check the resort's website for "golf passport" packages that include local lodging.

The adjacent **Jekyll Island Tennis Center** (400 Captain Wylly Rd., 912/635-3154, www.gate.net/~jitc, $25 per hour) boasts 13 courts, seven of them lighted, as well as a pro shop (daily 9am-6pm).

If a different kind of golf is your thing, try **Jekyll Island Miniature**

Fishing

On Beachview Drive, at the very top of the island is the well-done **Clam Creek Picnic Area** (daily dawn-dusk, free). This facility on the Colonial Coast Birding Trail has a spacious fishing pier over the Jekyll River and a trailhead through the woods and out onto the beach. About a 20-minute walk on the sand gets you to Driftwood Beach from the other side.

A good local fishing charter company is Captain Vernon Reynolds's **Coastal Expeditions** (3202 E. 3rd St., 912/265-0392, www.coastalcharterfishing.com), departing from the Jekyll Harbor Marina. Half-day and full-day trips are available; call for rates.

Kayaking and Boating

Most kayaking activity in the area centers on St. Simons across the sound. But **Tidelands 4-H Nature Center** (100 Riverview Dr., 912/635-5032, www.tidelands4h.org) offers Jekyll-oriented guided kayak tours and also rents kayaks and canoes March-October.

Water Parks

Summer Waves (210 S. Riverview Dr., 912/635-2074, www.jekyllisland.com, Memorial Day-Labor Day, $20 adults, $16 children under 48 inches tall) is just what the doctor ordered for kids with a surplus of energy. The 11-acre facility has a separate section for toddlers to splash around in, with the requisite more daring rides for hard-charging preteens. Hours vary, so call ahead.

Horseback Riding and Carriage Tours

Victoria's Carriages and Trail (100 Stable Rd., 912/635-9500, Mon.-Sat. 11am-4pm) offers numerous options, both on horseback as well as in a horse-drawn carriage, including carriage tours of the island (Mon.-Sat. every hour 11am-4pm, $15 adults, $7 children). There's a 6pm-8pm night ride ($38 per couple). Horseback rides include a one-hour beach ride ($55) that leaves at 11am, 1pm, and 3pm and a sunset ride (6:30pm, $65) that lasts a little over an hour. Victoria's is at the entrance to the Clam Creek Picnic Area on the north end of the island directly across the street from the Jekyll Island Campground.

Tours

The **Tidelands 4-H Center** (100 Riverview Dr., 912/635-5032, www.tidelands4h.org) gives 1.5- to 2-hour Marsh Walks (Mon. 9am, $5 adults, $3 children) leaving from Clam Creek Picnic Area, as well as Beach Walks ($5 adults, $3 children) leaving Wednesdays at 9am from the St. Andrews Picnic area and Fridays at 9am from South Dunes Picnic Area.

Captain Vernon Reynolds's **Coastal Expeditions** (3202 E. 3rd St., 912/265-0392, www.coastalcharterfishing.com, $24 adults, $10 children) provides dolphin tours March-May Tuesday-Saturday at 1:30pm, and there are three trips daily June-August.

Accommodations
Under $150

While most bargain lodging on Jekyll is sadly subpar, the old **Days Inn** (60 S. Beachview Dr., 912/635-9800, www.daysinnjekyll.com, $100) has undergone remodeling and is the best choice if budget is a concern and you don't want to camp. It has a good location on the south side of the island with nice ocean views.

$150-300

Any discussion of lodging on Jekyll Island begins with the legendary ★ **Jekyll Island Club** (371 Riverview Dr., 800/535-9547, www.jekyllclub. com, $199-490), which is reasonably priced considering its history, post-card-perfect setting, and delightful guest rooms. Some of its 157 guest rooms in the club and annex areas are available for under $200 per night, and even the finest, the Presidential Suite, tops out at less than $500 in high season (Mar.-Oct.). There are 60 guest rooms in the main club building, and several outlying cottages, chief among them the Crane, Cherokee, and Sans Souci Cottages, are also available. All rates include use of the big outdoor pool overlooking the river, and a neat amenity is a choice of meal plans for an extra daily fee.

Despite its auspicious beginnings, the club has not been a total success story. The state tried to run it as a resort in the 1950s and 1960s but gave up in 1971. With Historic Landmark District status coming in 1978, restoration wasn't far behind, and the club was reopened as a Radisson. Now operated by Landmark, the club is one of the "Historic Hotels of America" as ranked by the National Trust for Historic Preservation. Keep in mind that not all the fixtures are original, and the present interior design scheme was done with an eye to current commercial taste (those crusty old millionaires would never have gone for pastels).

The first hotel built on the island in 35 years, the ★ **Hampton Inn & Suites Jekyll Island** (200 S. Beachview Dr., 912/635-3733, www.hamptoninn.com, $180-210) was built according to an exacting set of conservation guidelines, conserving much of the original tree canopy and employing various low-impact design and building techniques. Quite simply, it's one of the best eco-friendly hotel designs I've experienced. An elevated wooden walkway to the beach preserves as much of the natural dune-scape as possible, though keep in mind that the tradeoff is that you can't see the ocean from the hotel. The beach isn't far away, and the walk-in saltwater pool is particularly enjoyable and relaxing.

One of the niftiest campgrounds in the entire area is the **Jekyll Island Campground** (197 Riverview Dr., 912/635-3021, tent sites $25, RV sites $32). It's a friendly place with an excellent location at the north end of the island—a short drive or bike ride from just about anywhere and directly across the street from the Clam Creek Picnic Area, with easy beach access. There are more than 200 sites, from tent to full-service pull-through RV sites. There's a two-night minimum on weekends and a three-night minimum on holiday and special event weekends; reservations are recommended.

Food

Cuisine offerings are few and far between on Jekyll. I'd suggest you patronize one of the three dining facilities at the **Jekyll Island Club** (371 Riverview Dr.), which are all open to nonguests. They're not only delicious but pretty reasonable as well, considering the swank setting. My favorite is the ★ **Courtyard at Crane** (912/635-2400, lunch Sun.-Fri. 11am-4pm and Sat. 11am-2pm, dinner Sun.-Thurs. 5:30pm-9pm, $27-38). Located in the circa-1917, beautifully restored Crane Cottage, one of the old tycoon villas, the Courtyard offers romantic evening dining (call for reservations) as well as tasty and stylish lunch dining in the alfresco courtyard area or inside. The lunch menu—a great deal for the quality—is Mediterranean heavy, with wraps, sandwiches, and soups. The dinner menu moves more toward wine-country casual chic, with a lot of pork, veal, and beef dishes to go with the requisite fresh seafood. As a plus, the coffee is great—not at all a given in Southern restaurants. Casual dress is acceptable.

For a real and figurative taste of history, make a reservation at the **Grand Dining Room** (912/635-2400, breakfast Mon.-Sat. 7am-11am and Sun. 7am-10am, lunch Mon.-Sat. 11:30am-2pm, brunch Sun. 10:45am-2pm, dinner daily 6pm-10pm, dinner $26-35), the club's full-service restaurant. Focusing on continental cuisine—ordered either à la carte or as a prix fixe "sunset dinner"—the Grand Dining Room features a pianist each evening and for Sunday brunch. Jackets or collared shirts are required for men.

For a tasty breakfast, lunch, or dinner on the go or at odd hours, check out **Café Solterra** (912/635-2600, daily 7am-10pm), great for deli-type food and equipped with Starbucks coffee. There are two places for seaside dining and cocktails at the historic Jekyll Island Club Wharf: **Latitude 31** (1 Pier Rd., 912/635-3800, www.crossoverjekyll.com, Tues.-Sun. 5:30pm-10pm, $15-25, no reservations) is an upscale seafood-oriented fine-dining place, while the attached **Rah Bar** (Tues.-Sat. 11am-close, Sun. 1pm-close, depending on weather) serves up oysters and shellfish in a very casual setting; try the Lowcountry boil or the crab legs.

Information and Services

The **Jekyll Island Visitor Center** (901 Downing Musgrove Causeway, 912/635-3636, daily 9am-5pm) is on the long causeway along the marsh before you get to the island. Set in a charming little cottage it shares with the Georgia State Patrol, the center has a nice gift shop and loads of brochures on the entire Golden Isles region. Don't hesitate to ask questions of the person taking your $5 entrance fee when you get to the island itself.

The **U.S. Postal Service** keeps an outpost at 18 South Beachview Drive (912/635-2625).

Getting There and Around

Jekyll Island is immediately south of Brunswick. Take I-95 exit 38 to the Golden Isles Parkway. Take a right onto U.S. 17 and keep going until you cross the huge Sidney Lanier Bridge over the Brunswick River. Take an immediate left at the foot of the bridge onto the Downing Musgrove Causeway (Jekyll Island Rd.). This long, scenic route over the beautiful marshes eventually takes you directly onto Jekyll, where you'll have to pay a $5 per vehicle fee to get onto the island. Once on the island, most sites are on the north end (a left as you reach the dead-end at Beachview Dr.). The main circuit route around the island is Beachview Drive, which suitably enough changes into Riverview Drive as it rounds the bend to landward at the north end.

Many visitors choose to bicycle around the island once they're here, which is certainly the best way to experience both the sights and the beach itself at low tide.

ST. SIMONS ISLAND

Despite a certain reputation for aloof affluence, the truth is that St. Simons Island is also very visitor-friendly, and there's more to do here than meets the eye. Think of St. Simons—with a year-round population of about 13,000—as a smaller, less-hurried Hilton Head and you've got the right idea. For those looking for island-style relaxation with no high-rise cookie-cutter development—but still all the modern amenities and luxuries—St. Simons fits the bill perfectly. A major difference from Hilton Head is that St. Simons respects much of its history, and a lot of it is still left to enjoy, particularly the expansive and archaeologically significant Fort Frederica National Monument.

History

St. Simons Island and its much smaller, symbiotic neighbor Sea Island (originally Long Island) were well known to Native Americans as hunting and fishing grounds. Eventually the Spanish would establish two missions on St. Simons, one at the south end and one at the north end, as well as a town for nonconverted native peoples called San Simon, which would eventually give the island its modern name. A lasting European influence didn't come until 1736 and General James Oglethorpe's construction of Fort Frederica. The fort and the surrounding town were a key base of operations for the

Golden Isles on the Page

Many authors have been inspired by their time in the Golden Isles, whether to pen flights of poetic fancy, page-turning novels, or politically oriented chronicles. Here are a few of the most notable names:

- **Sidney Lanier:** Born in Macon, Georgia, Lanier was a renowned linguist, mathematician, and legal scholar. Fighting as a Confederate during the Civil War, he was captured while commanding a blockade runner and taken to a POW camp in Maryland, where he came down with tuberculosis. After the war, he stayed at his brother-in-law's house in Brunswick to recuperate, and it was during that time that he took up poetry, writing the famous "Marshes of Glynn," the end of which is quoted above.

- **Eugenia Price:** Although not originally from St. Simons, Price remains the best-known local cultural figure, having set her *St. Simons Trilogy* here. After relocating to the island in 1965, she stayed here until her death in 1996. She's buried in the Christ Church cemetery on Frederica Road.

- **Tina McElroy Ansa:** Probably the most notable literary figure currently living on St. Simons Island is award-winning African American author Tina McElroy Ansa. Few of her books deal with the Golden Isles region, but they all deal with life in the South, and Ansa is an ardent devotee of St. Simons and its relaxed, friendly ways.

- **Fanny Kemble:** In 1834, this renowned English actress married Georgia plantation heir Pierce Butler, who would become one of the largest slave owners in the United States. Horrified by the treatment of Butler's slaves at Butler Island, just south of Darien, Georgia, Kemble penned one of the earliest antislavery chronicles, *Journal of a Residence on a Georgian Plantation in 1838-1839.* Kemble's disagreement with her husband over slavery hastened their divorce in 1849.

British struggle to evict the Spanish from Georgia—which culminated in 1742 in the decisive Battle of Bloody Marsh south of the fort—but fell into decline after the Spanish threat subsided.

In the years after American independence, St. Simons woke up from its slumber as acre after acre of virgin live oak was felled to make the massive timbers of new warships for the U.S. Navy, including the USS *Constitution*. In their place was planted a new crop—cotton. The island's antebellum plantations boomed to world-class heights of profit and prestige when the superior strain of the crop known as Sea Island cotton came in the 1820s.

On St. Simons in 1803, one of the most poignant chapters in the dark history of American slavery was written. In one of the first documented slave uprisings in North America, a group of slaves from the Igbo region of West Africa escaped custody and took over the ship that was transporting them to St. Simons from Savannah. But rather than do any further violence, immediately upon reaching shore on the west side of St. Simons, the slaves essentially committed mass suicide by walking into the swampy

Clockwise from top left: the historic lighthouse on St. Simons; Palm Coast Coffee, Cafe, and Pub; Fort Frederica National Monument.

waters nearby, which forever after would be known as Ebo Landing (a corruption of the original Igbo).

The Civil War came to St. Simons in late 1861 with a Union blockade and invasion, leading Confederate troops to dynamite the island's lighthouse. Initially St. Simons was a sanctuary for freed slaves from the island's 14 plantations, and by late 1862 over 500 former slaves lived on St. Simons, including Susie King Taylor, who began a school for African American children. But in November of that year all former slaves were dispersed to Hilton Head and Fernandina, Florida. St. Simons was chosen as one of the implementation sites for General William Sherman's Special Field Order No. 15, the famous "40 acres and a mule" order. The order granted the Sea Islands of South Carolina and Georgia to freed slaves. However, Sherman's order was quickly rescinded by President Andrew Johnson.

The next landmark development for St. Simons didn't come until the building of the first causeway in 1924, which led directly to the island's resort development by the mega-rich industrialist Howard Coffin of Hudson Motors fame, who also owned nearby Sapelo Island to the north. By 1928, Coffin had completed the Sea Island Golf Club on the grounds of the old Retreat Plantation on the south end of St. Simons Island. He would move on to develop the famous Cloisters resort on Long Island (later Sea Island) itself.

Orientation

Because it's only a short drive from downtown Brunswick on the Torras Causeway, St. Simons has much less of a remote feel than most other Georgia barrier islands and is much more densely populated than any other Georgia island except for Tybee. Most visitor-oriented activity on this 12-mile-long, heavily residential island about the size of Manhattan is clustered at the south end, where St. Simons Sound meets the Atlantic. The main reasons to travel north on the island are to golf or to visit the historic site of Fort Frederica on the landward side.

Sights

★ The Village

Think of "The Village" at the extreme south end of St. Simons as a mix of Tybee's downscale accessibility and Hilton Head's upscale exclusivity. This compact, bustling area only a few blocks long offers not only boutique shops and stylish cafés but vintage stores and busking musicians. While visitors and residents here tend toward the affluent, they also tend not to be as flashy about it as in some other locales. You'll find the vast majority of quality eating spots here, along with most worthwhile lodging. It's fun to meander down Mallory Drive, casually shopping or noshing, and then make your way out onto the short but fun **St. Simons Pier** to enjoy the breeze and occasional spray coming off the sound. The long, low, sprawling building immediately to the north overlooking the expanse of Massengale

Park is the old casino building, now used for local government offices and community meetings.

St. Simons Lighthouse Museum

Unlike at many East Coast lighthouses, which tend to be in hard-to-reach places, anyone can walk right up to the **St. Simons Lighthouse Museum** (101 12th St., 912/638-4666, www.saintsimonslighthouse.org, Mon.-Sat. 10am-5pm, Sun. 1:30pm-5pm, $10 adults, $5 children). Once inside, you can enjoy the museum's exhibit and take the 129 steps up to the top of the 104-foot beacon—which is, unusually, still active—for a gorgeous view of the island and the ocean beyond.

The first lighthouse on the spot came about after planter John Couper sold this land, known as Couper's Point, to the government in 1804 for $1. This original beacon was destroyed by retreating Confederate troops in 1862 to hinder Union navigation on the coast. Traces of its foundations are near the current facility. The existing lighthouse dates from 1872, built by Irishman Charles Cluskey, who was responsible for a lot of Greek Revival architecture up and down the Georgia coast. Attached to the lighthouse is the oldest brick structure in Glynn County, the 1872 lighthouse keeper's cottage, now a museum and gift shop run by the Coastal Georgia Historical Society.

Maritime Center

A short walk from the lighthouse and also administered by the Coastal Georgia Historical Society, the **Maritime Center** (4201 1st St., 912/638-4666, www.saintsimonslighthouse.org, Mon.-Sat. 10am-5pm, Sun. 1:30pm-5pm, $10 adults, $5 children) is at the historic East Beach Coast Guard Station. Authorized by President Franklin Roosevelt in 1933 and completed in 1937 by the Works Progress Administration, the East Beach Station took part in military action in World War II, an episode chronicled in exhibits at the Maritime Center. On April 8, 1942, the German U-boat U-123 torpedoed and sank two cargo ships off the coast of St. Simons Island. The Coast Guard of East Beach station mounted a full rescue effort, saving many crewmen of the merchant ships, including one ship's canine mascot. The Coast Guard's tenure on East Beach ended after a 1993 fire burned down their boathouse. Two years later the station was decommissioned, and the Coasties moved to a new station in Brunswick.

★ Fort Frederica National Monument

The expansive and well-researched **Fort Frederica National Monument** (Frederica Rd., 912/638-3639, www.nps.gov/fofr, daily 9am-5pm, $3 adults, free under age 15) lies on the landward side of the island. Established by General James Oglethorpe in 1736 to protect Georgia's southern flank from the Spanish, the fort (as well as the village that sprang up around it, in which the Wesley brothers preached for a short time) was named for Frederick Louis, the Prince of Wales. The feminine suffix -*a* was added to distinguish it from the older Fort Frederick in South Carolina.

You don't just get to see a military fort here (actually the remains of the old powder magazine; most of the fort itself eroded into the river long ago); this is an entire colonial town site a mile in circumference, originally modeled after a typical English village. A self-guided walking tour through the beautiful grounds—the oak trees here have the longest, most luxurious Spanish moss I've ever seen—shows foundations of building sites that have been uncovered, including taverns, shops, and the private homes of influential citizens. Closer to the river is the large tabby structure of the garrison barracks.

As for the actual fort itself, from its location astride a bend in the Frederica River you can instantly see why this was such a strategic location, guarding the approach to the great Altamaha River. The Frederica garrison took part in an unsuccessful attack on St. Augustine, Florida, in 1740 and was also the force that sallied out of the fort and southward to repulse the Spanish at Bloody Marsh two years later.

Take in the accompanying exhibits in the visitors center, including a 23-minute film shown every half hour 9am-4pm that is actually quite good. A park ranger also gives informative talks throughout the day, and there are occasional reenactments by uniformed colonial "soldiers."

Bloody Marsh Battlefield

There's not a lot to see at the site of the **Battle of Bloody Marsh** (Frederica Rd., 912/638-3639, www.nps.gov/fofr, daily 8am-4pm, free), but—as with the similarly stirring site of Custer's Last Stand at the Little Bighorn—your imagination fills in the gaps, giving it perhaps more emotional impact than other, more substantial historic sites.

Essentially just a few interpretive signs overlooking a beautiful piece of salt marsh, the site is believed to be near the place where British soldiers from nearby Fort Frederica ambushed a force of Spanish regulars on their way to besiege the fort. Frederica's garrison, the 42nd Regiment of Foot, was augmented by a company of tough Scottish Highlanders from Darien, Georgia, who legend says attacked to the tune of bagpipes. The battle wasn't actually that bloody—some accounts say the Spanish lost only seven men—but the stout British presence convinced the Spanish to leave St. Simons a few days later, never again to project their once-potent military power that far north in the New World.

While the Battle of Bloody Marsh site is part of the National Park Service's Fort Frederica unit, it's not at the same location. Get to the battlefield from the fort by taking Frederica Road south, and then turn left (east) on Demere Road. The site is on your left as Demere Road veers right, in the 1800 block.

Just down the road from Fort Frederica is historic **Christ Church** (6329 Frederica Rd., 912/638-8683, www.christchurchfrederica.org, daily 2pm-5pm). The first sanctuary dates from 1820, but the original congregation at the now-defunct town of Frederica held services under the oaks at the site as early as 1736. The founder of Methodism, John Wesley, and his brother Charles both ministered to island residents during 1736-1737.

The original church was rendered unusable by Union occupation during the Civil War. A handsome new church, the one you see today, was funded and built in 1883 by a local mill owner, Anson Dodge, as a memorial to his first wife. But Christ Church's claim to fame in modern culture is as the setting of local novelist Eugenia Price's *The Beloved Invader,* the first work in her Georgia trilogy. The late Price, who died in 1996, is buried in the church cemetery.

Tours
St. Simons Island Trolley Tours (912/638-8954, www.stsimonstours.com, daily 11am, $22 adults, $10 ages 4-12, free under age 4) offers just that, a ride around the island in comparative comfort, leaving from the pier.

Entertainment and Events
Nightlife
St. Simons is far from Savannah's league when it comes to partying, but there is a fairly active nightlife scene, with a strong dose of island casual. Unlike in some areas this far south on the Georgia coast, there's usually a sizable contingent of young people out looking for a good time. The island's premier club, **Rafters Blues and Raw Bar** (315½ Mallory St., 912/634-9755, www.raftersblues.com, Mon.-Sat. 4:30pm-2am), known simply as "Rafters," brings in live music most every night Thursday-Saturday, focusing on the best acts on the regional rock circuit.

My favorite spot on St. Simons for a drink or an espresso—or a panini for that matter—is **Palm Coast Coffee, Cafe, and Pub** (316 Mallory St., 912/634-7517, www.palmcoastssi.com, daily 8am-10pm). This handy little spot, combining a hip, relaxing coffeehouse with a hearty menu of brunchy items, is in the heart of the village. The kicker, though, is the cute little bar the size of a large walk-in closet right off the side of the main room—a little bit of Key West on St. Simons. Mondays are open mic nights.

Inside the Village Inn is the popular nightspot the **Village Pub** (500 Mallory St., 912/634-6056, www.villageinnandpub.com, Mon.-Sat. 5pm-midnight, Sun. 5pm-10pm). Slightly more upscale than most watering holes on the island, this is the best place for a quality martini or other premium cocktail.

Performing Arts
Because of its close proximity to Brunswick, a short drive over the bridge, St. Simons has a symbiotic relationship with that larger city in areas of art

and culture. Each summer, beginning Memorial Day weekend and continuing into September, there are several **Jazz in the Park** concerts by regional artists. The shows are usually Sunday 7pm-9pm on the lawn of the St. Simons Lighthouse, and the beautiful setting and calming breeze are delightful. Admission is charged; bring a chair or blanket if you like.

Cinema
The island has its own multiplex, **Island Cinemas 7** (44 Cinema Ln., 912/634-9100, www.georgiatheatrecompany.com).

Shopping
Most shopping on St. Simons is centered in the Village and is a typical beach town mix of hardware and tackle, casual clothing, and souvenir stores. A funky highlight is **Beachview Books** (215 Mallory St., 912/638-7282, Mon.-Sat. 10:30am-5:30pm, Sun. 11:30am-3pm), a rambling used bookstore with lots of regional and local goodies, including books by the late great local author Eugenia Price. Probably the best antiques shop in this part of town is **Village Mews** (504 Beachview Dr., 912/634-1235, Mon.-Sat. 10am-5pm).

The closest thing to a mall is farther north on St. Simons at **Redfern Village,** with some cute indie stores like **Beach Cottage Linens** (912/634-2000, Mon.-Fri. 10am-5:30pm, Sat. 10am-5pm), **Thomas P. Dent Clothiers** (912/638-3118, Mon.-Sat. 9:30am-6pm), and the craftsy **Rarebbits and Pieces** (912/638-2866, Mon.-Sat. 10am-5:30pm). Redfern Village is on Frederica Road, one traffic light past the corner of Frederica Road and Demere Road.

Sports and Recreation
Beaches
Keep going from the pier past the lighthouse to find **Massengale Park** (daily dawn-dusk), with a playground, picnic tables, and restrooms right off the beach on the Atlantic side. The beach itself on St. Simons is underwhelming compared to some in these parts, but nonetheless it's easily accessible from the pier area and good for a romantic stroll if it's not high tide. There's a great playground, Neptune Park, right next to the pier overlooking the waterfront.

Kayaking and Boating
With its relatively sheltered landward side nestled in the marsh and an abundance of wildlife, St. Simons Island is an outstanding kayaking site, attracting connoisseurs from all over. A good spot to put in on the Frederica River is the **Golden Isles Marina** (206 Marina Dr., 912/634-1128, www.gimarina.com), which is actually on little Lanier Island on the Torras Causeway right before you enter St. Simons proper. For a real adventure, put in at the ramp at the end of South Harrington Street off Frederica Road, which will take you out Village Creek on the seaward side of the island.

Undoubtedly the best kayaking outfitter and tour operator in this part of the Golden Isles is **SouthEast Adventure Outfitters** (313 Mallory St., 912/638-6732, www.southeastadventure.com, daily 10am-6pm), which also has a location in nearby Brunswick. Michael Gowen and company offer an extensive range of guided tours all over the St. Simons marsh and sound area as well as trips to undeveloped Little St. Simons Island to the north. Prices vary, so call or go to the website for information.

Hiking and Biking

Like Jekyll Island, St. Simons is a great place for bicyclists. Bike paths go all over the island, and a special kick is riding on the beach almost the whole length of the island (but only at low tide). There are plenty of bike rental spots, with rates generally $15-20 per day depending on the season. The best place to rent bikes is **Monkey Wrench Bicycles** (1700 Frederica Rd., 912/634-5551). You can rent another kind of pedal-power at **Wheel Fun Rentals** (532 Ocean Blvd., 912/634-0606), which deals in four-seat pedaled carts with steering wheels.

Golf and Tennis

A popular place for both sports is the **Sea Palms Golf and Tennis Resort** (5445 Frederica Rd., 800/841-6268, www.seapalms.com, greens fees $70-80) in the middle of the island, with three nine-hole public courses and three clay courts. The **Sea Island Golf Club** (100 Retreat Rd., 800/732-4752, www.seaisland.com, greens fees $185-260) on the old Retreat Plantation as you first come onto the island has two award-winning 18-hole courses, the Seaside and the Plantation. Another public course is the 18-hole **Hampton Club** (100 Tabbystone Rd., 912/634-0255, www.hamptonclub.com, greens fees $95) on the north side of the island, part of the King and Prince Beach and Golf Resort.

Accommodations
Under $150

A charming and reasonable place a stone's throw from the Village is ★ **Queens Court** (437 Kings Way, 912/638-8459, $85-135), a traditional roadside motel from the late 1940s, with modern upgrades that include a nice outdoor pool in the central courtyard area. Despite its convenient location, you'll feel fairly secluded.

One of the most interesting lodgings in the Lowcountry and Georgia coast is **Epworth by the Sea** (100 Arthur J. Moore Dr., 912/638-8688, www.epworthbythesea.org, $90-100). This Methodist retreat in the center of the island boasts an entire complex of freestanding motels and lodges on its grounds, in various styles and configurations. Cafeteria-style meals are the order of the day, and there are plenty of recreational activities on-site, including tennis, volleyball, baseball, football, soccer, and basketball. They also rent bikes, which is always a great way to get around St. Simons.

Everyone loves the **Lovely Lane Chapel,** a picturesque sanctuary that is a favorite spot for weddings and holds services Sunday at 8:45am (casual dress OK). Researchers can utilize the resources of the **Arthur J. Moore Methodist Museum and Library** (Tues.-Sat. 9am-4pm).

You couldn't ask for a better location than the **St. Simons' Inn by the Lighthouse** (609 Beachview Dr., 912-638-1101, www.saintsimonsinn.com, $120-300), which is indeed in the shadow of the historic lighthouse and right next to the hopping Village area. It's a so-called "condo-hotel," so each of the standard and deluxe suites at the inn is individually owned by off-site owners. However, each guest gets full maid service and a complimentary breakfast.

$150-300

The best-known lodging on St. Simons Island is the ★ **King and Prince Beach and Golf Resort** (201 Arnold Rd., 800/342-0212, $249-320). Originally opened as a dance club in 1935, the King and Prince brings a swank old-school glamour similar to the Jekyll Island Club (though less imposing). And like the Jekyll Island Club, the King and Prince is also designated as one of the Historic Hotels of America. Its nearly 200 guest rooms are spread over a complex that includes several buildings, including the historic main building, beach villas, and freestanding guesthouses. Some standard rooms can go for under $200 even in the spring high season. Winter rates for all guest rooms are appreciably lower and represent a great bargain. For a dining spot overlooking the sea, try the **Blue Dolphin** (lunch daily 11am-4pm, dinner daily 5pm-10pm, $15-30). The resort's Hampton Club provides golf for guests and the public.

An interesting B&B on the island that's also within walking distance of most of the action on the south end is the 28-room **Village Inn & Pub** (500 Mallory St., 912-634-6056, www.villageinnandpub.com, $160-245), nestled among shady palm trees and live oaks. The pub, a popular local hangout in a renovated 1930 cottage, is a nice plus.

Over $300

Affiliated with the Sea Island resort, the **Lodge at Sea Island Golf Club** (100 Retreat Ave., 912-638-3611, $650-2,500) is actually on the south end of St. Simons Island on the old Retreat Plantation. Its 40 grand guest rooms and suites all have great views of the Atlantic Ocean, the associated Plantation Course links, or both. Full butler service makes this an especially pampered and aristocratic stay.

Food

While the ambience at St. Simons has an upscale feel, don't feel like you have to dress up to get a bite to eat—the emphasis is on relaxation and having a good time.

★ **Palmer's Village Cafe** (223 Mallory St., 912/634-5515, www.palmersvillagecafe.com, Tues.-Sun. 7:30am-2pm, $10-15), formerly called Dressner's, is right in the middle of the Village's bustle. It's one of the island's most popular places but still has enough seats that you usually don't have to wait. Sandwiches and burgers are great, but breakfast all day is the real attraction and includes lovingly crafted omelets, hearty pancakes, and a "build your own biscuit" menu.

Seafood

Despite its somewhat unappetizing name, **Mullet Bay** (512 Ocean Blvd., 912/634-9977, daily 11:30am-10pm, $7-18) in the Village is a favorite good old-fashioned Southern seafood place, the kind where you get a big fried platter with two sides and hushpuppies. A popular seafood place right in the action in the Village is **Barbara Jean's** (214 Mallory St., 912/634-6500, www.barbarajeans.com, Sun.-Thurs. 11am-9pm, Fri.-Sat. 11am-10pm, $7-20), which also has a great variety of imaginative veggie dishes to go along with their formidable seafood menu, including some excellent she-crab soup and crab cakes. They also have plenty of good landlubber treats for those not inclined to the marine critters.

Fine Dining

★ **J. Mac's Island Restaurant** (407 Mallory St., 912/634-0403, www.jmacsislandrestaurant.com, Tues.-Sat. 6pm-9pm, $20-30) is the Village's high-end restaurant, one that wouldn't be out of place in downtown Savannah. Owner J. Mac Mason and head chef Connor Rankin conspire to bring a fresh take on Southern and seafood classics, with adventurous entrées like seared "Creamsicle" marlin with jumbo asparagus or sweet corn puree-seared filet with gorgonzola and herb gratin.

Inside the King and Prince Resort, you'll find the old-school glory of the **Blue Dolphin** (201 Arnold Rd., 800/342-0212, lunch daily 11am-4pm, dinner daily 5pm-10pm, $15-30), redolent of the *Great Gatsby* era. The Blue Dolphin claims to be the only oceanfront dining on the island, and the views are certainly magnificent.

Information and Services

The **St. Simons Visitors Center** (530-B Beachview Dr., 912/638-9014, www.bgivb.com, daily 9am-5pm) is in the St. Simons Casino Building near Neptune Park and the Village. The main newspaper in St. Simons is the *Brunswick News* (www.thebrunswicknews.com). The **post office** (800/275-8777) is at 620 Beachview Drive.

Getting There and Around

Get to St. Simons through the gateway city of Brunswick. Take I-95 exit 38 for Golden Isles, which will take you to the Golden Isles Parkway. Take a

Immediately as you cross the Frederica River onto the island, look for
a quick right onto Kings Way to take you directly to the Village area. You
can also take a quick left onto Demere Road to reach Frederica Road and
the more northerly portion of the island, where you'll find Fort Frederica
and Christ Church.

The main roads to remember are Kings Way, which turns into Ocean
Boulevard as it nears the active south end of the island, called "The Village";
Demere ("DEM-er-ee") Road, which loops west-east around the little island
airport and then south, joining up with Ocean Boulevard down near the
lighthouse; Frederica Road, the dominant north-south artery; and Mallory
Street, which runs north-south through the Village area and dead-ends at
the pier on St. Simons Sound. (You'll notice that Mallory Street is sometimes spelled "Mallery," which is actually the correct spelling of the avenue's namesake: Mallery King, child of Thomas King, owner of the historic
Retreat Plantation.)

Little St. Simons Island

This 10,000-acre privately owned island, accessible only by water, is almost
totally undeveloped—thanks to its salt-stressed trees, which discouraged
timbering—and boasts seven miles of beautiful beaches. All activity centers
on the circa-1917 ★ **Lodge on Little St. Simons Island** (1000 Hampton
Point Dr., 888/733-5774, www.littlestsimonsisland.com, from $625), named
by *Condé Nast Traveler* as the top U.S. mainland resort in 2007. Within it
lies the famed Hunting Lodge, where meals and cocktails are served. With
15 ultra-plush guest rooms and suites in an assortment of historic buildings, all set amid gorgeous natural beauty—there are five full-time naturalists on staff—the Lodge is a reminder of what St. Simons proper used to
look like. The guest count is limited to 30 people.

Getting There and Around

Unless you enlist the aid of a local kayaking charter company, you have
to be a guest of the Lodge on Little St. Simons Island to have access to the
island. The ferry, a 15-minute ride, leaves from a landing at the northern
end of St. Simons at the end of Lawrence Road. Guests have full use of bicycles once on the island and can also request shuttle transportation just
about anywhere.

Sea Island

The only way to enjoy Sea Island—basically a tiny appendage of St. Simons
facing the Atlantic Ocean—is to be a guest at the ★ **Sea Island resort**
(888/732-4752, www.seaisland.com, from $700). And guests visiting now
are truly lucky; the legendary facility, routinely ranked as one of the best resorts on the planet, completed extensive renovations in 2008. The economic

downturn combined with financial mismanagement sent the institution into bankruptcy followed by a sale in 2010. Guests won't notice, however. The rooms at the resort's premier lodging institution, **The Cloister,** nearly defy description—enveloped in Old World luxury, they also boast 21st-century technology. And the service at The Cloister is equally world-class, featuring 24-hour butler service in the European tradition. There are cottages for rental on Sea Island as well, all of which grant temporary membership in the Sea Island club and full use of its many amenities and services.

Getting There and Around

Get to Sea Island by taking Torras Causeway onto the island and then making a left onto Sea Island Causeway, which takes you all the way to the gate marking the only land entrance to Sea Island.

DARIEN AND MCINTOSH COUNTY

It doesn't get near the attention or the number of visitors as Savannah to the north or the St. Simons-Jekyll area to the south, but the small fishing and shrimping village of Darien in McIntosh County has an interesting and historic pedigree of its own. It is centrally located near some of the best treasures the Georgia coast has to offer, including the Harris Neck National Wildlife Refuge, the beautiful Altamaha River, and the sea island of Sapelo, and it also boasts what many believe to be the best traditional seafood restaurants in the state.

History

Unlike Anglophilic Savannah to the north, the Darien area has had a distinctly Scottish flavor from the beginning. In 1736, Scottish Highlanders established a settlement at the mouth of the Altamaha River at the bequest of General James Oglethorpe, who wanted the tough Scots protecting his southern border from the Spanish. The colony was at the site of an earlier English effort, the abandoned Fort King George, but the Scots came up with a new name, Darien, honoring a failed 1697 settlement in Panama. Leading them was John McIntosh Mohr, who would go on to father several sons who would become famous in their own right and eventually lend his surname to the county. The Scots brought a singularly populist sentiment to the New World. When Georgia planters lobbied to legalize slavery, which was outlawed by Oglethorpe, the Scots of Darien signed a petition against them in 1739—believed to be the first organized protest against slavery in America. The Darien settlers were also known for keeping more cordial relations with the Native Americans than the area's English settlements did. Of course, they were a frugal bunch too.

Darien's heyday was unquestionably in that antebellum period, when for a brief time the town was the world's largest exporter of cotton, floated down the Altamaha on barges and shipped out through the town's port. The Bank of Darien was the largest bank south of Philadelphia in the early 1800s. A prosperous rice culture grew up around the Altamaha estuary as

Clockwise from top left: the Smallest Church in North America; Gould Cemetery at Harris Neck National Wildlife Refuge; reenactors at Fort King George State Historic Site.

well, relying on the tidal flow of the area's acres and acres of marsh. Almost nothing from this period remains, however, because on June 11, 1863, a force of mostly African American Union troops under the command of Colonel Robert G. Shaw (portrayed in the movie *Glory*) burned Darien to the ground, with all its homes and warehouses going up in smoke.

After the Civil War, lumber became the new cash crop, and Darien once again became a thriving seaport and mill headquarters. The late 1800s saw a new reliance on shrimping and oystering, industries that survive to this day. A different kind of industry prospered in the years after World War II. In those pre-interstate highway days, U.S. 17 was the main route south to booming Florida. McIntosh County got a bad reputation for "clip joints," which would fleece gullible travelers with a variety of illegal schemes. This period is recounted in the best-seller *Praying for Sheetrock* by Melissa Fay Greene.

Sights
Smallest Church in North America
While several other churches also claim that title, in any case fans of the devout and of roadside kitsch alike will enjoy the tiny and charming little **Memory Park Christ Chapel** (U.S. 17, daily 24 hours). Built in 1949 by local grocer Agnes Harper, the church—which contains a pulpit and chairs for a dozen people—was intended as a round-the-clock travelers' sanctuary on what was then the main coastal road, U.S. 17. Upon her death, Harper simply willed the church to Jesus Christ. The stained glass windows are imported from England, and there's a guestbook so you can leave a note of appreciation. Get there by taking I-95 exit 67 and going south a short way on U.S. 17; the church is on the east side of the road.

★ Harris Neck National Wildlife Refuge
Literally a stone's throw away from the "Smallest Church" is the turnoff east onto the seven-mile Harris Neck Road leading to the **Harris Neck National Wildlife Refuge** (912/832-4608, www.fws.gov/harrisneck, daily dawn-dusk, free). In addition to being one of the single best sites in the South from which to view wading birds and waterfowl in their natural habitat, Harris Neck also has something of a poignant backstory. For generations after the Civil War, an African American community descended from the area's original slaves quietly struggled to eke out a living here by fishing and farming.

The settlers' land was taken by the federal government during World War II to build a U.S. Army Air Force base, primarily to train pilots on the P-40 Tomahawk fighter, the same plane used by the famed Flying Tigers. After the war, the base was decommissioned and given to McIntosh County as a municipal airport. But the notoriously corrupt local government so mismanaged the facility that the feds once again took it over, eventually transferring it to the forerunner of the U.S. Fish and Wildlife Service.

Now a nearly 3,000-acre nationally protected refuge, Harris Neck gets about 50,000 visitors a year to experience its mix of marsh, woods, and grassland ecosystems and for its nearly matchless **bird-watching**. Its former life as a military base has the plus of leaving behind a decent system of roads, many of them based on old runways. Most visitors use the four-mile "wildlife drive" to travel through the refuge, stopping occasionally for hiking or bird-watching. In the summer, look for egrets, herons, and wood storks nesting in rookeries. In the winter, waterfowl like mallards and teal flock to the brackish and freshwater pools. You can see painted buntings late April-late September.

Kayaks and canoes can put in at the public boat ramp on the Barbour River. Near the landing is **Gould Cemetery,** an old African American cemetery that is publicly accessible. It has some charming handmade tombstones that evoke the post-Civil War era of Harris Neck before the displacement of local citizens to build the airfield.

To get here, take I-95 exit 67 and go south on U.S. 17 about one mile, then east on Harris Neck Road (Hwy. 131) for seven miles to the entrance gate on the left.

Shellman Bluff

Just northeast of Darien is the old oystering community of **Shellman Bluff.** It's notable not only for the stunning views from the high bluff, but also for fresh seafood. Go to **Shellman's Fish Camp** (1058 River Rd., 912/832-4331, call ahead) to put in for a kayak or canoe ride. Save room for some food; there are some great seafood places here.

To get to Shellman Bluff, take I-95 exit 67 for South Newport and get on U.S. 17 south. There are two easy ways to get to Shellman Bluff from U.S. 17: east on Minton Road and then left onto Shellman Bluff Road, or east on Pine Harbor Road followed by an immediate left onto Shellman Bluff Road. In either case, take Shellman Bluff Road until it dead-ends, then make a right onto Sutherland Bluff Drive.

Darien Waterfront Park

Right where U.S. 17 crosses the Darien River, you'll find the **Darien Welcome Center** (U.S. 17 and Fort King George Dr., 912/437-6684, daily 9am-5pm). From there it's a short walk down some steps to the newly re-furbished little **Darien Waterfront Park**. This small but charming area on a beautiful bend of the Darien River—a tributary of the mighty Altamaha River just to the south—features some old tabby warehouse ruins, some of the only remnants of Darien's glory days as a major seaport and old enough to have century-old live oaks growing around them. To the east are the picturesque docks where the town shrimp boat fleet docks.

McIntosh Old Jail Art Center

Within Darien proper is the **McIntosh Old Jail Art Center and Welcome Center** (404 North Way, 912/437-7711, www.visitdarien.com, Tues.-Sat.

10am-4pm), which also hosts several small art galleries and the McIntosh County History Museum.

Vernon Square

Right around the corner from the welcome center on Washington Street is **Vernon Square,** a charming little nook of live oaks and Spanish moss that was the social center of Darien in the town's antebellum heyday. The **Darien Methodist Church** on the square was built in 1843, damaged during the Civil War, and then rebuilt in 1884 using materials from the first church. The nearby **St. Andrews Episcopal Church,** built in 1878, was once the site of the powerful Bank of Darien. Nearby is the affiliated and equally historic **St. Cyprian's Episcopal Church** (Fort King George Rd. and Rittenouse St.), built by an African American congregation and one of the largest tabby structures still in use anywhere.

Fort King George State Historic Site

The oldest English settlement in what would become Georgia, **Fort King George State Historic Site** (1600 Wayne St., 912/437-4770, www.gastate-parks.org/fortkinggeorge, Tues.-Sun. 9am-5pm, $5 adults, $2.50 children) for a short time protected the Carolinas from attack, from its establishment in 1721 to its abandonment in 1727. Walking onto the site, with its restored 40-foot-tall cypress blockhouse fort, instantly reveals why this place was so important: It guards a key bend in the wide Altamaha River, vital to any attempt to establish transportation and trade in the area. In addition to chronicling the ill-fated English occupation of the area—plagued by insects, sickness, danger, and boredom—the site also has exhibits about other aspects of local history, including the Guale Indians, the Spanish missionary presence, and the era of the great sawmills. Nature lovers will enjoy the site as well, as it offers gorgeous vistas of the marsh. Fort King George holds regular reenactments, living history demonstrations, and cannon firings; go to the website for details.

To get here, take U.S. 17 to the Darien River Bridge, and then go east on Fort King George Drive. There's a bike route to the fort if you want to park in town and pedal here.

Butler Island

South of Darien is the Altamaha River, Georgia's largest watershed and only undammed river as well as one of the country's great estuarine habitats, with the second-largest watershed on the East Coast. It's a paradise for outdoors enthusiasts, one that amazed and delighted famed naturalist William Bartram on his journey here in the late 1700s. Over 30,000 ducks visit each year mid-October to mid-April on this key stop on the **Colonial Coast Birding Trail.**

A great place to enjoy the river ecosystem is the **Altamaha Waterfowl Management Area** (912/262-3173, http://georgiawildlife.dnr.state.ga.us). This was the site of Butler Island Plantation, one of the largest and most successful tidewater plantations in the antebellum era. (The 75-foot brick chimney just off U.S. 17 is part of an old rice mill belonging to the plantation.) In 1834, planter Pierce Butler II married English actress Fanny Kemble, who would go on to write one of the earliest antislavery chronicles, *Journal of a Residence on a Georgian Plantation in 1838-39,* about what she saw during her short stay at Butler Island. Just past the chimney is a large plantation house, which now contains offices of the Nature Conservancy. There's a picnic ground nearby. The dominance of the plantation culture in this area is proved by the dikes and gates throughout the marsh, still plainly visible from the road. Many are still used by the Georgia Department of Natural Resources to maintain bird habitat. Birds you can see throughout the area include endangered wood storks, painted bunting, white ibis, all types of ducks, and even bald eagles.

Some of the best hiking and birding in the area is just south of the chimney on U.S. 17. Park on the east side of the road at an old dairy barn, and from there you'll find the trailhead for a four-mile round-trip hike on the Billy Cullen Memorial Trail, which offers great bird-watching opportunities and interpretive signage. On the other side of U.S. 17 is the entrance to the Ansley Hodges Memorial, where a 0.25-mile hike takes you to an observation tower. Be aware that hunting goes on near this area on some Saturdays during the year.

Kayaks and canoes can easily put in at the state-run landing at **Champney River Park** right where U.S. 17 crosses the Champney River. There are fish camps up and down this entire riverine system, providing fairly easy launching and recovery.

Tours

Altamaha Coastal Tours (229 Ft. King George Rd., 912/437-6010, www.altamaha.com) is your best bet for taking a guided kayak tour (from $50) or renting a kayak (from $20 per day) to explore the beautiful **Altamaha River.**

Accommodations

If you want to stay in McIntosh County, I strongly recommend booking one of the five charming guest rooms at ★ **Open Gates Bed and Breakfast** (301 Franklin St., Darien, 912/437-6985, www.opengatesbnb.com, $125-140). This lovingly restored and reasonably priced inn is on historic and relaxing Vernon Square in downtown Darien. Owners Kelly and Jeff Spratt are not only attentive innkeepers who rustle up a mean breakfast, they're also biologists who can hook you up with the best nature-oriented experiences and tours on this part of the coast.

Food

McIntosh County is a powerhouse in the food department, and as you might expect, fresh and delicious seafood in a casual atmosphere is the order of the day here.

The Old School Diner (1080 Jesse Grant Rd. NE, Townsend,

912/832-2136, http://oldschooldiner.com, Wed.-Fri. 5:30pm-9:30pm, Sat.-Sun. noon-9:30pm, $15-30, cash only) is located in a whimsical semirural compound seven miles off U.S. 17 just off Harris Neck Road on the way to the wildlife refuge. Run by the gregarious comfort-food culinary genius Jerome Brown, the restaurant is a reflection of the man himself—warm, inviting, eccentric, and full of life. The draw here is succulent fresh seafood in the coastal Georgia tradition—delicately fried and imbued with the subtle, inviting flavors of soul food. Old School's prices aren't so old school, but keep in mind that the portions are huge, rich, and filling.

Even farther off the main roads than the Old School Diner, the community of Shellman Bluff is well worth the drive. Find ★ **Hunters Cafe** (Shellman Bluff, 912/832-5771, http://hunterscafe.com, lunch Mon.-Fri. 11am-2pm, dinner Mon.-Fri. 5pm-10pm, Sat.-Sun. 7am-10pm, $10-20) and get anything that floats your boat—it's all fresh and local. Wild Georgia shrimp are a particular specialty, as is the hearty cream-based crab stew. Take a right off Shellman Bluff Road onto Sutherland Bluff Drive, then a left onto New Shellman Road. Take a right onto the unpaved River Road and you can't miss it.

Another Shellman Bluff favorite is ★ **Speed's Kitchen** (Shellman Bluff, 912/832-4763, Thurs.-Sat. 5pm-close, Sun. noon-close, $10-20), where people move anything but fast and the fried fish and crab-stuffed flounder are out of this world. Take a right off of Shellman Bluff Road onto Sutherland Bluff Drive. Take a right onto Speed's Kitchen Road.

On the Darien waterfront, you'll find **Skipper's Fish Camp** (85 Screven St., Darien, 912/437-3579, www.skippersfishcamp.com, daily 11am-9pm, $15-25), which, as is typical for this area, also hosts a marina. Try the fried wild Georgia shrimp, fresh from local waters. South of Darien just off U.S. 17 on the Altamaha River, try **Mudcat Charlie's** (250 Ricefield Way, 912/261-0055, daily 8am-2pm, $10-20), where fresh seafood is served in a friendly and very casual atmosphere, yes, right in the middle of a busy fish camp.

Information and Services

The **Darien Welcome Center** (1111 Magnolia Bluff Way, www.visitdarien.com, Mon.-Sat. 10am-8pm, Sun. 11am-6pm) is within the Preferred Outlets mall just off I-95 at exit 49.

The closest hospital is the Brunswick campus of **Southeast Georgia Health System** (2415 Parkwood Dr., Brunswick, 912/466-7000, http://sghs.org).

Getting There and Around

U.S. 17 goes directly through Darien. The closest I-95 exit is exit 49. Once you get off U.S. 17, Darien is a pretty bike-friendly place; you can park the car downtown and ride your bike east on Fort King George Drive to visit Fort King George.

Sapelo Island

Another of those amazing, undeveloped Georgia barrier islands that can only be reached by boat, Sapelo also shares with some of those islands a link to the Gilded Age.

History

The Spanish established a Franciscan mission on the north end of the island in the 1500s. Sapelo didn't become fully integrated into the Lowcountry plantation culture until its purchase by Thomas Spalding in the early 1800s. After the Civil War, many of the nearly 500 former slaves on the island remained, with a partnership of freedmen buying land as early as 1871.

Hudson Motors mogul Howard Coffin bought all of Sapelo, except for the African American communities, in 1912, building a palatial home and introducing a modern infrastructure. Among Coffin's visitors were two presidents, Calvin Coolidge and Herbert Hoover, and aviator Charles Lindbergh. Coffin hit hard times in the Great Depression and in 1934 sold Sapelo to tobacco heir R. J. Reynolds, who consolidated the island's African Americans into the single Hog Hammock community. By the mid-1970s the Reynolds family had sold the island to the state, again with the exception of the 430 acres of Hog Hammock, which at the time had slightly more than 100 residents. Today most of the island is administered for marine research purposes under the designation of **Sapelo Island National Estuarine Research Reserve** (www. sapelonerr.org).

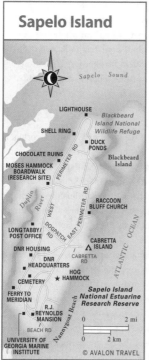

Sights

Once on the island, you can take guided tours under the auspices of the Georgia Department of Natural Resources. Wednesday 8:30am-12:30pm there's a tour of the island that includes the **R. J. Reynolds Mansion** (www.reynoldsonsapelo. com) on the south end as well as Hog Hammock and the Long Tabby ruins. Saturday 9am-1pm there's a tour of the historic **Sapelo Lighthouse** on the north end along with the rest of the island. June-Labor Day there's an extra lighthouse and island tour Friday 8:30am-12:30pm. March-October on the last Tuesday of the month they do an extra-long day trip,

8:30am-3pm. Tours cost $10 adults, $6 children, free under age 6. Call 912/437-3224 for reservations. You can also arrange private tours.

Another key sight on Sapelo is a 4,500-year-old **Native American shell ring** on the north end, one of the oldest and best preserved anywhere. Beach lovers will especially enjoy the unspoiled strands on Sapelo, including the famous **Nannygoat Beach.**

Accommodations

While it's theoretically possible to stay overnight at the **R. J. Reynolds Mansion** (www.reynoldsonsapelo.com), it is limited to groups of at least 16 people. Realistically, to stay overnight on Sapelo you need a reservation with one of the locally owned guesthouses. One recommendation is Cornelia Bailey's six-room **The Wallow** (912/485-2206, call for rates) in historic Hog Hammock. The Baileys also run a small campground, **Comyam's Campground** (912/485-2206, $10 pp). Another option is **The Weekender** (912/485-2277, call for rates).

Getting There

Visitors to Sapelo must embark on the ferry at the **Sapelo Island Visitors Center** (912/437-3224, www.sapelonerr.org, Tues.-Fri. 7:30am-5:30pm, Sat. 8am-5:30pm, Sun. 1:30pm-5pm, $10 adults, $6 ages 6-18) in little Meridian, Georgia, on Highway 99 north of Darien. The visitors center actually has a nice nature hike of its own as well as an auditorium where you can see an informative video. From here it's a half-hour trip to Sapelo over the Doboy Sound. Keep in mind you must call in advance for reservations before showing up at the visitors center. April-October it's recommended to call at least a week in advance.

St. Catherine's Island

The interior of this beautiful island off the coast of Midway, Georgia, is off-limits to the public, but you can visit the beach up to the high-water mark by boat, enjoy its beautiful unspoiled beaches, and spy on local wildlife. While that's about all you can do, it's important to know a little of the interesting background of this island. Owned and administered by the St. Catherine's Island Foundation, it's unusual in that it has a 25-foot-high bluff on the northern end, an extraordinarily high geographic feature for a barrier island in this part of the world.

Once central to the Spanish missionary effort on the Georgia coast, St. Catherine's was found to be home to over 400 graves of Christianized Native Americans (a large shell ring also exists on the island). Declaration of Independence signer Button Gwinnett made a home here for a while until his death from a gunshot wound suffered in a duel in Savannah in 1777. After General Sherman's famous "40 acres and a mule" order, a freed slave named Tunis Campbell was governor of the island, living in Gwinnett's home. But when the order was rescinded, all former slaves had to leave for the mainland. In 1986, American Museum of Natural History archaeologist David Hurst Thomas began extensive research on Spanish artifacts left behind from the Santa Catalina de Guale mission, including foundations of living quarters, a kitchen, and a church—possibly the first church in what is now the United States. Today, however, the island, a National Historic Landmark, is better known as host to a New York Zoological Society project to recover injured or sick animals of endangered species and nurse them back to health for a possible return to the wild.

The closest marinas for the trip to the island's peaceful beaches are **Shellman Fish Camp** (1058 River Rd. NE, Townsend, 912/832-4331) in McIntosh County and **Halfmoon Marina** (171 Azalea Rd., Midway, 912/884-5819) in Liberty County.

Blackbeard Island

While no one is positive if the namesake of Blackbeard Island actually landed here, the legends tell us he used it as a layover—even leaving some treasure here. Now federally administered as **Blackbeard Island National Wildlife Refuge** (912/652-4415, www.fws.gov/blackbeardisland), the island is accessible to the public by boat and gets about 10,000 visitors a year. Plenty of hiking trails exist, and the bird-watching is fantastic. It's also a major nesting ground for the endangered loggerhead turtle. Cycling is permitted, but overnight camping is not. For charters to Blackbeard, I recommend **SouthEast Adventure Outfitters** (313 Mallory St., St. Simons, 912/638-6732, www.southeastadventure.com, daily 10am-6pm) on St. Simons Island.

CUMBERLAND ISLAND AND ST. MARYS

Actually two islands—Great Cumberland and Little Cumberland—Cumberland Island National Seashore is the largest and one of the oldest of Georgia's barrier islands, and also one of its most remote and least developed. Currently administered by the National Park Service, it's accessible only by ferry or private boat. Most visitors to Cumberland get here from the gateway town of St. Marys, Georgia, a nifty little fishing village.

St. Marys

Much like Brunswick to the north, the fishing town of St. Marys plays mostly a gateway role, in this case to the Cumberland Island National Seashore. That being said, it's a very friendly little waterfront community with undeniable charms of its own and a historic pedigree going back to the very beginnings of the nation.

History

As early as 1767, once the Spanish threat subsided, plans were made to establish a town, then known as Buttermilk Bluff, in the area near the Florida border. But it wasn't until 20 years later that a meeting was held

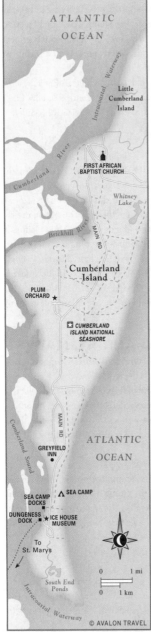

Cumberland Island

ATLANTIC OCEAN

Little Cumberland Island

Intracoastal Waterway

Cumberland River

FIRST AFRICAN BAPTIST CHURCH

Whitney Lake

Brickhill River

MAIN RD

Cumberland Island

PLUM ORCHARD ★

☆ CUMBERLAND ISLAND NATIONAL SEASHORE

MAIN RD

ATLANTIC OCEAN

Cumberland Sound

GREYFIELD INN ●

SEA CAMP DOCKS ▲ SEA CAMP

DUNGENESS DOCK ■ ★ ICE HOUSE MUSEUM

To St. Marys

South End Ponds

0   1 mi

0   1 km

Intracoastal Waterway

© AVALON TRAVEL

on Cumberland Island to close the deal with Jacob Weed to purchase the tract—acquired by confiscation from two loyalist landowners—for the grand sum of $38. The first influx of immigration to the area came as French Canadian refugees from Acadia (who would become known as Cajuns in Louisiana) came to St. Marys after being deported by the British. Another group of French speakers followed, fleeing Toussaint Louverture's slave rebellion in Haiti.

During the colonial period, St. Marys was the southernmost U.S. city and enjoyed not only importance as a seaport but military significance as well. Ironically, this strategic importance came into play more during the conflict with Great Britain than with anything to do with the Spanish. In 1812 a British force took over Cumberland Island and St. Marys, with a contingent embarking up the St. Marys River to track down the customs collector. However, in a bloody skirmish they were ambushed by American troops firing from the riverbanks. They vowed to avenge their loss by burning every building between the St. Marys and the Altamaha Rivers, but the ensuing peace treaty ending the War of 1812 brought a ceasefire.

Unlike towns such as Darien, which was put to the torch by Union troops, St. Marys was saved from destruction in the Civil War. The lumber industry boomed after that conflict as well as the local fishing and shrimping industries. A hotel was built in 1916 (and hosted Marjorie Kinnan Rawlings, author of *The Yearling*), but tourists didn't discover the area until the 1970s. It was also then that the U.S. Navy built the huge nuclear submarine base at Kings Bay, currently the area's largest employer with almost 10,000 workers. Development has increased in the area, with suburban sprawl beginning to cover the area like mushrooms after a heavy rain. Indeed, there's so much growth in the St. Marys-Camden County area that it's increasingly considered an outpost of the huge Jacksonville, Florida, metropolitan area to the south.

Orientation

As in Brunswick, the waterfront faces opposite the ocean and is instead oriented west, toward a river, in this case the St. Marys River. Most activity in downtown St. Marys happens up and down Osborne Street, which perhaps not coincidentally is also how you get to the **Cumberland Island Visitor Center** (113 St. Marys St., 912/882-4335, daily 8am-4:30pm) and from there board the *Cumberland Queen* for the trip to the island. (Note: The Cumberland Island Visitor Center and the Cumberland Island National Seashore Museum are in two different places, about a block apart.)

Sights

Tying the past to the present, it's only fitting that the home of the Kings Bay Submarine Base (which is not open to the public) has a museum dedicated to the "Silent Service." The **St. Marys Submarine Museum** (102 St. Marys St., 912/882-2782, www.stmaryswelcome.com, Tues.-Sat. 10am-4pm, Sun. 1pm-5pm, $5 adults, $3 children) on the riverfront has exhibits honoring the contribution of American submariners, including a bunch of cool models. There's a neat interactive exhibit where you can look through the genuine sub periscope that sticks out of the roof of the museum. Interpretation isn't a strong point—those without some previous knowledge won't find much help—but for military and nautical buffs the sheer number of artifacts is amazing.

A block down Osborne Street from the waterfront—and *not* at the actual Cumberland Island Visitor Center or the actual ferry dock—is the handsome little **Cumberland Island National Seashore Museum** (129 Osborne St., 912/882-4336, www.stmaryswelcome.com, Wed.-Sun. 1pm-4pm, free). It has several very informative exhibits on the natural and human history of Cumberland, as well as a room devoted to the short but fascinating role the island played in the War of 1812.

The most notable historic home in St. Marys is the **Orange Hall House Museum** (311 Osborne St., 912/576-3644, www.orangehall.org, Tues.-Sat. 9am-4pm, Sun. 1pm-4pm, $3 adults, $1 children). This beautiful Greek Revival home, circa 1830, survived the Civil War and was the center of town social life during the Roaring '20s, when it was owned by a succession of socialites from up north. The home is gorgeous inside and out, particularly during the holidays when it gets the full decorative treatment.

As a nod to its Cajun history, St. Marys hosts a heck of a **Mardi Gras Festival** each February, closing down six blocks of the riverfront for a parade. There's also live entertainment, vendors, and a costume ball.

For outdoor recreation near St. Marys, go to **Crooked River State Park** (6222 Charlie Smith Sr. Hwy., 912/882-5256, www.gastateparks.org, office Fri.-Wed. 8am-10pm, Thurs. 8am-5pm), which is not only a great place to put in for kayaking trips, including jaunts to Cumberland Island, but also has a wide range of lodging options. A key stop on the **Colonial Coast Birding Trail,** Crooked River features its own nature center and is near a historic site just upriver, the tabby ruins of the McIntosh Sugar Works—actually a lumber mill from the early 1800s. The easiest way to get here is to take I-95 exit 3 and go about eight miles east. To rent kayaks or book kayak and ecotours, try **Up the Creek Xpeditions** (111 Osborne St., 912/882-0911, www.upthecreekx.com), which can take you all around the area, including out to Cumberland Island.

Accommodations

Don't even think about staying at a chain hotel when you're in St. Marys. Stay at one of these cute historic inns, all within easy walking distance of the waterfront, for a song.

The most notable lodging for historic as well as economic value is the 18-room **Riverview Hotel** (105 Osborne St., 912/882-3242, www.riverviewhotelstmarys.com, under $100). The waterfront locale, like many old hotels in this area, has a great retro feel. It was built in the 1920s and has hosted such notables as author Marjorie Rawlings, John Rockefeller, poet Sidney Lanier, and Andrew Carnegie. ★ **Emma's Bed and Breakfast** (300 W. Conyers St., 912/882-4199, www.emmasbedandbreakfast.com, under $200) is situated on four beautiful acres in downtown St. Marys in a grand Southern-style mansion with all the trappings and hospitality you'd expect. You can also hang out on the stunning veranda at the historic ★ **Goodbread House** (209 Osborne St., 912/882-7490, www.goodbreadhouse.com, under $200), which offers rates below $100 in the off-season. The 1870 house features sumptuous interiors, including a classic dining room in which awesome breakfasts are served.

More outdoorsy visitors can stay at cottage, tent, or RV sites at **Crooked River State Park** (6222 Charlie Smith Sr. Hwy., 912/882-5256, www.gastateparks.org). There are 62 tent and RV sites (about $22) and 11 cottages ($85-110) as well as primitive camping ($25).

Food

St. Marys cannot compete in culinary sophistication with Savannah, but it does have some of the freshest seafood around. One of the best places to eat seafood on the waterfront in St. Marys is at **Lang's Marina Restaurant** (307 W. St. Marys St., 912/882-4432, lunch Tues.-Fri. 11am-2pm, dinner

Wed.-Sat. 5pm-9pm, $15-20). Two more good waterfront spots, right next to each other, are **The Shark Bite** (104 W. St. Marys St., 912/576-6993, Tues.-Sat. 11am-9pm, $12-20), which has great burgers and live music, and **Riverside Café** (106 W. St. Marys St., 912/882-3466, Tues.-Sat. 11am-9pm, $15-20), which specializes in Greek favorites.

Information and Services

The **St. Marys Convention and Visitors Bureau** (406 Osborne St., 912/882-4000, www.stmaryswelcome.com) is a good source of information not only for the town but for Cumberland Island, but keep in mind that this is not actually where you catch the ferry to the island.

Getting There and Around

Take I-95 exit 3 for Kingsland-St. Marys Road (Hwy. 40). This becomes Osborne Road, the main drag of St. Marys, as it gets closer to town. The road by the waterfront is St. Marys Street.

★ Cumberland Island National Seashore

Not only one of the richest estuarine and maritime forest environments in the world, **Cumberland Island National Seashore** (912/882-4335, reservations 877/860-6787, www.nps.gov/cuis) is quite simply one of the most beautiful and romantic places on the planet, as everyone learned when the "it" couple of their day, John F. Kennedy Jr. and Carolyn Bessette, were wed on the island in 1996. With more than 16 miles of gorgeous beach and an area of over 17,000 acres, there's no shortage of beauty either, and the island's already remote feel is further enhanced by the efforts that have been taken to protect it from development.

Cumberland is far from pristine: It has been used for timbering and cotton, is dotted with evocative abandoned ruins, and hosts a band of beautiful but voracious wild horses. But it is still a remarkable island paradise in a world where those kinds of locations are getting harder and harder to find.

There are two ways to enjoy Cumberland: day trip or overnight stay. An early arrival and departure on the late ferry, combined with bike rental and a tour, still leaves plenty of time for day-trippers to relax. Camping overnight on Cumberland is quite enjoyable, but it's a bit rustic and probably isn't for novices.

Important note: Distances on the map can be deceiving. Cumberland is very narrow but also very long—about 18 miles tip to tip. You can walk the width of the island in minutes, but you will not be able to hike its length even in a day.

You can have a perfectly enjoyable time on Cumberland just hanging out on the more populated south end, but those who want to explore the island fully should consider renting a bike or booking seats on the new National Park Service van tour around the island.

Like modern-day Americans, the Timucuan Indians also revered this site, visiting it often for shellfish and for sassafras, a medicinal herb common on the island. Cumberland's size and great natural harbor made it a perfect base for Spanish friars, who established the first mission on the island, San Pedro Mocama, in 1587. In fact, the first Christian martyr in Georgia was created on Cumberland, when Father Pedro Martinez was killed by the Indians.

As part of his effort to push the Spanish back into Florida for good, General James Oglethorpe established Fort William at the south end of Cumberland—the remains of which are now underwater—and a hunting lodge named Dungeness, an island place-name that persists today. While land grants were made in the 1760s, they saw little follow-through, and by the time of naturalist William Bartram's visit in 1774, Cumberland Island was almost uninhabited. But inevitably, the Lowcountry planters' culture made its way down to Cumberland, which was soon the site of 15 thriving plantations and small farms. After the Revolution, the heirs of one of its heroes, General Nathanael Greene, established Dungeness Plantation in 1802, its central building a now-gone tabby structure built on top of an ancient shell mound.

Actual military action wouldn't come to Cumberland until the War of 1812, when the British came in force and occupied the island for two months, using Dungeness as their headquarters. In the process they freed 1,500 slaves, who would then emigrate to various British colonies. In 1818, Revolutionary War hero General "Light-Horse" Harry Lee—father of Robert E. Lee—arrived on Cumberland's shore, in failing health and determined to see the home of his old friend General Greene one last time. He died a month later and was buried here, his son returning later to erect a gravestone. Light-Horse Harry remained on Cumberland until 1913, when his remains were taken to Lexington, Virginia, to rest beside those of his son. His gravestone on Cumberland remains.

The Civil War—and another freeing of slaves—came again in the 1860s, when Union troops occupied the island. At war's end Cumberland was set aside as a home for freed African Americans—part of the famous and ill-fated "40 acres and a mule" proposal—but politics intervened: Most of Cumberland's slaves were rounded up and taken to Amelia Island, Florida, although some remained and settled at Cumberland's north end (the "Settlement" area today).

As elsewhere on the Georgia coast, the Industrial Revolution came to Cumberland in the form of a vacation getaway for a mega-tycoon, in this case Thomas Carnegie, industrialist and brother of the better-known Andrew Carnegie of Carnegie Library fame. Carnegie built a new, even grander Dungeness, which suffered the same fate as its predecessor in a 1959 fire.

Cumberland Island narrowly avoided becoming the next Hilton Head—literally—in 1969 when Hilton Head developer Charles Fraser bought the

Wild Horses of Cumberland

the wild horses of Cumberland Island

Contrary to popular opinion, Cumberland Island's famous wild horses are not actually direct descendants of the first horses brought to the island by Spanish and English settlers, although feral horses have certainly ranged the island for most of recorded history. The current population of about 140 or so is actually descended from horses brought to the island by the Carnegie family in the 1920s. Responding to overwhelming public opinion, the National Park Service leaves the herd virtually untended and unsupervised. The horses eat, live, fight, grow up, give birth, and pass away largely without human influence, other than euthanizing animals who are clearly suffering and have no hope of recovery.

You're not guaranteed to see wild horses on Cumberland, but the odds are very heavily in your favor. They often congregate to graze around the Dungeness ruins, and indeed any open space. Over the years they've made trails through the forest and sand dunes, and can often be seen cavorting on the windy beach in the late afternoon and early evening.

Each stallion usually acquires a "harem" of dependent mares, and occasionally you might even witness spirited competition between stallions for mares and/or territory.

Gorgeous and evocative though these magnificent animals are, they have a big appetite for vegetation and frankly are not the best thing for this sensitive barrier island ecosystem. But their beauty and visceral impact on the visitor are undeniable, which means the horses are likely to stay as long as nature will have them.

And yes, these really are *wild* horses, meaning you should never try to feed or pet them, and you certainly won't be riding them.

northern tip of the island and began bulldozing a runway. The dwindling but still influential Carnegies joined with the Georgia Conservancy to broker an agreement that resulted in dubbing Cumberland a national seashore in 1972, saving it from further development. A $7.5 million gift from the Mellon Foundation enabled the purchase of Fraser's tract and the eventual incorporation of the island within the national park system.

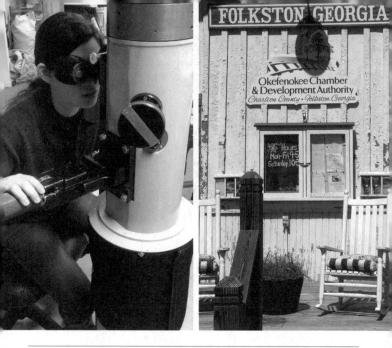

Clockwise from top left: St. Mary's Submarine Museum; Folkston Railroad Transportation Museum; alligator in the Okefenokee Swamp.

To learn more about Cumberland's fascinating history, visit the **Cumberland Island National Seashore Museum** (129 Osborne St., 912/882-4336, www.stmaryswelcome.com, Wed.-Sun. 1pm-4pm, free) while you're in St. Marys, a block away from the actual ferry docks.

Sights

The ferry typically stops at two docks a short distance from each other, the Sea Camp dock and the Dungeness dock. At 4pm, rangers offer a "dock-side" interpretive program at the Sea Camp. A short way farther north at the Dungeness dock, rangers lead a highly recommended "Dungeness Footsteps Tour" at 10am and 12:45pm, concentrating on the historic sites at the southern end of the island. Also at the Dungeness dock is the little **Ice House Museum** (912/882-4336, daily 9am-5pm, free), containing a range of exhibits on the island's history from Native American times to the present day.

Down near the docks is also where you'll find the stirring, almost spooky **Dungeness Ruins** and the nearby grave marker of Light-Horse Harry Lee. (You're very likely to see some wild horses around this area too.) The cause of the 1866 fire that destroyed the old Dungeness home is still unknown. Another even grander home was built on the same site during the Victorian era but also fell victim to fire in the 1950s while uninhabited (the rangers say it's the result of a dispute with locals over hunting rights). It's these Victorian ruins you see today.

A very nice addition to the National Park Service offering is a daily **Lands and Legacies van tour** (reservations 877/860-6787, $15 adults, $12 seniors and children) that takes you all around the island, eliminating the need for lengthy hikes. It's ideal for day-trippers—if a bit long at six hours—but anyone can take the ride. It leaves from the Sea Camp Ranger Station soon after the first morning ferry arrives. Reservations are strongly recommended.

Moving north on the main road (Grand Ave.)—a dirt path and the only route for motor vehicles—you come to the **Greyfield Inn** (904/261-6408, www.greyfieldinn.com). Because it is a privately owned hotel, don't trespass through the grounds. A good way farther north, just off the main road, you'll find the restored, rambling 20-room mansion **Plum Orchard,** another Carnegie legacy. Guided tours of Plum Orchard are available on the second and fourth Sunday of the month ($6 plus ferry fare); reserve a space at 912/882-4335.

At the very north end of the island, accessible only by foot or by bicycle, is the former freedmen's community simply known as **The Settlement,** featuring a small cemetery and the now-famous **First African Baptist Church** (daily dawn-dusk)—a 1937 version of the 1893 original—a humble and rustic one-room church made of whitewashed logs and in which the 1996 Kennedy-Bessette wedding took place.

There are more than 50 miles of hiking trails all over Cumberland, about 15 miles of nearly isolated beach to comb, and acres of maritime forest to explore—the latter an artifact of Cumberland's unusually old age for a barrier island. Upon arrival, you might want to rent a bicycle at the **Sea Camp dock** (no reservations, arrange rentals on the ferry, adult bikes $16 per day, youth bikes $10, $20 overnight). The only catch with the bikes is that you shouldn't plan on taking them to the upcountry campsites.

Shell-and-shark-teeth collectors might want to explore south of Dungeness Beach as well as between the docks. Unlike in some parks, you are allowed to take shells and fossils off the island.

Wildlife enthusiasts will be in heaven. More than 300 species of birds have been recorded on the island, which is also a favorite nesting ground for female loggerhead turtles in the late summer. Of course, the most iconic image of Cumberland Island is of its famous **wild horses,** a free-roaming band of feral equines who traverse the island year-round, grazing as they please.

The rangers warn you about it, and I will too: Cumberland Island is home to some creepy-crawlies, including mosquitoes, gnats, and, ticks. Ticks are especially prevalent throughout the maritime forest as you work your way north. Bring high-strength insect repellent with you, or buy some at the camp store. Rangers recommend you do a frequent "tick check" on yourself and your companions.

Accommodations

The only "civilized" lodging on Cumberland is the 13-room ★ **Greyfield Inn** (Grand Ave., 904/261-6408, www.greyfieldinn.com, $475), ranked by the American Inn Association as one of the country's "Ten Most Romantic Inns." Opened in 1962 as a hotel, the Greyfield was originally built in 1900 as the home of the Carnegies. The room rates include meals, transportation, tours, and bicycle usage.

Many visitors opt to camp on Cumberland (reservations 877/860-6787, limit of seven nights, $4) in one of three basic ways: at the **Sea Camp,** which has restrooms and shower facilities and allows fires; at the remote but pleasant **Stafford Beach,** a vigorous three-mile hike from the docks and with a basic restroom and shower; or pure wilderness camping farther north at **Hickory Hill, Yankee Paradise,** and **Brickman Bluff,** all of which are a several-mile hike away, do not permit fires, and have no facilities of any kind. Reservations are required for camping. All trash must be packed out on departure, as there are no refuse facilities on the island. Responsible alcohol consumption is limited to those 21 and over.

Insect life is abundant. Bring heavy-duty repellent or purchase some at the camp store.

The most vital information about Cumberland is how to get ashore in the first place. Most visitors do this by purchasing a ticket on the *Cumberland Queen* at the **Cumberland Island Visitor Center** (113 St. Marys St., St. Marys, 877/860-6787, www.cumberlandislandferry.com, daily 8am-4:30pm, $20 adults, $18 seniors, $12 under age 13) on the waterfront in St. Marys. I strongly suggest calling or faxing ahead. Be aware that there are often very long hold times by phone.

The ferry ride is 45 minutes each way. You can call for reservations Monday-Friday 10am-4pm. The ferry does not transport pets, bicycles, kayaks, or cars. However, you can rent bicycles at the Sea Camp dock once you're there. Every visitor to Cumberland over age 16 must pay a $4 entry fee, including campers.

March-November, the ferry leaves St. Marys daily at 9am and 11:45am, returning from Cumberland at 10:15am and 4:45pm. March-September Wednesday-Saturday, there's an additional 2:45pm departure from Cumberland back to St. Marys. December-February the ferry operates only Thursday-Monday. Make sure you arrive and check in at least 30 minutes before your ferry leaves.

One of the quirks of Cumberland, resulting from the unusual way in which it passed into federal hands, is the existence of some private property on which you mustn't trespass, except where trails specifically allow it. Also, unlike the general public, these private landowners are allowed to use vehicles. For these reasons, it's best to make sure you have a map of the island, which you can get before you board the ferry at St. Marys or at the ranger station at the Sea Camp dock.

There are no real stores and very few facilities on Cumberland. *Bring whatever you think you'll need,* whether it be food, water, medicine, suntan lotion, insect repellent, toilet paper, or otherwise.

THE OKEFENOKEE SWAMP

Scientists often refer to Okefenokee as an "analogue," an accurate representation of a totally different epoch in the earth's history. In this case it's the Carboniferous period, about 350 million years ago, when the living plants were lush and green and the dead plants simmered in a slow-decaying peat that would one day end up as the oil that powers our civilization.

But for the casual visitor, Okefenokee might also be simply a wonderful place to get almost completely away from human influence and witness firsthand some of the country's most interesting wildlife in its natural habitat. Despite the enormous wildfires of the spring of 2007 and the summer of 2011—some of the largest the Southeast has seen in half a century, so large they were visible from space—the swamp has bounced back, for the most part, and is once again hosting visitors who wish to experience its timeless beauty.

It's nearly the size of Rhode Island and just a short drive off I-95, but the massive and endlessly fascinating **Okefenokee National Wildlife Refuge** (912/496-7836, www.fws.gov/okefenokee, Mar.-Oct. daily dawn-7:30pm, Nov.-Feb. daily dawn-5:30pm, $5 per vehicle) is one of the lesser-visited national public lands. Is it that very name "swamp" that keeps people away, with its connotations of fetid misery and lurking danger? Or simply its location, out of sight and out of mind in south Georgia?

In any case, while it long ago entered the collective subconscious as a metaphor for the most untamed, darkly dangerous aspects of the American South—as well as the place where Pogo the Possum lived in Walt Kelly's comic strip *Pogo*—the Okefenokee remains one of the most intriguing natural areas on the planet. The nearby old rail town of Folkston is the gateway to the swamp for most visitors off I-95, which is to say most of them. In true Georgia fashion, the town is insular but friendly, slow but sincere.

History

The Okefenokee Swamp was created by an accident of geology. About 250,000 years ago, the Atlantic Ocean washed ashore about 70 miles farther inland from where it does today. Over time, a massive barrier island formed off this primeval Georgia coastline, running from what is now Jesup, Georgia, south to Starke, Florida. When the ocean level dropped during the Pleistocene era, this sandy island became a topographical feature known today as the Trail Ridge, its height effectively creating a basin to its west. Approximately 90 percent of the Okefenokee's water comes from rainfall into that basin, which drains slowly via the Suwannee and St. Marys Rivers.

Ordinarily, what the summer heat evaporates from the Okefenokee is more than replenished by rain, unless there's a severe drought like the one that caused the recent wildfires. But even the fires can't hold the swamp back. In fact, the Okefenokee is a fire ecosystem, meaning some plant species, like the cypress, depend on heat generated by wildfires to open their seed cones and perpetuate their lifecycle. Indeed, the particularly combustible peat that forms most of the swamp takes a long time to burn and sometimes remains smoldering under the surface, meaning that fire is never far away—sometimes it's right under your feet!

The massive Honey Prairie Fire of 2011 in the swamp's southwestern area, caused by a lightning strike, left scars that are visible to this day. Because of constant rejuvenation by water and fire, biologists estimate that the oldest portion of this supposedly "ancient" swamp is actually no older than 7,000 years—the faintest blink of an eye in geological terms. Unlike Florida's Everglades, which are actually a single large and very slow-moving river, the Okefenokee is a true swamp.

Native Americans used the swamp as a hunting ground and gave us its current name, which means "land of the trembling earth," a reference to the floating peat islands, called "houses," that dominate the landscape.

The Okefenokee Swamp

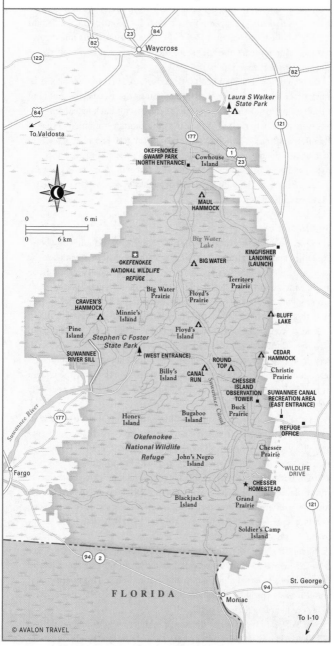

© AVALON TRAVEL

The Spanish arrived about 1600, calling the swamp Laguna de Oconi (Lake Oconi) and establishing at least two missions in the area near two Timucuan villages. During the Seminole Wars of the 1830s, the Timucua took refuge within the swamp for a time before continuing south into Florida. While trade had occurred on the swamp's outskirts for nearly a century prior, it wasn't until the 1850s that the first nonnative settlers set up camp inside the swamp itself.

It's a common mistake to call the Okefenokee "pristine," because like much of the heavily timbered and farmed southeastern coast, it is anything but. The swamp's ancient cypress stands and primordial longleaf pine forests were heavily harvested in the early 20th century. About 200 miles of old railbed through the swamp remain as a silent testament to the scope of that logging operation. In 1918 the Okefenokee Society, the first organized attempt to protect the habitat, was formed in nearby Waycross, Georgia. In 1937, President Franklin Roosevelt brought the area within the federal wildlife refuge system.

Sights

The Okefenokee features a wide variety of ecosystems, including peat bogs, sand hills, and black gum and bay forests. Perhaps most surprising are the wide-open vistas of the swamp's many prairies or extended grasslands, 22 in all, which besides being stirring to the eye are also great places to see birds. So you see, not all of the Okefenokee is wet. There is water aplenty here, though, with over 60 named lakes and 120 miles of boating trails.

And as you kayak or canoe on one of the water trails or on the old **Suwanee Canal** (a relic of the logging era), you'll notice the water is all very dark. This blackwater is not due to dirt or silt but to natural tannic acid released into the water from the decaying vegetation that gave the swamp its name. While I don't recommend that you drink the water, it's actually very clean despite its color.

As you'd expect in a national wildlife refuge, the Okefenokee hosts a huge variety of animal life—more than 400 species of vertebrates, including over 200 varieties of birds and more than 60 types of reptiles. Birders get a special treat late November-early December when sandhill cranes come south to winter in the swamp. In January their colonies are at their peak, and the swamp echoes with their loud cries. Other common bird species you'll see are herons, egrets, and endangered wood storks and red-cockaded woodpeckers. The white ibis has seen a big spike in population in the refuge recently, as has the bald eagle.

A great way to see the sandhill cranes and other birds of the Okefenokee is to hike the 0.75-mile boardwalk out to the 50-foot **Chesser Island Observation Tower** on the eastern end of the swamp. This boardwalk is brand-new, a byproduct of the huge 2011 fire; you can see the charred piers of the old boardwalk as you stroll.

You can get to the tower by driving or biking the eight-mile round-trip **Wildlife Drive,** which also takes you by the old **Chesser Homestead,** the remnants of one of the oldest settlements in the swamp and a very interesting look back into early-20th-century rural homestead life. You can also hike out to Chesser; indeed, there are many miles of hiking trails through the upland areas of the swamp near the East Entrance.

Probably the first creature one thinks of when one thinks of a swamp is the alligator. Certainly Okefenokee has plenty of them, and no one who has heard the roar of a male alligator break the quiet of the night will ever forget the experience. Most of the time, though, alligators are quite shy, and spotting them is an acquired skill. They often look like floating logs. Conversely, in warm weather you might see them out in the open sunning themselves. While no one can remember an incident of a gator attacking a human in the refuge, whatever you do, don't feed alligators in the wild.

As a Fish and Wildlife ranger in Okefenokee once told me: "If a gator attacks a human, at some point in the past someone has fed that gator. Gators get used to being fed. Unfortunately, they can't tell the difference between the person and the food."

Believe it or not, the alligator is not even the top predator in the Okefenokee; that title belongs to the black bear. Biologists estimate that as many as 90 percent of alligator eggs laid in the refuge are eaten by the local black bear population. And as with the gators, don't feed the bears.

Recreation and Accommodations
For most visitors, the best way to enjoy the Okefenokee is to book a guided tour through **Okefenokee Adventures** (866/843-7926, www.okefenokeeadventures.com), the designated concessionaire of the refuge. They offer a 90-minute guided boat tour ($18.50 adults, $11.25 children) that leaves each hour, and a 2.5-hour reservation-only sunset tour ($25 adults, $17 children) that takes you to see the gorgeous sunset over Chesser Prairie. Extended or custom tours, including multiday wilderness excursions, are also available. They also rent bikes, canoes, and camping gear, and even run a decent little café where you can either sit down and have a meal or take it to go out on the trail.

If fire and water levels permit, it's possible to stay the night in the swamp, canoeing to one of the primitive camping "islands" in the middle of the refuge. You need to make reservations up to two months in advance, however, by calling **U.S. Fish and Wildlife** (912/496-3331, Mon.-Fri. 7am-10am). A nonrefundable fee of $10 per person (which also covers your entrance fee) must be received 16 days before you arrive (mailing address: Okefenokee National Wildlife Refuge, Route 2, Box 3330, Folkston, GA 31537). Campfires are allowed only at Canal Run and Floyds Island. A camp stove is required for cooking at all other shelters. (Keep in mind that in times of extreme drought or fire threat, boat trips may not be allowed. Always check the website for the latest announcements.)

Privately owned canoes and boats with motors under 10 horsepower may put in with no launch fee, but you must sign in and out. No ATVs are allowed on the refuge, and bicycles are allowed only on designated bike trails. Keep in mind that some hunting goes on in the refuge at designated times. Pets must be leashed at all times.

At **Stephen Foster State Park** (17515 Hwy. 177, 912/637-5274, fall-winter daily 7am-7pm, spring-summer daily 6:30am-8:30pm), aka the **West Entrance,** near Fargo, Georgia, there are 66 tent sites ($24) and nine cottages ($100). This part of the Okefenokee is widely considered the best way to get that "true swamp" experience.

Several miles away, the state has recently opened the **Suwanee River Visitor Center** (912/637-5274, www.gastateparks.org, Wed.-Sun. 9am-5pm), a "green" building featuring an orientation video and exhibits.

Getting There and Around

For anyone using this guide as a travel resource, the best way to access the Okefenokee—and the one I recommend—is the **East Entrance** (912/496-7836, www.fws.gov/okefenokee, Mar.-Oct. daily dawn-7:30pm, Nov.-Feb. daily dawn-5:30pm, $5 per vehicle), otherwise known as the **Suwanee Canal Recreation Area.** This is the main U.S. Fish and Wildlife Service entrance and the most convenient way to hike, rent boating and camping gear, and observe nature. The **Richard S. Bolt Visitor Center** (912/496-7836) has some cool nature exhibits and a surround-sound orientation video. Get to the East Entrance by taking I-95 exit 3 for Kingsland onto Highway 40 west. Go through Kingsland and into Folkston until Highway 40 dead-ends. Take a right, and then an immediate left onto Main Street. At the third light, make a left onto Okefenokee Drive (Hwy. 121) south.

Families with kids may want to hit the **North Entrance** at the privately run **Okefenokee Swamp Park** (U.S. 1, 912/283-0583, www.okeswamp. com, daily 9am-5:30pm, $12 adults, $11 ages 3-11) near Waycross, Georgia. (Fans of the old comic strip *Pogo* will recall Waycross from the comic strip; yes, there's a real "Fort Mudge" nearby.) Here you will find a more touristy vibe, with a reconstructed pioneer village, a serpentarium, and animals in captivity. From here you can take various guided tours for an additional fee.

There's camping at the nearby but unaffiliated **Laura S. Walker State Park** (5653 Laura Walker Rd., 800/864-7275, www.gastateparks.org). Be aware the state park is not in the swamp and isn't very swampy, but it does have a nice manmade lake where you can rent canoes. Get to the North Entrance by taking I-95 exit 29 and going west on U.S. 82 about 45 miles to Highway 177 (Laura Walker Rd.). Go south through Laura S. Walker State Park; Okefenokee Swamp Park is several miles farther.

If you really want that cypress-festooned, classic swamp look, take the long way around the Okefenokee to **Stephen Foster State Park** (17515 Hwy. 177, 912/637-5274, fall-winter daily 7am-7pm, spring-summer daily 6:30am-8:30pm), aka the **West Entrance,** near Fargo, Georgia. Guided tours are available. Get to Stephen Foster State Park by taking I-95 exit 3 and following the signs to Folkston. Get on Highway 121 south to St. George, and then go west on Highway 94.

Folkston

The chief attraction in Folkston and its main claim to fame is the viewing depot for the **Folkston Funnel** (912/496-2536, www.folkston.com), a veritable train-watcher's paradise. This is the spot where the big CSX double-track rail line—following the top of the ancient Trail Ridge—hosts 60 or more trains a day. They say 90 percent of all freight trains to and from Florida use this track.

Railroad buffs from all over the South congregate here, anticipating the next train by listening to their scanners. The first Saturday each April brings buffs together for the all-day Folkston RailWatch.

The old Atlantic Coast Line depot across the track from the viewing platform has been converted into the very interesting **Folkston Railroad Transportation Museum** (3795 Main St., 912/496-2536, www.charlton-countyga.us, Mon.-Fri. 9am-5pm, Sat. 10am-3pm, free), with lots of history, maps, and technical stuff for the hardcore rail buff and novice alike.

To fuel up in Folkston for your trek in the swamp, go no farther than the friendly ★ **Okefenokee Restaurant** (1507 3rd St., 912/496-3263, daily 11am-8pm, $10-20) across from the handsome county courthouse. Their huge buffet is a steal at under $10; come on Friday night for a massive seafood buffet (mostly fried) for under $20 per person. In any case don't miss the fried catfish, featured at both buffets. It's some of the best I've had anywhere in the South.

For a bit of luxury in town, right outside the refuge's East Entrance is the excellent ★ **Inn at Folkston Bed and Breakfast** (509 W. Main St., 888/509-6246, www.innatfolkston.com, $120-170). There is nothing like coming back to its cozy Victorian charms after a long day out in the swamp. The four-room inn boasts an absolutely outstanding breakfast, an extensive reading library, and a whirlpool tub.

Background

The Landscape

GEOGRAPHY

The area covered by this guide falls within the **Coastal Plain** region of the southeastern United States, which contains some of the most unique ecosystems in North America. It's a place where water is never far away and features large in the daily lives, economy, and folkways of the region's people.

Although it's hundreds of miles away, the Appalachian mountain chain has a major influence on the southeastern coast. It's in Appalachia where so much of the coast's freshwater—in the form of rain—comes together and flows southeast—in the form of rivers—to the Atlantic Ocean. Moving east, the next level down from the Appalachians is the hilly **Piedmont** region, the eroded remains of an ancient mountain chain.

At the Piedmont's eastern edge is the **fall line,** so named because it's where rivers make a drop toward the sea, generally becoming navigable. Around the fall line zone in the **Upper Coastal Plain** you can sometimes spot **sand hills,** usually only a few feet in elevation, generally thought to be the vestigial remains of primordial sand dunes and offshore sandbars. Well beyond the fall line and the sometimes nearly invisible sand hills lies the **Lower Coastal Plain,** gradually built up over a 150-million-year span by sedimentary runoff from the Appalachian Mountains, which at that time were as high or even higher than the modern-day Himalayas.

The Coastal Plain was sea bottom for much of the earth's history, and in some eroded areas you can see dramatic proof of this in the form of prehistoric shells, shark's teeth, and fossilized whale bones and oyster beds, often many miles inland. Sea level has fluctuated wildly with climate and geological changes through the eons. At various times over the last 50 million years, the Coastal Plain has submerged, surfaced, and submerged again. At the height of the last major ice age, when global sea levels were very low, the east coast of North America extended out nearly 100 miles farther than the present shoreline. (We now call this former coastal region the **continental shelf.**) The Coastal Plain has been roughly in its current form for about the last 15,000 years.

Rivers

Visitors from drier climates are sometimes shocked to see how huge the rivers can get in coastal Georgia. Wide and voluminous as they saunter to the sea, their seemingly slow speed belies the massive power they contain. Georgia's big **alluvial,** or sediment-bearing, rivers originate in the region of the Appalachian mountain chain.

The headwaters of the Savannah River, for example, are near Tallulah

---

Previous: azaleas in the spring; Reynolds Square.

Gorge in extreme north Georgia. Some rivers form out of the confluence of smaller rivers, such as Georgia's mighty Altamaha River, actually the child of the Ocmulgee and Oconee Rivers in the middle of the state. Others, like the Ashley and Cooper Rivers in South Carolina, originate much closer to the coast in the Piedmont.

The **blackwater river** is a particularly interesting Southern phenomenon, duplicated only in South America and in one example each in New York and Michigan. While alluvial rivers generally originate in highlands and carry with them a large amount of sediment, blackwater rivers originate in low-lying areas and move slowly toward the sea, carrying with them very little sediment. Rather, their dark tea color comes from the tannic acid of decaying vegetation all along their banks, washed out by the slow, inexorable movement of the river toward the sea. Blackwater courses featured prominently in this guide are Ebenezer Creek near Savannah and Georgia's Suwannee River, which originates in the Okefenokee Swamp and empties into the Gulf of Mexico. Georgia's Altamaha River is a hybrid of sorts because it is partially fed by the blackwater Ohoopee River.

The Intracoastal Waterway

You'll often see its acronym, ICW, on signs—and sadly you'll probably hear the locals mispronounce it "intercoastal"—but the casual visitor might actually find the Intracoastal Waterway difficult to spot. Relying on a natural network of interconnected estuaries and channels, combined with artificial **cuts,** the ICW often blends in rather subtly with the region's already extensive network of creeks and rivers.

Mandated by Congress in 1919 and maintained by the U.S. Army Corps of Engineers, the Atlantic portion of the ICW runs from Key West, Florida, to Boston, Massachusetts, and carries recreational and barge traffic away from the perils of offshore currents and weather. Even if they don't use it specifically, kayakers and boaters often find themselves on it at some point during their nautical adventures.

Estuaries

Most biologists will tell you that the Coastal Plain is where things get interesting. The place where a river interfaces with the ocean is called an estuary, and it's perhaps the most interesting place of all. Estuaries are heavily tidal in nature (indeed, the word derives from *aestus,* Latin for "tide") and feature brackish water and heavy silt content. This portion of the U.S. coast typically has about a 6- to 8-foot tidal range, and the coastal ecosystem depends on this steady ebb and flow for life. At high tide, shellfish open and feed. At low tide, they literally clam up, keeping saltwater inside their shells until the next tide comes. Waterbirds and small mammals feed on shellfish and other animals at low tide, when their prey is exposed. High tide brings an influx of fish and nutrients from the sea, in turn drawing predators like dolphins, who often come into tidal creeks to feed. In the region covered by this guide, key estuaries from north to south are: May River, Calibogue

Clockwise from top left: alligator in Okefenokee Swamp; waterfowl along the coast; boat docks along a grass marsh.

Sound, Savannah River, Wilmington River, Midway River, Altamaha River, and the Brunswick River.

Salt Marsh

All this water action in both directions—freshwater coming from inland, saltwater encroaching from the Atlantic—results in the phenomenon of the salt marsh, the single most recognizable and iconic geographic feature of the Georgia and South Carolina coast, also known simply as "wetlands." (Freshwater marshes are rarer, with Florida's Everglades being perhaps the premier example.) Far more than just a transitional zone between land and water, marsh is also nature's nursery. Plant and animal life in marshes not only tends to be diverse but encompasses multitudes.

You may not see its denizens easily, but on close inspection you'll find the marsh absolutely teeming with creatures. Visually, the main identifying feature of a salt marsh is its distinctive, reedlike marsh grasses, adapted to survive in brackish water. Like estuaries, marshes and all life in them are heavily influenced by the tides, which bring in nutrients.

The marsh has also played a key role in human history as well, for it was here that the massive rice and indigo plantations grew their signature crops, aided by the natural ebb and flow of the tides. While most marsh you see will look quite undisturbed, very little of it could be called pristine. In the heyday of the rice plantations, much of the coastal salt marsh was criss-crossed by the canal-and-dike system of the paddy fields.

You can still see evidence almost everywhere in this area if you look hard enough (the best time to look is right after takeoff or before landing in an airplane, since many approaches to regional airports take you over wetlands). Anytime you see a low, straight ridge running through a marsh, that's likely the eroded, overgrown remnant of an old paddy field dike. Kayakers occasionally find old wooden sluice gates on their paddles.

In the Lowcountry, you'll often hear the term **pluff mud.** This refers to the area's distinctive variety of soft, dark mud in the salt marsh, which often has an equally distinctive odor that locals love but some visitors have a hard time getting used to. Extraordinarily rich in nutrients, pluff mud helped make rice such a successful crop in the marshes of the Lowcountry.

In addition to their vital role as wildlife incubators and sanctuaries, wetlands are also one of the most important natural protectors of the health of the coastal region. They serve as natural filters, cleansing runoff from the land of toxins and pollutants before it hits the ocean. They also help humans by serving as natural hurricane barriers, their porous nature helping to ease the brunt of the damaging storm surge.

Beaches and Barrier Islands

The beautiful, broad beaches of Georgia and South Carolina are almost all situated on barrier islands, long islands parallel to the shoreline and separated from the mainland by a sheltered body of water. Because they're formed from the deposit of sediment by offshore currents, they change shape over the years, with the general pattern of deposit going from north to south (meaning the northern end will begin eroding first). Most of the barrier islands are geologically quite young, only having formed within the last 25,000 years or so. Natural erosion by currents and by storms, combined with the accelerating effects of dredging for local port activity, has quickened the decline of many barrier islands. Many beaches in the area are subject to a mitigation of erosion called **beach renourishment,** which generally involves redistributing dredged material closely offshore so that it will wash up on and around the beach.

As the name indicates, barrier islands are another of nature's safeguards against hurricane damage. Historically, the barrier islands have borne the vast bulk of the damage done by hurricanes in the region. Tybee Island near Savannah was completely under water in the hurricane of 1898. More recently, Sullivan's Island near Charleston was submerged by 1989's Hurricane Hugo. Like the marshes, barrier islands also help protect the mainland by absorbing the brunt of the storm's wind and surging water.

Though barrier islands are ephemeral by nature, they have played an important role in the area's geography from the beginning of time. In fact, nearly every major settlement on the Georgia coast today—including Savannah, Darien, and Brunswick—is built on the vestiges of massive barrier islands that once guarded a primordial shoreline many miles inland from the present one. By far the largest of these ancient barrier islands, now on dry land, is the fabled **Trail Ridge,** which runs from Jesup, Georgia, to Starke, Florida. The Trail Ridge's height all along its distance made it a favorite route first for Native Americans and then for railroads, which still run along its crest today. The Trail Ridge is such a dominant geographical feature even today that it's actually responsible for the formation of the Okefenokee Swamp. The ridge effectively acts as a levee on the swamp's eastern side, preventing its drainage to the sea.

CLIMATE

One word comes to mind when one thinks about Southern climate: *hot.* That's the first word that occurs to Southerners as well, but virtually every survey of why residents are attracted to the area puts the climate at the top of the list. Go figure. How hot is hot? The average high for July, the region's hottest month, is about 92°F. While that's nothing compared to Tucson or Death Valley, when coupled with the region's notoriously high **humidity** it can have an altogether miserable effect.

Heat aside, there's no doubt that one of the most difficult things for an outsider to adjust to in the South is the humidity. The average annual humidity in Savannah is about 55 percent in the afternoons and a whopping 85 percent in the mornings. The most humid months are August and September. There is no real antidote to humidity—other than air conditioning, that is—although many film crews and other outside workers swear by the use of Sea Breeze astringent. If you and your traveling companions can deal with the strong minty odor, dampen a hand towel with the astringent, drape it across the back of your neck, and go about your business.

Don't assume that because it's humid you shouldn't drink fluids. Just as in any hot climate, you should drink lots of water if you're going to be out in the Southern heat.

August and September are by far the wettest months in terms of rainfall, with averages well over six inches for each of those months. July is also quite wet, coming in at over five inches on average.

Winters here are pretty mild but can seem much colder than they actually are because of the dampness in the air. The coldest month is January, with a high of about 58°F for the month and 42°F the average low. You're highly unlikely to encounter snow in the area, and if you do, it will likely be only skimpy flurries that a resident of the Great Lakes region wouldn't even notice as snow. But don't let this lull you into a false sense of security.

If such a tiny flurry were to hit, be aware that most people down here have no clue how to drive in rough weather and will not be prepared for even such a small amount of snowfall. Visitors from snow country are often surprised, sometimes bordering on shock, by how completely a Southern city will shut down when that once-in-a-decade few tenths of an inch of snow finally hits.

Hurricanes

The major weather phenomenon of concern for residents and visitors alike is the mighty hurricane. These massive storms, with counterclockwise-rotating bands of clouds and winds that can push 200 mph, are an ever-present danger to the southeast coast June-November each year. While the South Carolina coast has had its share of hurricane strikes, historically the Georgia coast has been relatively safe, if not immune, from major hurricane activity. In fact, as of this writing the last major storm to hit the Georgia coast directly was in 1898.

Meteorologists chalk this up to the Georgia coast's relatively sheltered, concave position relative to the rest of the southeastern coastline, as well as prevailing pressure and wind patterns that tend to deflect the oncoming storms. In any case, as most everyone is aware of now from the horrific, well-documented damage from such killer storms as Hugo, Andrew, and Katrina, hurricanes are not to be trifled with. Old-fashioned drunken "hurricane parties" are a thing of the past for the most part, the images of cataclysmic destruction everyone has seen on TV having long since eliminated any lingering romanticism about riding out the storm.

Tornadoes—especially those that come in the "back door" through the Gulf of Mexico and overland to the Georgia or Carolina coast—are a very present danger with hurricanes. As hurricanes die out over land, they can spawn dozens of tornadoes, which in many cases prove more destructive than the hurricanes that produced them.

Local TV, websites, and print media can be counted on to give more than ample warning in the event a hurricane is approaching the area during your visit. Whatever you do, do not discount the warnings; it's not worth it. If the locals are preparing to leave, you should too. Typically when a storm is likely to hit the area, there will first be a suggested evacuation. But if authorities determine there's an overwhelming likelihood of imminent hurricane damage, they will issue a **mandatory evacuation order.** What this means in practice is that if you do choose to stay behind, you cannot count on any type of emergency services or help whatsoever.

Generally speaking, the most lethal element of a hurricane is not the wind but the **storm surge,** the wall of ocean water that the winds drive before them onto the coast. During 1989's Hurricane Hugo, Charleston's Battery was inundated with a storm surge of over 12 feet, with an amazing 20 feet reported farther north at Cape Romain.

In the wake of such devastation, local governments have dramatically improved their once tepid disaster-response plans. For example, the large red traffic barriers you see stowed in their ready positions at many exits along I-16 in Georgia are a direct result of the chaos of the botched evacuation during Hurricane Floyd in 1999. Learning from that lesson, Georgia officials decided to make all four lanes of I-16 westbound in the event of a major evacuation, and those red barriers are there today to reroute traffic should they ever be needed.

ENVIRONMENTAL ISSUES

The coast of Georgia is currently experiencing a double whammy, environmentally speaking: Not only are its distinctive wetlands extraordinarily sensitive to human interference, but this is one of the most rapidly developing parts of the country. New and often poorly planned subdivisions and resort communities are popping up all over the place. Vastly increased port activity is also taking a devastating toll on the salt marsh and surrounding barrier islands. Combine all that with the South's often skeptical attitude toward environmental activism and you have a recipe for potential ecological disaster.

Thankfully, there are some bright spots. More and more communities are seeing the value of responsible planning and not green-lighting every new development sight unseen. Land trusts and other conservation organizations are growing in size, number, funding, and influence. The large number of marine biologists in these areas at various research and educational institutions means there's a wealth of education and talent available to advise local governments and citizens on how best to conserve the area's natural beauty.

Here's a closer look at some of the most urgent environmental issues facing the region today.

Marsh Dieback

The dominant species of marsh grass, *Spartina alterniflora* (pronounced spar-TINE-uh) and *Juncus roemerianus,* thrive in the typically brackish water of the coastal marsh estuaries, their structural presence helping to stem erosion of banks and dunes. While drought and blight have taken their toll on the grass, increased coastal development and continued channel deepening have also led to a steady creep of ocean saltwater farther and farther into remaining marsh stands.

Effects of Dredging

When General James Oglethorpe first sailed up the Savannah River, it was less than 20 feet deep. Today the Savannah River has been dredged to an average depth of 42 feet—and another deepening is planned, to nearly 50 feet.

Port activity is economically vital—and becoming more so—to the coastal cities. The downside of such large-scale industrial dredging is threefold:

- The deeper the channel, the farther upstream salty ocean water is able to infiltrate. This destroys freshwater and brackish habitats such as the salt marsh.

- Deepening the channel increases both the volume and the velocity of the river, quickening erosion of the riverbanks.

- Too much dredging risks the intrusion of ocean saltwater into underground freshwater aquifers that provide drinking water to millions of people in the area.

Currently the debate over harbor deepening has hit home in Savannah, one of the country's busiest ports. As of this writing the state of Georgia is pursuing deepening at the city's port, much to the consternation of local environmentalists.

The Paper Industry

Early in the 20th century, the Southeast's abundance of cheap undeveloped land and plentiful free water led to the establishment of massive pine tree farms to feed coastal pulp and paper mills. Chances are, if you used a paper grocery bag recently, it was made in a paper mill in the South.

But in addition to making a whole lot of paper bags and providing lots of employment for residents through the decades, the paper industry also gave the area lots of air and water pollution, stressed local rivers (it takes a lot of freshwater to make paper from trees), and took away natural species diversity from the area by devoting so much acreage to a single crop, pine trees.

When driving near rivers in this region, anytime you see a large industrial facility on the riverside it's probably a paper mill. The rotten egg smell that comes next is from the sulfurous discharge from its smokestacks.

Aquifers

Unlike parts of the western United States, where individuals can enforce private property rights to water, the South has generally held that the region's water is a publicly held resource. The upside of this is that everybody has equal claim to drinking water without regard to status or income or how long they've lived here. The downside is that industry also has the same free claim to the water that citizens do—and they use a heck of a lot more of it.

Currently most of coastal region gets its water from aquifers, which are basically huge underground caverns made of limestone. Receiving **groundwater** drip by drip, century after century, from rainfall farther inland, the aquifers essentially act as massive sterile warehouses for freshwater, accessible through wells.

The aquifers have human benefit only if their water remains fresh. Once saltwater from the ocean begins intruding into an aquifer, it doesn't take much to render all of it unfit for human consumption—forever. What keeps that freshwater fresh is natural water pressure, keeping the ocean at bay.

But nearly a century ago, paper mills began pumping millions and millions of gallons of water out of coastal aquifers. Combined with the dramatic rise in coastal residential development and a continuing push to deepen existing shipping channels, the natural water pressure of the aquifers has decreased, leading to measurable saltwater intrusion at several points under the coast.

Currently, local and state governments in both states are increasing their reliance on **surface water** (treated water from rivers and creeks) to relieve the strain on the underground aquifer system. But it's too soon to tell if that has contained the threat from saltwater intrusion.

Air Pollution

Despite growing awareness of the issue, air pollution is still a big problem in the coastal region. Paper mills still operate, putting out their distinctive rotten-eggs odor, and auto emissions standards are notoriously lax. The biggest culprits, though, are coal-powered electric plants, which are the norm throughout the region and which continue to pour large amounts of toxins into the atmosphere.

Plants and Animals

PLANTS

Probably the most iconic plant life of the coastal region is the **southern live oak** (*Quercus virginiana*), the official state tree of Georgia. Named because of its evergreen nature, a live oak is technically any of a number of evergreens in the *Quercus* genus, many of which reside on the coast, but in local practice the term almost always refers to the southern live oak.

Capable of living over 1,000 years and possessing wood of legendary resilience, the southern live oak is one of nature's most magnificent creations. The timber value of live oaks has been well known since the earliest days of the American shipbuilding industry—when the oak dominated the entire coast inland of the marsh—but their value as a canopy tree has finally been widely recognized by local and state governments.

Fittingly, the other iconic plant life of the coastal region grows on the branches of the live oak. Contrary to popular opinion, **Spanish moss** (*Tillandsia usneoides*) is neither Spanish nor moss. It's an air plant, a wholly indigenous cousin to the pineapple. Also contrary to folklore, Spanish moss is not a parasite nor does it harbor parasites while living on an oak tree—although it can after it has already fallen to the ground.

Also growing on the bark of a live oak, especially right after a rain shower, is the **resurrection fern** (*Polypodium polypodioides*), which can stay dormant for amazingly long periods of time, only to spring back to life with the introduction of a little water. You can find live oak, Spanish moss, and resurrection fern anywhere in the **maritime forest** ecosystem of coastal Georgia and South Carolina, a zone generally behind the **interdune meadows,** which is right behind the beach zone.

The oak may be Georgia's state tree, but far and away its most important commercial tree is the pine, used for paper, lumber, and turpentine. Rarely seen in the wild today due to tree farming, which has covered most of southern Georgia, the dominant species is now the **slash pine** (*Pinus elliottii*), often seen in long rows on either side of rural highways. Before the introduction of large-scale monoculture tree farming, however, a rich variety of native pines flourished in the **upland forest** inland from the maritime forest, including **longleaf** (*Pinus palustris*) and **loblolly** (*Pinus taeda*) pines.

Right up there with live oaks and Spanish moss in terms of instant recognition would have to be the colorful, ubiquitous **azalea,** a flowering shrub of the *Rhododendron* genus. Over 10,000 varieties have been cultivated through the centuries, with quite a wide range of them on display during blooming season, March-April, on the coast.

The area's other great floral display comes from the **camellia** (*Camellia japonica*), a large, cold-hardy evergreen shrub that generally blooms in late winter (Jan.-Mar.). An import from Asia, the southeastern coast's camellias are close cousins to *Camellia sinensis,* also an import and the plant from which tea is made.

Other colorful ornamentals of the area include the ancient and beautiful **southern magnolia** (*Magnolia grandiflora*), a native plant with distinctive large white flowers that evolved before the advent of bees; and the **flowering dogwood** (*Cornus florida*), which, despite its very hard wood—great for daggers, hence its original name "dagwood"—is actually quite fragile. An ornamental imported from Asia that has now become quite obnoxious in its aggressive invasiveness is the **mimosa** (*Albizia julibrissin*), which blooms March-August.

Moving into watery areas, you'll find the remarkable **bald cypress** (*Taxodium distichum*), a flood-resistant conifer recognizable by its tufted top, its great height (up to 130 feet), and its distinctive "knees," parts of the root that project above the waterline and which are believed to help stabilize the tree in lowland areas. Cypress is much prized for its beautiful pest-resistant wood, and great stands of ancient cypress once dominated the marsh along the coast; sadly, overharvesting and destruction of wetlands have made the magnificent sight of this ancient, dignified species much less common. The acres of **smooth cordgrass** for which the Golden Isles are named are plants of the *Spartina alterniflora* species. (A cultivated cousin, *Spartina anglica*, is considered invasive.) Besides its simple natural beauty, *Spartina* is also a key food source for marsh denizens. Playing a key environmental role on the coast are **sea oats** (*Uniola paniculata*). This wispy, fast-growing perennial grass anchors sand dunes and hence is a protected species on the Georgia coast (it's a misdemeanor to pick them).

Palm varieties are not as common up here as in Florida, but you'll definitely encounter several types along the coast. The **cabbage palm** (*Sabal palmetto*) is the largest variety, up to 50-60 feet tall. Its "heart of palm" is an edible delicacy, which coastal Native Americans boiled in bear fat to make porridge. In dunes and sand hills you'll find clumps of the low-lying **saw palmetto** (*Serenoa repens*). The **bush palmetto** (*Sabal minor*) has distinctive fan-shaped branches. The common **Spanish bayonet** (*Yucca aloifolia*) looks like a palm, but it's actually a member of the agave family.

ANIMALS
On the Land

Perhaps the most iconic land animal—or semi-land animal, anyway—of this coastal region is the legendary **American alligator** (*Alligator mississippiensis*), the only species of crocodilian native to the area. Contrary to their fierce reputation, these massive reptiles, 6-12 feet long as adults, are quite shy. If you come in the colder months, you won't see them at all, since alligators require an outdoor temperature over 70°F to become active and feed (indeed, the appearance of alligators was once a well-known symbol of spring in the area).

Often all you'll see is a couple of eyebrow ridges sticking out of the water, and a gator lying still in a shallow creek can easily be mistaken for a floating log. But should you see one or more gators basking in the sun—a favorite activity on warm days for these cold-blooded creatures—it's best to admire them from afar. A mother alligator, in particular, will destroy anything that comes near her nest. Despite the alligator's short, stubby legs, it can run amazingly fast on land—faster than you, in fact.

If you're driving on a country road at night, be on the lookout for **white-tailed deer** (*Odocoileus virginianus*), which, besides being quite beautiful, also pose a serious road hazard. Because coastal development has dramatically reduced the habitat—and therefore the numbers—of their natural predators, deer are very plentiful throughout the area, and as you read this they are hard at work devouring vast tracts of valuable vegetation. No one wants to hurt poor little Bambi, but the truth is that area hunters perform a valuable service by culling the local deer population, which is in no danger of extinction anytime soon.

The coast hosts fairly large populations of playful **river otters** (*Lontra canadensis*). Not to be confused with the larger sea otters of the West Coast, these fast-swimming members of the weasel family inhabit inland waterways and marshy areas, with dominant males sometimes ranging as much as 50 miles within a single waterway. While you're unlikely to encounter an otter, if you're camping you might easily run into the **raccoon** (*Procyon lotor*), an exceedingly intelligent and crafty relative of the bear, sharing that larger animal's resourcefulness in stealing your food. Though nocturnal, raccoons will feed whenever food is available. Rabies is prevalent in the raccoon population, and you should always, always keep your distance.

Another common campsite nuisance, the **opossum** (*Didelphis virginiana*) is a shy, primitive creature that is much more easily discouraged. It's North America's only marsupial, and an opossum's usual "defense" against predators is to play dead. That said, however, they have an immunity to snake venom and often feed on the reptiles, even the most poisonous ones.

While you're unlikely to actually see a **red fox** (*Vulpes vulpes*), you might very well see their distinctive footprints in the mud of a marsh at low tide. These nocturnal hunters, a nonnative species introduced by European settlers, range the coast seeking mice, squirrels, and rabbits.

Once fairly common in this region, the **black bear** (*Ursus americanus*) has suffered from hunting and habitat destruction. Of the regions in this guide, the Okefenokee Swamp area is the only place in which you'll be close to one.

In the Water

Without a doubt the most magnificent denizen—if only part-time—of the southeastern coast is the **North Atlantic right whale** (*Eubalaena glacialis*), which can approach 60 feet in length. Each year December-March the mothers give birth to their calves and nurse them in the warm waters off the Georgia coast in an eons-old ritual. (In the summer they like to hang around the rich fishing grounds off the New England coast, although biologists still can't account for their whereabouts at other times of the year.) Their numbers were so abundant in past centuries that the Spanish name for Jekyll Island, Georgia, was Isla de las Ballenas (Island of the Whales). Whaling and encounters with ship propellers have taken their toll, and numbers of this endangered species are dwindling fast now, with fewer than 500 estimated left in the world.

Another of humankind's aquatic cousins, the **bottlenose dolphin** (*Tursiops truncatus*) is a well-known and frequent visitor to the coast, coming far upstream into creeks and rivers to feed. Children, adults, and experienced sailors alike all delight in encounters with the mammals, sociable creatures who travel in family units. They will gather near boats, surfacing often with the distinctive chuffing sound of air coming from their blowholes. Occasionally they'll even lift their heads out of the water to have a look at you; consider yourself lucky indeed to have such a close encounter. Don't be fooled by their cuteness, however. Dolphins live life with gusto and aren't scared of much. They're voracious eaters of fish, energetic lovers, and will take on an encroaching shark in a heartbeat.

Another beloved part-time marine creature of the barrier islands is the **loggerhead turtle** (*Caretta caretta*). Though the species prefers to stay well offshore most of the year, females weighing up to 300 pounds come out of the sea each May-July to dig a shallow hole in the dunes and lay more than 100 leathery eggs, returning to the ocean and leaving the eggs to hatch on their own after two months.

Interestingly, the mothers prefer to nest at the same spot on the same island year after year. After hatching, the baby turtles then make a dramatic, extremely dangerous (and extremely slow) trek to the safety of the waves, at the mercy of various predators. Dedicated research and conservation efforts, like the Caretta Project based on Wassaw Island, Georgia, are working hard to protect the loggerheads' traditional nursery grounds to ensure survival of this fascinating, loveable, and threatened species.

Of course, the coastal waters and rivers are chockablock with fish. The most abundant and sought-after recreational species in the area is the **spotted sea trout** (*Cynoscion nebulosus*), followed by the **red drum** (*Sciaenops ocellatus*). Local anglers also pursue many varieties of **bass, bream, sheepshead,** and **crappie.** It may sound strange to some accustomed to considering it a "trash" fish, but many types of **catfish** are not only plentiful here but are a common and well-regarded food source. Many species of **flounder** inhabit the silty bottoms of estuaries all along the coast. Farther offshore are game and sport fish like **marlin, swordfish, shark, grouper,** and **tuna.**

Each March, anglers jockey for position on coastal rivers for the yearly running of the **American shad** (*Alosa sapidissima*) upstream to spawn. This large (up to eight pounds) catfish-like species is a regional delicacy as a seasonal entrée as well as for its tasty roe. There's a catch limit of eight shad per person per season. One of the more interesting fish species in the area is the endangered **shortnose sturgeon** (*Acipenser brevirostrum*). A fantastically ancient species that has evolved little in hundreds of millions of years, this small freshwater fish is known to exist in the Altamaha, Savannah, and Ogeechee Rivers of Georgia. Traveling upriver to spawn in the winter, the sturgeons remain around the mouths of waterways the rest of the year, venturing near the ocean only sparingly.

Crustaceans and shellfish have been a key food staple in the area for thousands of years, with the massive shell middens of the coast being testament to Native Americans' healthy appetite for them. The beds of the local variant, the **eastern oyster** (*Crassostrea virginica*), aren't what they used to be due to overharvesting, water pollution, and disruption of habitat. In truth, these days most local restaurants import the little filter-feeders from the Gulf of Mexico. Oysters spawn May-August, hence the old folk wisdom about eating oysters only in months with the letter *r* so as not to disrupt the breeding cycle.

Each year April-January, shrimp boats up and down the southeastern coast trawl for **shrimp,** most commercially viable in two local species, the white shrimp (*Litopenaeus setiferus*) and the brown shrimp

(*Farfantepenaeus aztecus*). Shrimp are the most popular seafood item in the United States and bring hundreds of millions of dollars in revenue into the coastal economy. While consumption won't slow down anytime soon, the region's shrimping industry is facing serious threats, from species decline due to pollution and overfishing as well as from competition from shrimp farms and the Asian shrimp industry.

Another important commercial crop is the **blue crab** (*Callinectes sapidus*), the species used in such Lowcountry delicacies as crab cakes. You'll often see floating markers bobbing up and down in rivers throughout the region. These signal the presence directly below of a crab trap, often of an amateur crabber.

A true living link to primordial times, the alien-looking **horseshoe crab** (*Limulus polyphemus*) is frequently found on beaches of the coast during the spring mating season (it lives in deeper water the rest of the year). More closely related to scorpions and spiders than crabs, the horseshoe has evolved hardly a lick in hundreds of millions of years.

Any trip to a local salt marsh at low tide will likely uncover hundreds of **fiddler crabs** (*Uca pugilator* and *Uca pugnax*), so-named for the way the males wave their single enlarged claw in the air to attract mates. (Their other, smaller claw is the one they actually eat with.) The fiddlers make distinctive burrows in the pluff mud for sanctuary during high tide, recognizable by the little balls of sediment at the entrances (the crabs spit out the balls after sifting through the sand for food).

One charming beach inhabitant, the **sand dollar** (*Mellita quinquiesperforata*), has seen its numbers decline drastically due to being entirely too charming for its own good. Beachcombers are now asked to enjoy these flat little cousins to the sea urchin in their natural habitat and to refrain from taking them home. Besides, they start to smell bad when they dry out.

The **sea nettle** (*Chrysaora quinquecirrha*), a less-than-charming beach inhabitant, is a jellyfish that stings thousands of people on the coast each year (although only for those with severe allergies are the stings potentially life-threatening). Stinging their prey before transporting it into their waiting mouths, the jellyfish also sting when disturbed or frightened. Most often, people are stung by stepping on the bodies of jellyfish washed up on the sand. If you're stung by a jellyfish, don't panic. You'll probably experience a stinging rash for about half an hour. Locals say applying a little baking soda or vinegar helps cut the sting. (Some also swear fresh urine will do the trick, and I pass that tip along to you purely in the interest of thoroughness.)

In the Air

When enjoying the marshlands of the coast, consider yourself fortunate to see a **wood stork** (*Mycteria americana*), very recently taken off the endangered species list. The only storks to breed in North America, these graceful long-lived birds (routinely living over 10 years) are usually seen on a low flight path across the marsh, although at some birding spots beginning in late summer you can find them at a **roost,** sometimes numbering over 100 birds. Resting at high tide, they fan out over the marsh to feed at low tide on foot. Old-timers sometimes call them "Spanish buzzards" or simply "the preacher."

Often confused with the wood stork is the gorgeous **white ibis** (*Eudocimus albus*), distinguishable by its orange bill and black wingtips. Like the wood stork, the ibis is a communal bird that roosts in colonies.

Other similar-looking coastal denizens are the white-feathered **great egret** (*Ardea alba*) and **snowy egret** (*Egretta thula*), the former distinguishable by its yellow bill and the latter by its black bill and the tuft of plumes on the back of its head. Egrets are in the same family as herons.

The most magnificent in that family is the **great blue heron** (*Ardea herodias*). Despite their imposing height—up to four feet tall—these waders are shy. Often you hear them rather than see them, as a loud shriek of alarm echoes over the marsh.

So how to tell the difference between all these wading birds at a glance? It's actually easiest when they're in flight. Egrets and herons fly with their necks tucked in, while storks and ibis fly with their necks extended.

Dozens of species of shorebirds comb the beaches, including **sandpipers, plovers,** and the wonderful and rare **American oystercatcher** (*Haematopus palliatus*), instantly recognizable for its prancing walk, dark-brown back, stark white underside, and long bright-orange bill. **Gulls** and **terns** also hang out wherever there's water. They can frequently be seen swarming around incoming shrimp boats, attracted by the catch of little crustaceans.

The chief raptor of the salt marsh is the fish-eating **osprey** (*Pandion haliaetus*). These large grayish birds of prey are similar to eagles but are adapted to a maritime environment, with a reversible outer toe on each talon (the better for catching wriggly fish) and closable nostrils so they can dive into the water after prey. Very common all along the coast, they like to build big nests on top of buoys and channel markers in addition to trees.

The **bald eagle** (*Haliaeetus leucocephalus*) is making a comeback in the area thanks to increased federal regulation and better education of trigger-happy locals. Apparently not as all-American as their bumper stickers might sometimes indicate, local farmers would often regard the national symbol as more of a nuisance and fire away anytime they saw one. Of course, as we all should have learned in school, the bald eagle is not actually bald but has a head adorned with white feathers. Like the osprey, bald eagles prefer fish, but unlike the osprey will settle for rodents and rabbits.

Inland among the pines you'll find the most common area woodpecker, the huge **pileated woodpecker** (*Dryocopus pileatus*) with its large crest. Less common is the smaller, more subtly marked **red-cockaded woodpecker** (*Picoides borealis*). Once common in the vast primordial pine forests of the Southeast, the species is now endangered, its last real refuge being the big tracts of relatively undisturbed land on military bases.

Down here they say that God invented bugs to keep the Yankees from completely taking over the South. And insects are probably the most unpleasant fact of life in the southeastern coastal region. The list of annoying indigenous insects must begin with the infamous **sand gnat** (*Culicoides furens*). This tiny and persistent nuisance, a member of the midge family, lacks the precision of the mosquito with its long proboscis. No, the sand gnat is more torture master than surgeon, brutally gouging and digging away its victim's skin until it hits a source of blood. Most prevalent in the spring and fall, the sand gnat is drawn to its prey by the carbon dioxide trail of its breath. While long sleeves and long pants are one way to keep gnats at bay, the only real antidote to the sand gnat's assault—other than never breathing—is the Avon skin-care product Skin So Soft, which has taken on a new and wholly unplanned life as the South's favorite anti-gnat lotion. In calmer moments, grow to appreciate the great contribution sand gnats make to the salt marsh ecosystem—as food for birds and bats.

Running a close second to the sand gnat are the over three dozen species of the highly aggressive **mosquito,** which breeds anywhere a few drops of water lie stagnant. Not surprisingly, massive populations blossom in the rainiest months, in late spring and late summer, feeding in the morning and late afternoon. Like the gnat, the mosquito—the biters are always female—homes in on its victim by trailing the plume of carbon dioxide exhaled in the breath. More than just a biting nuisance, mosquitoes are now carrying West Nile disease to the Lowcountry and Georgia coast, signaling a possibly dire threat to public health. Alas, Skin So Soft has little effect on the mosquito. Try over-the-counter sprays, anything smelling of citronella, and wearing long sleeves and long pants when weather permits.

But undoubtedly the most viscerally loathed of all pests on the Lowcountry and Georgia coasts is the so-called "palmetto bug," or **American cockroach** (*Periplaneta americana*). These black, shiny, and sometimes grotesquely massive insects—up to two inches long—are living fossils, virtually unchanged over hundreds of millions of years. And perfectly adapted as they are to life in and among wet, decaying vegetation, they're unlikely to change a bit in 100 million more years. While they spend most of their time crawling around, usually under rotting leaves and tree bark, American cockroaches can indeed fly—sort of. There are few more hilarious sights than a room full of people frantically trying to dodge a palmetto bug that has just clumsily launched itself off a high point on the wall. Because the cockroach doesn't know any better than you do where it's going, it can be a particularly bracing event—though the insect does not bite and poses few real health hazards.

Popular regional use of the term *palmetto bug* undoubtedly has its roots in a desire for polite Southern society to avoid using the ugly word *roach* and its connotations of filth and unclean environments. But the colloquialism actually has a basis in reality. Contrary to what anyone tells you, the natural habitat of the American cockroach—unlike its kitchen-dwelling, much-smaller cousin the German cockroach—is outdoors, often up in trees. They only come inside human dwellings when it's especially hot, especially cold, or especially dry outside. Like you, the palmetto bug is easily driven indoors by extreme temperatures and by thirst.

Other than visiting the Southeast during the winter, when the roaches go dormant, there's no convenient antidote for their presence. The best way to keep them out of your life is to stay away from decaying vegetation and keep doors and windows closed on especially hot nights.

History

BEFORE THE EUROPEANS

Based on artifacts found throughout the state, anthropologists know the first humans arrived on the coasts of South Carolina and Georgia at least 13,000 years ago, at the tail end of the last ice age. During this **Paleo-Indian period,** sea levels were over 200 feet lower than present levels, and large mammals such as woolly mammoths, horses, and camels were hunted for food and skins. However, rapidly increasing temperatures, rising sea levels, and efficient hunting techniques combined to quickly kill off these large mammals, relics of the Pleistocene era, ushering in the **Archaic period.** Still hunter-gatherers, Archaic period inhabitants began turning to small game such as deer, bears, and turkeys, supplemented with fruit and nuts. The latter part of the Archaic period saw more habitation on the coasts, with an increasing reliance on fish and shellfish. It's to this time that the great **shell middens** of the coastal region trace their origins. Basically serving as trash heaps for discarded oyster shells, as the middens grew in size they also took on a ceremonial status, often being used as sites for important rituals and meetings. Such sites are often called **shell rings,** and the largest yet found was over nine feet high and 300 feet in diameter.

The introduction of agriculture and improved pottery techniques about 3,000 years ago led to the **Woodland period** of Native American settlement. Extended clan groups were much less migratory, establishing year-round communities of up to 50 people, who began the practice of clearing land to grow crops. The ancient shell middens of their ancestors were not abandoned, however, and were continually added onto. Native Americans had been cremating or burying their dead for years, a practice that eventually gave rise to the construction of the first **mounds** during the Woodland period. Essentially built-up earthworks sometimes marked with spiritual symbols, often in the form of animal shapes, mounds contained not only the remains of the deceased but items like pottery to accompany the deceased into the afterlife.

Increased agriculture led to increased population, and with that population growth came competition over resources and a more formal notion of warfare. This period, about AD 800-1600, is termed the **Mississippian period.** It was the Mississippians who would be the first Native Americans in what's now the continental United States to encounter European explorers and settlers after Columbus. The Native Americans who would later be called **Creek Indians** were the direct descendants of the Mississippians in lineage, language, and lifestyle. Native American social structure north of Mexico reached its apex with the Mississippians, who were not only prodigious mound builders but constructed elaborate wooden villages and evolved a top-down class system. The defensive palisades surrounding some of the villages attest to the increasingly martial nature of the groups and their chieftains, or *micos*.

Described by later European accounts as a tall, proud people, the Mississippians often wore elaborate body art and, like the indigenous inhabitants of Central and South America, used the practice of **head shaping**, whereby an infant's skull was deliberately deformed into an elongated shape by tying the baby's head to a board for about a year.

THE SPANISH ARRIVE

The first known contact by Europeans on the southeastern coast came in 1521, roughly concurrent with Cortés's conquest of Mexico. A party of Spanish slavers ventured into what's now Port Royal Sound, South Carolina, from Santo Domingo in the Caribbean. Naming the area Santa Elena, they kidnapped a few Indian slaves and left, ranging as far north as the Cape Fear River in present-day North Carolina.

The first serious exploration of the coast came in 1526, when Lucas Vázquez de Ayllón and about 600 colonists made landfall at Winyah Bay in South Carolina, near present-day Georgetown. They didn't stay long, however, immediately moving down the coast and trying to set down roots in the St. Catherine's Sound area of modern-day Liberty County, Georgia.

That colony—called San Miguel de Gualdape—was the first European settlement in North America since the Vikings (the continent's oldest continuously occupied settlement, St. Augustine, Florida, wasn't founded until 1565). The colony also brought with it the seed of a future nation's dissolution: slaves from Africa. While San Miguel lasted only six weeks due to political tension and a slave uprising, artifacts from its brief life have been discovered in the area.

Hernando de Soto's ill-fated trek of 1539-1543 from Florida through Georgia to Alabama (where De Soto died of a fever) did not find the gold he anticipated, nor did it enter the coastal region covered in this guide. But De Soto's legacy was indeed soon felt there and throughout the Southeast in the form of various diseases for which the Mississippian people had no immunity whatsoever: smallpox, typhus, influenza, measles, yellow fever, whooping cough, diphtheria, tuberculosis, and bubonic plague.

While the cruelties of the Spanish certainly took their toll, these deadly diseases were far more damaging to a population totally unprepared for them. Within a few years, the Mississippian people—already in a state of internal decline—were losing a huge percentage of their population to disease, echoing what had already happened on a massive scale to the indigenous people of the Caribbean after Christopher Columbus's expeditions. As the viruses they introduced ran rampant, the Europeans themselves stayed away for a couple of decades after the ignominious end of De Soto's fruitless quest.

During that quarter-century, the once-proud Mississippian culture continued to disintegrate, dwindling into a shadow of its former greatness. In all, disease would claim the lives of at least 80 percent of all indigenous inhabitants of the Western Hemisphere.

THE FRENCH MISADVENTURE

The next European presence on the Georgia and South Carolina coast was another ill-fated attempt, the establishment of Charlesfort in 1562 by French Huguenots under Jean Ribault on present-day Parris Island, South Carolina. Part of a covert effort by the Protestant French admiral Gaspard II de Coligny to send Huguenot colonists around the globe, Ribault's crew of 150 first explored the mouth of the St. Johns River near present-day Jacksonville, Florida, before heading north.

After establishing Charlesfort, Ribault returned to France for supplies. In his absence, religious war had broken out in his home country. Ribault sought sanctuary in England but was clapped in irons anyway. Meanwhile, most of Charlesfort's colonists grew so demoralized they joined another French expedition led by René Laudonnière at Fort Caroline on the St. Johns River. The remaining 27 built a ship to sail from Charlesfort back to France; 20 of them survived the journey, which was cut short in the English Channel when they had to be rescued.

Ribault himself was dispatched to reinforce Fort Caroline, but was headed off by a contingent from the new Spanish settlement at St. Augustine. The fate of the French presence on the southeast coast was sealed when not only did the Spanish take Fort Caroline but a storm destroyed Ribault's reinforcing fleet; Ribault and all survivors were killed as soon as they came ashore. To keep the French away for good and cement Spain's hold on this northernmost part of their province of La Florida, the Spanish built the fort of Santa Elena directly on top of Charlesfort. Both layers are currently being excavated and studied.

THE MISSION ERA

With Spanish dominance of the region ensured for the near future, the lengthy mission era began. It's rarely mentioned as a key part of U.S. history, but the Spanish missionary presence on the Georgia coast was longer and more comprehensive than its much more widely known counterpart in California. St. Augustine's governor, Pedro Menéndez de Avilés—sharing "biscuits with honey" on the beach at St. Catherine's Island with a local *mico*—negotiated for the right to establish a system of Jesuit missions in two coastal chiefdoms: the Mocama on and around Cumberland Island, and the Guale (pronounced "wallie") to the north. Those early missions, the first north of Mexico, were largely unsuccessful. But a renewed, organized effort by the Franciscan Order came to fruition during the 1580s. Starting with Santa Catalina de Guale on St. Catherine's Island, missions were established all along the Georgia coast.

The looming invasion threat to St. Augustine from English adventurer and privateer Sir Francis Drake was a harbinger of trouble to come, as was a Guale uprising in 1597. The Spanish consolidated their positions near St. Augustine, and Santa Elena was abandoned. As Spanish power waned, in 1629 Charles I of England laid formal claim to what is now the Carolinas, Georgia, and much of Florida but made no effort to colonize the area. Largely left to their own devices and facing an indigenous population dying from disease, the missions in the Georgia interior nonetheless carried on. A devastating Indian raid in 1661 on a mission at the mouth of the Altamaha River, possibly aided by the English, persuaded the Spanish to pull the mission effort to the barrier islands. But even as late as 1667, right before the founding of Charles Towne far to the north, there were 70 missions still extant in the old Guale kingdom.

Pirate raids and slave uprisings finished off the Georgia missions for good by 1684. By 1706 the Spanish mission effort in the Southeast had fully retreated to St. Augustine. In an interesting postscript, 89 Native Americans—the only surviving descendants of Spain's Georgia missions—evacuated to Cuba with the final Spanish exodus from Florida in 1763.

ENTER THE ENGLISH

With the native populations in steep decline due to disease and a wholesale retrenchment by European powers, a sort of vacuum came to the southeastern coast. Into the vacuum came the first English-speaking settlers of South Carolina. The first attempt was an expedition by a Barbadian colonist, William Hilton, in 1663. While he didn't establish a new colony, he did leave his name on the most notable geographic feature he saw—Hilton Head Island.

In 1665 King Charles II gave a charter to eight **Lords Proprietors** to establish a colony, generously to be named Carolina after the monarch himself. Remarkably, none of the Proprietors ever set foot in the colony they established for their own profit. Before their colony was even set up, the Proprietors themselves set the stage for the vast human disaster that would eventually befall it. They encouraged slavery by promising that each colonist would receive 20 acres of land for every black male slave and 10 acres for every black female slave brought to the colony within the first year.

In 1666 explorer Robert Sandford officially claimed Carolina for the king. The Proprietors then sent out a fleet of three ships from England, only one of which, the *Carolina,* would make it the whole way. After stops in the thriving English colonies of Barbados and Bermuda, the ship landed in Port Royal. The settlers were greeted without violence, but the fact that the local indigenous people spoke Spanish led the colonists to conclude that perhaps the site was too close for comfort to Spain's sphere of influence.

A Kiawah chief, eager for allies against the fierce, slave-trading Westo people, invited the colonists north to settle instead. So the colonists—148 of them, including three African slaves—moved 80 miles up the coast and in 1670 pitched camp on the Ashley River at a place they dubbed Albemarle Point after one of their lost ships. Living within the palisades of the camp, the colonists farmed 10-acre plots outside the walls.

A few years later some colonists from Barbados, which was beginning to suffer the effects of overpopulation, joined the Carolinians. The Barbadian influence, with an emphasis on large-scale slave labor and a caste system, would have an indelible imprint on the colony. Indeed, within a generation a majority of settlers in the new colony would be African slaves.

By 1680, however, Albemarle Point was feeling growing pains as well, and the Proprietors ordered the site moved to Oyster Point at the confluence of the Ashley and Cooper Rivers (the present-day Battery). Within a year Albemarle Point was abandoned, and the walls of Charles Towne were built a few hundred yards up from Oyster Point on the banks of the Cooper River.

The original Anglican settlers were quickly joined by various **Dissenters**, among them French Huguenots, Quakers, Congregationalists, and Jews. A group of Scottish Presbyterians established the short-lived Stuart Town near Port Royal in 1684. Recognizing this diversity, the colony in 1697 granted religious liberty to all "except Papists," meaning Catholics. The Anglicans attempted a crackdown on Dissenters in 1704, but two years later Queen Anne stepped in and ensured religious freedom for all Carolinians (again with the exception of Catholics, who wouldn't be a factor in the colony until after the American Revolution).

THE YAMASEE WAR

Within 20 years the English presence had expanded throughout the Lowcountry to include Port Royal and Beaufort. Charles Towne became a thriving commercial center, dealing in deerskins with traders in the interior and with foreign concerns from England to South America. Its success was not without a backlash, as the local **Yamasee** people became increasingly disgruntled at the settlers' growing monopolies on deerskin and the trade in Native American slaves.

As rumors of war spread, on Good Friday, 1715, a delegation of six Carolinians went to the Yamasee village of Pocataligo to address some of the Native Americans' grievances in the hopes of forestalling violence. Their effort was in vain, however, as warriors murdered four of them in their sleep; the remaining two escaped to sound the alarm.

The treacherous attack signaled the beginning of the two-year Yamasee War, which would claim the lives of nearly 10 percent of the colony's population and an unknown number of Native Americans—making it one of the bloodiest conflicts fought on American soil.

Energized and ready for war, the Yamasee attacked Charles Towne itself

Henry Woodward, Colonial Indiana Jones

He's virtually unsung in the history books, and there are no movies made about him, but Dr. Henry Woodward, the first English settler in South Carolina, lived a life that is the stuff of novels and screenplays. Educated in medicine in London, Woodward first tried his hand in the colony of Barbados. Still in his teens, Woodward left Barbados in Captain Robert Sandford's 1664 expedition to Carolina. In 1666, in what is perhaps the New World's first "cultural exchange program," Woodward volunteered to stay behind while the rest of the expedition returned to England.

Woodward learned the local language and established relations with Native Americans, actions for which the Lords Proprietors granted him temporary "formall possession of the whole Country to hold as Tennant att Will." The Spanish kidnapped the young Englishman, taking him to the Spanish stronghold of St. Augustine in Florida. Woodward was popular and treated well. During that time, he studied the Spanish government, commerce, and culture, with the same diligence with which he had studied the Indians a year earlier. In 1668, Woodward was "rescued" by English pirates under the command of Robert Searle. Woodward's sojourn with the pirates would last two years, during which he was kept on board as ship's surgeon.

In 1670 Woodward was rescued when the pirates shipwrecked on the Caribbean island of Nevis. His rescuers were none other than settlers on their way to found Charles Towne. Woodward used his previous experi-

and killed almost all the white traders in the interior, effectively ending commerce in the area. As Charles Towne began to swell with refugees from the hinterland, water and supplies ran low, and the colony's very existence was in peril.

After an initially poor performance by the Carolina militia, a professional army—including armed African slaves—was raised. Well trained and well led, the new army more than held its own despite being outnumbered. A key alliance with local Cherokees was all the advantage the colonists needed to turn the tide. While the Cherokee never received the overt military backing from the settlers that they sought, they did garner enough supplies and influence to convince their Creek rivals, the Yamasee, to begin the peace process. The war-weary settlers, eager to get back to life and to business, were anxious to negotiate with them, offering goods as a sign of their earnest intent. By 1717 the Yamasee threat had subsided and trade in the region began flourishing anew.

No sooner had the Yamasee War ended, however, than a new threat emerged: the dreaded pirate Edward Teach, aka Blackbeard. Entering Charleston harbor in May 1718 with his flagship *Queen Anne's Revenge* and three other vessels, he promptly plundered five ships and began a full-scale blockade of the entire settlement. He took a number of prominent citizens hostage before finally departing northward.

ence to direct the colonists to an area of less Spanish influence. That same year he began a series of expeditions to contact Native Americans in the Carolina interior—the first non-Spanish European to set foot in the area. Using information gained from the Spanish, Woodward's goal was to jump-start the trade in deerskins that would be the bulwark of the Charles Towne colony. Woodward's 1674 alliance with the aggressive Westo people was instrumental in this burgeoning trade. As if all this weren't enough, in 1680 Woodward, now with property of his own on Johns Island, would introduce local farmers to a certain crop recently imported from Madagascar: rice.

Woodward made enemies of settlers who were envious of his growing affluence and suspicious of his friendship with the Westo. His outspoken disgust with the spread of Indian slavery brought a charge against him of undermining the interests of the crown. But Woodward, by now a celebrity of sorts, returned to England to plead his case directly to the Lords Proprietors. They not only pardoned him but made him their official Indian agent—with a 20 percent share of the profits.

Woodward returned to the American colonies to trek inland, making alliances with groups of Creek Indians in Spanish-held territory. Hounded by Spanish troops, Woodward fell ill of a fever somewhere in the Savannah River valley. He made it to Charleston and safety but never fully recovered and died around 1690.

SLAVERY

For the colonists, the Blackbeard episode was the final straw. Already disgusted by the lack of support from the Lords Proprietors during the Yamasee War, the humiliation of the pirate blockade was too much to take. To almost universal agreement in the colony, the settlers threw off the rule of the Proprietors and lobbied in 1719 to become a crown colony, an effort that came to final fruition in 1729.

While this outward-looking and energetic Charleston was originally built on the backs of merchants, with the introduction of the rice and indigo crops in the early 1700s it would increasingly be built on the backs of slaves. For all the wealth gained through the planting of rice and cotton seeds, another seed was sown by the Lowcountry plantation culture. The area's total dependence on slave labor would ultimately lead to a disastrous war, a conflict signaled for decades to those smart enough to read the signs.

By the early 18th century Savannah and Charleston were firmly established as the key American ports for the importation of African slaves, with about 40 percent of the trade centered in Charleston alone. As a result, the black population of the coast outnumbered the white population by more than three to one, and much more than that in some areas. The fear of violent slave uprisings had great influence over not only politics but day-to-day affairs.

These fears were eventually realized in the **Stono Rebellion** on

September 9, 1739. Twenty African American slaves led by an Angolan known only as Jemmy met near the Stono River near Charleston. Marching with a banner that read "Liberty," they seized guns with the plan of marching all the way to Spanish Florida and finding sanctuary in the wilderness. On the way they burned seven plantations and killed 20 more whites. A militia eventually caught up with them, killing 44 escaped slaves while losing 20 of their own. The prisoners were decapitated and had their heads spiked on every milepost between the spot of that final battle and Charleston. Inspired by the rebellion, at least two other uprisings would take place over the next two years in South Carolina and Georgia.

OGLETHORPE'S VISION

In 1729, Carolina was divided into north and south. In 1731, a colony to be known as Georgia, after the new English king, was carved out of the southern part of the Carolina land grant. A young general, aristocrat, and humanitarian named James Edward Oglethorpe gathered together a group of Trustees—similar to Carolina's Lords Proprietors—to take advantage.

While Oglethorpe would go on to found Georgia, his wasn't the first English presence in the area. A garrison built Fort King George in modern-day Darien, Georgia, in 1721, which you can visit today. A cypress blockhouse surrounded by palisaded earthworks, the fort defended the southern reaches of England's claim for seven years before being abandoned in 1728.

On February 12, 1733, after stops in Beaufort and Charleston, the ship *Anne* with its 114 passengers made its way to the highest bluff on the Savannah River. The area was controlled by the peaceful Yamacraw people, who had been encouraged by the powers-that-be in Charleston to settle on this vacant land 12 miles up the Savannah River to serve as a buffer for the Spanish. Led by an elderly chief, or *mico,* named Tomochichi, the Yamacraw enjoyed the area's natural bounty of shellfish, fruit, nuts, and small game.

A deft politician, Oglethorpe struck up a treaty and eventually a genuine friendship with Tomochichi. To the Yamacraw, Oglethorpe was a rare bird—a white man who behaved with honor and was true to his word. The Native Americans reciprocated by helping the settlers and pledging fealty to the crown. Oglethorpe reported to the Trustees that Tomochichi personally requested "that we would Love and Protect their little Families."

In negotiations with local tribes using Mary Musgrove, a Creek-English settler in the area, as translator, the persuasive Oglethorpe convinced the coastal Creek to cede to the crown all Georgia land to the Altamaha River. Oglethorpe's impact was soon felt farther down the Georgia coast, as St. Simons Island, Jekyll Island, Darien, and Brunswick were settled in rapid succession, and with them the entrenchment of the plantation system and slave labor.

While the Trustees' utopian vision was largely economic in nature, like Carolina the Georgia colony also emphasized religious freedom. While to modern ears Charleston's antipathy toward "papists" and Oglethorpe's original ban of Catholics from Georgia might seem incompatible with

Clockwise from top left: horse on the grounds of Hilton Head's Coastal Discovery Museum; Savannah Cotton Exchange; Fort Pulaski.

this goal, the reason was a coldly pragmatic one for the time: England's two main global rivals, France and Spain, were both staunchly Catholic countries.

SPAIN VANQUISHED

Things heated up on the coast in 1739 with the so-called **War of Jenkins' Ear,** which despite its seemingly trivial beginnings over the humiliation of a British captain by Spanish privateers was actually a proxy struggle emblematic of changes in the European balance of power. A year later Oglethorpe cobbled together a force of settlers, Indian allies, and Carolinians to reduce the Spanish fortress at St. Augustine, Florida. The siege failed, and Oglethorpe retreated to St. Simons Island to await the inevitable counterattack. In 1742, a Spanish force invaded the island but was eventually turned back for good at the **Battle of Bloody Marsh.** That clash marked the end of Spanish overtures on England's colonies in what is now the United States.

Though Oglethorpe returned to England a national hero, things fell apart in Savannah. The settlers became envious of the success of Charleston's slave-based rice economy and began wondering aloud why they couldn't also make use of free labor. With Oglethorpe otherwise occupied in England, the Trustees of Georgia—distant in more ways than just geographically from the new colony—bowed to public pressure and relaxed the restrictions on slavery and rum. By 1753 the Trustees voted to return their charter to the crown, officially making Georgia the 13th and final colony of England in America. With first the French and then the Spanish effectively shut off from the American East Coast, the stage was set for an internal battle between England and its burgeoning colonies across the Atlantic.

REVOLUTION AND INDEPENDENCE

The population of the colonies swelled in the mid-1700s, not only from an influx of slaves but a corresponding flood of European immigrants. The interior began filling up with Germans, Swiss, Scottish, and Irish settlers. Their subsequent demands for political representation led to tension between them and the coastal inhabitants, typically depicted through the years as an Upcountry versus Lowcountry competition. It is a persistent but inaccurate myth that the affluent elite on the southeastern coast were reluctant to break ties with England. While the Lowcountry's cultural and economic ties to England were certainly strong, the **Stamp Act** and the **Townshend Acts** combined to turn public sentiment against the mother country here as elsewhere in the colonies.

South Carolinian planters like Christopher Gadsden, Henry Laurens, John Rutledge, and Arthur Middleton were early leaders in the movement for independence. Planters in what would be called Liberty County, Georgia, also strongly agitated for the cause. War broke out between the colonists and the British in New England and soon made its way southward. The British failed to take Charleston—the fourth-largest city in the colonies—in June 1776, an episode that gave South Carolina its "Palmetto State" moniker when redcoat cannonballs bounced off the palm tree-lined walls of Fort Moultrie. The British under General Sir Henry Clinton successfully took the city in 1780, however, occupying it until 1782.

The British, under General Archibald Campbell, took Savannah in 1778. Royal Governor Sir James Wright returned from exile to Georgia to reclaim it for the crown, the only one of the colonies to be subsumed again into the British Empire. A polyglot force of colonists, Haitians, and Hessians attacked the British fortifications on the west side of Savannah in 1779 but were repulsed with heavy losses. Although the area's two major cities had fallen to the British, the war raged on throughout the surrounding area.

Indeed, throughout the Lowcountry, fighting was as vicious as anything yet seen on the North American continent. With over 130 known military engagements occurring there, South Carolina sacrificed more men during the war than any other colony—including Massachusetts, the "Cradle of the Revolution."

The struggle became a guerrilla war of colonists versus the British as well as a civil war between patriots and loyalists, or Tories. Committing what would today undoubtedly be called war crimes, the British routinely burned homes, churches, and fields and massacred civilians. Using Daufuskie Island as a base, British soldiers staged raids on Hilton Head plantations.

In response, patriots of the Lowcountry bred a group of deadly guerrilla soldiers under legendary leaders such as Francis Marion, "the Swamp Fox," and Thomas Sumter, "the Gamecock," who attacked the British in daring hit-and-run raids staged from swamps and marshes. A covert group of patriots called the Sons of Liberty met clandestinely throughout the Lowcountry, plotting revolution over pints of ale. Sometimes their efforts transcended talk, however, and atrocities were committed against area loyalists.

In all, four South Carolinians signed the Declaration of Independence (Thomas Heyward Jr., Thomas Lynch Jr., Arthur Middleton, and Edward Rutledge), as did three Georgians (Button Gwinnett, Lyman Hall, and George Walton).

HIGH COTTON

True to form, the new nation wasted no time in asserting its economic strength. Rice planters from Georgetown north of Charleston on down to the Altamaha River in Georgia built on their already impressive wealth, becoming the new nation's richest men by far—with fortunes built on the backs of the slaves working in their fields.

In 1786, a new crop was introduced that would only enhance the financial clout of the coastal region: cotton. A former loyalist colonel, Roger Kelsal, sent some seed from the West Indies to his friend James Spaulding, owner of a plantation on St. Simons Island, Georgia. This crop, soon to be known as Sea Island cotton and considered the best in the world, would supplant rice as the crop of choice for coastal plantations. At the height of

Nathanael Greene and Mulberry Grove

Nathanael Greene's time in Savannah was short and mostly unfortunate. One of the American Revolution's greatest heroes, Greene rose from the rank of private in the Continental Army to become George Washington's right-hand man. As a brigadier general in the Rhode Island militia, Greene's innate military prowess caught Washington's eye during the siege of Boston, whereupon the future president gave Greene command of the entire Southern theater of the fight for independence. Greene's guerrilla tactics forced the English contingent to divide and hence weaken itself. It was Greene who sent General "Mad Anthony" Wayne in 1782 to free Savannah from the British. Greene insisted that no revenge be taken on Savannah's loyalists, instead welcoming them into the new nation as partners. For his service, Washington granted Greene a large estate on the banks of the Savannah River known as Mulberry Grove, known to history as the place where Eli Whitney would later invent the cotton gin while serving as tutor to the Greene children.

Mulberry Grove was less productive for Greene, who as a lifelong abolitionist refused to use slave labor on the plantation, and hence paid a steep financial price. The 44-year-old Greene had spent less than a year at Mulberry Grove, mostly worrying about finances, when he caught sunstroke on a particularly brutal June day in 1786 and died shortly thereafter.

At some point Greene's remains were said to have been lost after a family vault in Colonial Cemetery was vandalized by Union troops. Then in 1900 the Society of the Cincinnati of Rhode Island appointed a search committee to find and properly inter the general's long-lost remains. The remains were indeed found—right in the vault in Colonial Cemetery where they were supposed to have been, which you can see to this day. However, they were underneath someone else: After removing the coffin of one Robert Scott, excavators found "a mass of rotten wood and human bones mixed with sand," along with a rusty coffin plate reading, "Nathanael Greene / Obit June 19, 1786 / Aetat [Age] 44 Years." In 1902, Greene's remains were put to rest under his monument in Johnson Square—dedicated to him by the Marquis de Lafayette in 1825.

All buildings at Mulberry Grove were razed by Sherman's troops in 1864. The area entered industrial use in 1975 and is currently occupied by the Georgia Ports Authority. No full-scale archaeological dig has ever been done at the site, although the nonprofit Mulberry Grove Foundation (www.mulberrygrove.org) is working toward that as well as a plan to make part of the 2,200-acre parcel a wildlife preserve.

the Southern cotton boom in the early 1800s, a single Sea Island cotton harvest on a single plantation might go for $100,000—in 1820 dollars. While Charleston was still by far the largest, most powerful, and most influential city on the southeastern coast of the United States, at the peak of the cotton craze Savannah was actually doing more business—a fact that grated to no end on the Holy City's elite. Unlike Charleston, where the planters themselves dominated city life, in Savannah it was cotton brokers called **factors** who were the city's leading class. During this time most of the grand homes of downtown Savannah's historic district were built. This boom period, fueled largely by cotton exports, was perhaps most iconically represented by the historic sailing of the SS *Savannah* from Savannah to Liverpool in 29 days, the first transatlantic voyage by a steamship.

During the prosperous antebellum period, the economy of Charleston, Savannah, and surrounding areas was completely dependent on slave labor, but the cities themselves boasted large numbers of African Americans who were active in business and agriculture. For example, the vending stalls at the City Markets of both Savannah and Charleston were predominantly staffed by African American workers, some of them free.

SECESSION

Much of the lead-in to the Civil War focused on whether slavery would be allowed in the newest U.S. territories in the West, but there's no doubt that all figurative roads eventually led to South Carolina. During Andrew Jackson's presidency in the 1820s, his vice president, South Carolina's John C. Calhoun, became a thorn in Jackson's side with his aggressive advocacy for **nullification**. In a nutshell, Calhoun said that if a state decided the federal government wasn't treating it fairly—in this case with regard to tariffs that were hurting the cotton trade in the Palmetto State—it could simply nullify the federal law, superseding it with law of its own.

As the abolition movement gained steam and tensions over slavery rose, South Carolina congressman Preston Brooks took things to the next level. On May 22, 1856, he beat fellow senator Charles Sumner of Massachusetts nearly to death with his walking cane on the Senate floor. Sumner had just given a speech criticizing pro-slavery forces—including a relative of Brooks—and called slavery "a harlot." (In a show of support, South Carolinians sent Brooks dozens of new canes to replace the one he broke over Sumner's head.)

In 1860, the national convention of the Democratic Party, then the dominant force in U.S. politics, was held in—where else?—Charleston. Rancor over slavery and states' rights was so high that they couldn't agree on a single candidate to run to replace President James Buchanan. Reconvening in Maryland, the party split along sectional lines, with the Northern wing backing Stephen A. Douglas. The Southern wing, fervently desiring secession, deliberately chose its own candidate, John Breckinridge, in order to split the Democratic vote and throw the election to Republican Abraham Lincoln, an outspoken opponent of the expansion of slavery. During that so-called **Secession Winter** before Lincoln took office, seven states seceded from the union, first among them the Palmetto State, followed by Mississippi, Florida, Alabama, Georgia, Louisiana, and Texas.

CIVIL WAR

Five days after South Carolina's secession on December 21, 1860, U.S. Army major Robert Anderson moved his garrison from Fort Moultrie on Sullivan's Island to nearby Fort Sumter in Charleston Harbor. Over the

Robert E. Lee and Savannah

Before reluctantly surrendering his commission to serve the Confederacy, Robert E. Lee was a bright up-and-comer with the U.S. Army Corps of Engineers. As a 22-year-old lieutenant, the talented Virginian spent a year and a half in and around Savannah overseeing the construction of Fort Pulaski, named for the brave Polish count who lost his life in 1779's Siege of Savannah. On Lee's arrival in Savannah, construction was on hiatus due to the stifling summer heat. The handsome and dashing young man made the most of his time off, making significant inroads into downtown Savannah's high society. He was heartily welcomed into the home of his old West Point roommate John Mackay, whose three daughters adored him. The same was true of the two Minis daughters who lived nearby and also frequently had the young lieutenant over (and all this while Lee was conducting a long-distance courtship with his future wife back home in Virginia).

Construction of the fort on Cockspur Island began in 1829 under Major Samuel Babcock, whose health problems soon forced Lee to take over. Most of Lee's work focused on draining and diking the marshy island and its blue clay soil, and much of his handiwork remains functional today. After Lee was reassigned in 1831, Lieutenant Joseph Mansfield completed construction of the fort in 1847. A mix of slave labor and paid artisans lived in a sprawling construction camp. Today only Fort Pulaski's brick structures remain.

Five years after the war, Robert E. Lee paid a final visit to Savannah at age 63, accompanied by his daughter Agnes, to see his old comrade-in-arms General Joseph E. Johnston, who lived at 105 East Oglethorpe Avenue. During his stay in town, Lee slept at the Andrew Low House (Andrew's wife, Mary, was Jack Mackay's niece). Lee died six months later.

Fort Pulaski National Monument is currently administered by the National Park Service, which maintains an excellent website (www.nps.gov) detailing the rich history and fascinating archaeology of this, one of Savannah's great must-see sights.

next few months and into the spring, Anderson would ignore many calls to surrender, and Confederate forces would prevent any Union resupply or reinforcement. The stalemate was broken and the Confederates finally got their *casus belli* when a Union supply ship successfully ran the blockade and docked at Fort Sumter. Shortly before dawn on April 12, 1861, Confederate batteries around Charleston—ironically none of which were at the famous Battery itself—opened fire on Fort Sumter for 34 straight hours, until Anderson surrendered on April 13.

In a classic example of why you should always be careful what you wish for, the secessionists had been too clever by half in pushing for Lincoln. Far from prodding the North to sue for peace, the fall of Fort Sumter instead caused the remaining states in the Union to rally around the previously unpopular tall man from Illinois. Lincoln's skillful management of the Fort Sumter standoff meant that from then on, the South would bear history's blame for initiating the conflict that would claim over half a million American lives.

After Fort Sumter, four more Southern states—Virginia, Arkansas, North Carolina, and Tennessee—seceded to join the Confederacy. The Old Dominion was the real prize for the secessionists, as Virginia had the South's only ironworks and by far the largest manufacturing base.

In November 1861, a massive Union invasion armada landed in Port Royal Sound in South Carolina, effectively taking the entire Lowcountry out of the war. Hilton Head was a Union encampment, and Beaufort became a major hospital center for the U.S. Army. The coast of Georgia was also blockaded, with Union forces using new rifled cannons in 1862 to quickly reduce Fort Pulaski at the mouth of the Savannah River. Charleston, however, did host two battles in the conflict. The **Battle of Secessionville** came in June 1862, when a Union force attempting to take Charleston was repulsed on James Island with heavy casualties.

The next battle, an unsuccessful Union landing on Morris Island in July 1863, was immortalized by the movie *Glory*. The 54th Massachusetts Regiment, an African American unit with white commanders, performed so gallantly in its failed assault on the Confederate **Battery Wagner** that it inspired the North and was cited by abolitionists as further proof that African Americans should be given freedom and full citizenship rights. Another invasion attempt on Charleston would not come, but the city was besieged and bombarded for nearly two more years (devastation made even worse by a massive fire, unrelated to the shelling, that destroyed much of the city in 1861).

Otherwise, the coast grew quiet. From Charleston to Brunswick, white Southerners evacuated the coastal cities and plantations for the hinterland, leaving behind only slaves to fend for themselves. In many coastal areas, African Americans and Union garrison troops settled into an awkward but peaceful coexistence. Many islands under Union control, such as Cockspur Island, where Fort Pulaski sat, became endpoints in the Underground Railroad.

General William Sherman concluded his **March to the Sea** in Savannah in 1864, famously giving the city to Lincoln as a Christmas present. While staunch Confederates, city fathers were wise enough to know what would happen to their accumulated wealth and fine homes should they be foolhardy enough to resist Sherman's army of war-hardened veterans.

The only military uncertainty left was in how badly Charleston, the "cradle of secession," would suffer for its sins. Historians and local wags have long debated why Sherman spared Charleston, the hated epicenter of the Civil War. Did he fall in love with the city during his brief posting there as a young lieutenant? Did he literally fall in love there, with one of the city's legendarily beautiful and delicate local belles? We may never know for sure, but it's likely that the Lowcountry's marshy, mucky terrain simply made it too difficult to move large numbers of men and supplies. So Sherman turned his army inland toward the state capital, Columbia, which would not be so lucky.

For the African American population of Savannah and Charleston, however, it was not a time of sadness but the great Day of Jubilee. Soon after the Confederate surrender, black Charlestonians held one of the largest parades the city has ever seen, with one of the floats being a coffin bearing the sign, "Slavery is dead."

As for the place where it all began, a plucky Confederate garrison remained underground at Fort Sumter throughout the war, as the walls above them were literally pounded into dust by the long Union siege. The garrison quietly left the fort under cover of night on February 17, 1865. Major Robert Anderson, who surrendered the fort at war's beginning, returned to Sumter in April 1865 to raise the same flag he'd lowered exactly four years earlier. Three thousand African Americans attended the ceremonies. Later that same night, Abraham Lincoln was assassinated in Washington DC.

RECONSTRUCTION

A case could be made that slavery need not have led the United States into Civil War. The U.S. government had banned the importation of slaves long before, in 1808. The great powers of Europe would soon ban slavery altogether (Spain in 1811, France in 1826, and Britain in 1833). Visiting foreign dignitaries in the mid-1800s were often shocked to find the practice in full swing in the American South. Even Brazil, the world center of slavery, where four out of every 10 slaves taken from Africa were brought (less than 5 percent came to the United States), would ban slavery in 1888, suggesting that slavery in the United States would have died a natural death. Still, the die was cast, the war was fought, and everyone had to deal with the aftermath.

For a brief time, Sherman's benevolent dictatorship on the coast held promise for an orderly postwar future. In 1865 he issued his sweeping "40 acres and a mule" order seeking dramatic economic restitution for coastal Georgia's free blacks. Politics reared its ugly head in the wake of Lincoln's assassination, however, and the order was rescinded, ushering in the chaotic Reconstruction era, echoes of which linger to this day.

Even as the trade in cotton and naval stores resumed to even greater heights than before, urban life and racial tension became more and more problematic. Urban populations swelled as freed blacks from all over the depressed countryside rushed into the cities. As one of them, his name lost to history, famously said: "Freedom was freer in Charleston."

RECONCILIATION

The opening of the exclusive Jekyll Island Club in 1886 marked the coming of the effects of the Industrial Revolution to the Deep South and the rejuvenation of regional economies. In Savannah, the Telfair Academy of Arts and Sciences, the South's first art museum, opened that same year. The cotton trade built back up to antebellum levels, and the South was on the long road to recovery.

The Spanish-American War of 1898 was a major turning point for the South, the first time since the Civil War that Americans were joined in patriotic unity. The southeastern coast felt this in particular, as it was a staging area for the invasion of Cuba. President William McKinley addressed the troops bivouacked in Savannah's Daffin Park, and Charlestonians cheered the exploits of their namesake heavy cruiser the USS *Charleston*, which played a key role in forcing the Spanish surrender of Guam.

Charleston would elect its first Irish American mayor, John Grace, in 1911, who would serve until 1923 (with a break 1915-1919). Although it wouldn't open until 1929, the first Cooper River Bridge joining Charleston with Mount Pleasant was the child of the Grace administration, credited today for modernizing the Holy City's infrastructure.

The arrival of the tiny but devastating boll weevil all but wiped out the cotton trade on the coast after the turn of the century, forcing the economy to diversify. Naval stores and lumbering were the order of the day at the advent of World War I, the combined patriotic effort for which did wonders in repairing the wounds of the Civil War, still vivid in many local memories. A major legacy of World War I that still greatly influences life in the Lowcountry is the Marine Corps Recruit Depot Parris Island, which began life as a small Marine camp in 1919.

RENAISSANCE AND DEPRESSION

In the Roaring '20s, that boom period following World War I, both Savannah and Charleston entered the world stage and made some of their most significant cultural contributions to American life. It was also the era of Prohibition. Savannah became notorious as a major import center for illegal rum from the Bahamas.

As elsewhere in the country, Prohibition ironically brought out a new appreciation for the arts and just plain having fun. The "Charleston" dance, originated on the streets of the Holy City and popularized in New York, would sweep the world. The Jenkins Orphanage Band, credited with the dance, traveled the world, even playing at President William Howard Taft's inauguration.

In the visual arts, the "Charleston Renaissance" took off, specifically intended to introduce the Holy City to a wider audience. Key work included the Asian-influenced art of self-taught painter Alice Ravenel Huger Smith and the etchings of Elizabeth O'Neill Verner. Edward Hopper was a visitor to Charleston during that time and produced several noted watercolors. The Gibbes Art Gallery, now the Gibbes Museum of Art, opened in 1905. Recognizing the cultural importance of the city and its history, in 1920 socialite Susan Pringle Frost and other concerned Charlestonians formed the Preservation Society of Charleston, the oldest community-based historic preservation organization in the country.

In 1924, lauded Charleston author DuBose Heyward wrote the locally set novel *Porgy*. With Heyward's cooperation, the book would soon be turned into the first American opera, *Porgy and Bess*, by George Gershwin, who labored over the composition in a cottage on Folly Beach. Ironically, *Porgy and Bess*, which premiered with an African American cast in New York in 1935, wouldn't be performed in its actual setting until 1970 because of segregation laws.

In Savannah, the Roaring '20s coincided with the rise of Johnny Mercer, who began his theater career locally in the Town Theater Group. In 1925, Flannery O'Connor was born in Savannah, and the quirky, Gothic nature of the city would mark her later writing indelibly.

The Depression hit the South hard, but since wages and industry were already behind the national average, the economic damage wasn't as bad as elsewhere in the country. As elsewhere in the South, the public works programs of President Franklin D. Roosevelt's New Deal not only helped to keep locals employed but contributed greatly to the cultural and archaeological record of the region. The Civilian Conservation Corps built much of the modern state park system in the area.

WORLD WAR II AND THE POSTWAR BOOM

With the attack on Pearl Harbor and the coming of World War II, life on the southeastern coast would never be the same. Military funding and facilities swarmed into the area, and populations and long-depressed living standards rose as a result. In many outlying Sea Islands of Georgia and South Carolina, electricity came for the first time.

The "Mighty Eighth" Air Force was founded and based in Savannah, and Camp Stewart, later Fort Stewart, was built in nearby Hinesville. In shipyards in Savannah and Brunswick, hundreds of Liberty ships were built to transport cargo to the citizens and allied armies of Europe.

The postwar U.S. infatuation with the automobile—and its troublesome child, the suburb—brought exponential growth to the great cities of the coast. The first bridge to Hilton Head Island was built in 1956, leading to the first of many resort developments, Sea Pines, in 1961. With rising coastal populations came pressure to demolish more and more fine old buildings to put parking lots and high-rises in their place. A backlash grew among the elite, aghast at the destruction of so much history.

The immediate postwar era brought about the formation of both the Historic Charleston Foundation and the Historic Savannah Foundation, which began the financially and politically difficult work of protecting historic districts from the wrecking ball. They weren't always successful, but the work of these organizations—mostly older women from the upper crust—laid the foundation for the successful coastal tourist industry to come and preserved important American history for the ages.

CIVIL RIGHTS

The ugly racial violence that plagued much of the country during the civil rights era rarely visited the Georgia coast. Whether due to the laid-back ambience or the fact that African Americans were simply too numerous there to be denied, cities like Savannah experienced little real unrest during that time.

Contrary to popular opinion, the civil rights era wasn't just a blip in the 1960s. The gains of that decade were the fruits of efforts begun decades earlier. Many of the exertions involved efforts to expand black suffrage. Though African Americans had secured the nominal right to vote years before, primary contests were not under the jurisdiction of federal law. As a result, Democratic Party primary elections—the de facto general elections because of that party's total dominance in the South at the time—were effectively closed to African American voters.

Savannah was at the forefront of expanding black suffrage, and Ralph Mark Gilbert, pastor of the historic First African Baptist Church, launched one of the first black voter registration drives in the South. In Charleston, the Democratic primary was opened to African Americans for the first time in 1947. In 1955, a successful black realtor, J. Arthur Brown, became head of the Charleston chapter of the NAACP and membership soared, bringing an increase in activism. In 1960, the Charleston Municipal Golf Course voluntarily integrated to avoid a court battle.

Martin Luther King Jr. visited South Carolina in the late 1960s, speaking in Charleston in 1967 and helping reestablish the Penn Center on St. Helena Island as not only a cultural center but a center of political activism as well. The hundred-day strike of hospital workers at the Medical University of South Carolina in 1969—right after King's assassination—got national attention and was the culmination of Charleston's struggle for civil rights. By the end of the 1960s, the city councils of Savannah and Charleston had elected their first black aldermen, and the next phase in local history began.

A COAST REBORN

The decade of the 1970s brought the seeds of the future success of the coastal region. Influential and long-serving mayor John P. Rousakis was elected. The Greek American would break precedents and forge key alliances, reviving the local economy.

In the years 1970-1976, Rousakis renovated the then-seedy riverfront district, making it the centerpiece of the city's burgeoning tourist trade. The Savannah College of Art and Design (SCAD) opened in 1979 and began the process of renovating dozens of the city's historic buildings, a process that continues today.

The coast's combination of beautiful scenery and cheap labor proved irresistible to the movie and TV industry, which would begin filming many series and films in the area in the 1970s and continuing to this day.

The economic boom of the 1990s was particularly good to Savannah, whose port saw a huge dividend from increasing globalization. Also in the 1990s came the *Midnight in the Garden of Good and Evil* phenomenon, which would put Savannah—already on the upswing—on the tourist map for good. Although not a Savannah native, the iconic Paula Deen brought a new national focus on the city through her long presence on the Food Network and through her local restaurant, The Lady and Sons, which continues to pack in visitors.

Today Savannah's tourism business is healthier than ever. Attracted by the coastal region, artists, writers, and entrepreneurs continue to flock, increasing the economic and social diversity of the area and taking it to new heights of livability.

People and Culture

Contrary to how the region is portrayed in the media, the coast from Charleston down to the Georgia-Florida border is hardly exclusive to natives with thick, flowery accents who still obsess over the Civil War and eat grits three meals a day. As you will quickly discover, the entire coastal area is heavily populated with transplants from other parts of the country, and in some areas you can actually go quite a long time without hearing even one of those Scarlett O'Hara accents. Some of this is due to the region's increasing attractiveness to professionals and artists, drawn by the temperate climate, natural beauty, and business-friendly environment. Part of it is due to its increasing attractiveness to retirees, most of them from the frigid Northeast. Indeed, in some places, chief among them Hilton Head, the most common accent is a New York or New Jersey one, and a Southern accent is rare.

In any case, don't make the common mistake of assuming you're coming to a place where footwear is optional and electricity is a recent development (though it's true that many of the islands didn't get electricity until the 1950s and 1960s). Because so much new construction has gone on in the South in the last quarter-century or so, you might find some aspects of the infrastructure—specifically the roads and the electrical utilities—actually superior to where you came from.

POPULATION

The Savannah Metropolitan Statistical Area (MSA), which includes Chatham, Bryan, and Effingham Counties, numbered about 347,000 people in the 2010 census. The city of Savannah itself has a population of about 136,000. The Hilton Head-Beaufort MSA includes Beaufort and Jasper Counties and comprised about 180,000 people in the 2010 census. The town of Hilton Head had about 37,000 residents in 2010, and Beaufort had about 13,000. The Brunswick MSA includes Brantley, Glynn, and McIntosh Counties and has about 100,000 people.

Racial Makeup

Its legacy as the center of the U.S. slave trade and plantation culture means that the Savannah region has a large African American population. The Savannah MSA is about 35 percent black. In the city proper, the black population percentage is higher, nearly 60 percent.

Voodoo and Hoodoo

The spiritual system called voodoo—the word is a corruption of various West African spellings—came to the Western Hemisphere with the importation of slaves. Voodoo is a clearly defined religion and is the dominant religion of millions of West Africans.

Like many ancient belief systems, voodoo is based on the veneration of ancestors and the possibility of continued communication with them. Up until fairly recently the African American Gullah and Geechee populations of the South Carolina and Georgia Sea Islands still had a common belief that the older slaves who were born in Africa could actually fly in spirit form to the continent of their birth and back again.

While voodoo has always been unfairly sensationalized—a notable recent example being the "voodoo priestess" Minerva in *Midnight in the Garden of Good and Evil*—it's not necessarily as malevolent in actual practice as in the overactive imaginations of writers and directors. The stereotypical practice of sticking pins in dolls to bring pain to a living person actually has its roots in European and Native American folklore.

Much of what the layperson thinks is voodoo is actually hoodoo, a body of folklore—not a religion—indigenous to the American South. Hoodoo combines elements of voodoo (communicating with the dead) and fundamentalist Christianity (extensive scriptural references). In the United States, most African American voodoo tradition was long ago subsumed within Protestant Christianity, but the Gullah populations of the Sea Islands of South Carolina and Georgia still keep alive the old ways. In the Gullah and Geechee areas of the Georgia and Carolina Sea Islands, the word *conjure* is generally the preferred terminology for this hybrid belief system, which has good sides and bad sides and borrows liberally from African lore and Christian folkways.

The old Southern practice of painting shutters and doors blue to ward off evil comes from hoodoo, where the belief in ghosts, or "haints," is largely a byproduct of poorly understood Christianity (Mediterranean countries also use blue to keep evil at bay, and the word *haint* is of Scots-Irish origin). You can still see this particular shade of "haint blue" on rural and vernacular structures throughout the Lowcountry.

Another element of hoodoo that you can still encounter today is the role of the "root doctor," an expert at folk remedies who blends together various indigenous herbs and plants in order to produce a desired effect or result. In *Midnight in the Garden of Good and Evil,* this role belongs to the fabled Dr. Buzzard, who teaches Minerva everything she knows about "conjure work." However, a root doctor is not to be confused with a "gifted reader," a fortune-teller born with the talent to tell the future. From the no-doubt embellished account in John Berendt's *Midnight,* scholars would put the late Minerva squarely into the category of root doctor or "conjurer" rather than the undeniably more compelling "voodoo priestess."

The Hispanic population, as elsewhere in the United States, is growing rapidly, but statistics can be misleading. Though Hispanics are growing at a triple-digit clip in the region, they still remain less than 3 percent of Georgia's population. Bilingual signage is becoming more common but is still quite rare.

RELIGION

This area is unusual in the Deep South for its wide variety of religious faiths. While Georgia remains overwhelmingly Protestant—at least three-quarters of all Christians in Georgia are members of some Protestant denomination, chief among them Southern Baptist and Methodist—Savannah's cosmopolitan, polyglot history has made it a real melting pot of faith.

Savannah was originally dominated by the Episcopal Church (known as the Anglican Church in other countries), but from early on it was also a haven for those of other faiths. Various types of Protestant offshoots soon arrived, including the Scottish Presbyterians and German Salzburger Lutherans. The seeds of Methodism and the "Great Awakening" were planted along the coast from Savannah up to Charleston.

Owing to vestigial prejudice from the European realpolitik of the founding era, the Roman Catholic presence on the coast was late in arriving, but once it came it was there to stay. Savannah has quite a large Roman Catholic population by Southern standards, mostly due to the influx of Irish in the mid-1800s.

But most unusually of all for the Deep South, Savannah and Charleston not only have large Jewish populations but ones that have been key participants in the cities from the very first days of settlement. Sephardic Jews of primarily Portuguese descent were among the first settlers of both Savannah and Charleston, and they kept up an energetic trade between the two cities for centuries afterward, continuing to the present day.

MANNERS

The prevalence and importance of good manners is the main thing to keep in mind about the South. While it's tempting for folks from more outwardly assertive parts of the world to take this as a sign of weakness, that would be a major mistake. Southerners use manners, courtesy, and chivalry as a system of social interaction with one goal above all: to maintain the established order during times of stress. A relic from a time of extreme class stratification, etiquette and chivalry are ways to make sure that the elites are never threatened—and, on the other hand, that even those on the lowest rungs of society are afforded at least a basic amount of dignity. But as a practical matter, it's also true that Southerners of all classes, races, and backgrounds rely on the observation of manners as a way to sum up people quickly. To any Southerner, regardless of class or race, your use or neglect of basic manners and proper respect indicates how seriously they should take you—not in a socioeconomic sense, but in the big picture overall.

The typical Southern sense of humor—equal parts irony,

Sephardic Jews in the South

Two of the oldest cities in the Anglo-Saxon Protestant South have rich and early histories of an active Jewish presence—specifically, Sephardic Jews (those with a Spanish or Portuguese background). Jews and Muslims on the Iberian Peninsula got along quite well while the Islamic Moors of North Africa dominated the area. But after Ferdinand and Isabella's completion of the Reconquista in 1492, the Jews of Spain went from being respected citizens to persecuted pariahs nearly overnight. Five years later, Portugal followed suit, expelling all Jews on pain of death unless they became "New Christians," or *conversos*. A sizable proportion of *conversos*, however, were actually so-called crypto-Jews, who publicly practiced Roman Catholicism while secretly remaining devout Jews. Many synagogues of Sephardic origin today have their floors covered in sand to remember that dark time when Jewish congregations practiced their faith in basements covered with sand to muffle the sounds of their feet.

The diaspora of the Sephardic Jews, ironically, contributed greatly to the health of the global Jewish community, as skilled tradesmen, doctors, and men of letters spread out to Spanish, Portuguese, English, and Dutch colonies where the Inquisition had little sway. It was primarily from the ranks of this Sephardic diaspora that the Jewish settlers of the Lowcountry and Georgia coast came.

Savannah wasn't the first colonial town to host Jewish settlers, but the group of 42 Sephardic Jews that arrived five months after Oglethorpe's landing in 1733 was by far the largest contingent to travel to North America up to that time. All but eight of this core group were Spanish and Portuguese Jews who immigrated to London after spending years as crypto-Jews in their home countries. Accepted without question by Oglethorpe, the Jews of Savannah quickly rose in power and influence. In fact, the first white male child born in Georgia was a Jewish boy, Philip "Uri" Minis.

The assimilation of the Jews into Southern society was so complete that the Secretary of State of the Confederate States of America, Judah Benjamin, was a practicing Jew of Sephardic origin. This assimilation also had a flip side, in that the Sephardic Jews were generally just as enthusiastic about owning slaves as any other white citizens of the area. In 1830 about 83 percent of Jewish households in Charleston had slaves, compared to an almost-identical percentage of 87 percent of white Christian Charlestonians.

In Savannah, the key Judaic attraction is Temple Mickve Israel (20 E. Gordon St., 912/233-1547, www.mickveisrael.org, 30-minute tours Mon.-Fri. 10am-12:30pm and 2pm-3:30pm, $6 suggested donation) the only Gothic synagogue in the country and the third-oldest Jewish congregation in North America.

self-deprecation, and good-natured teasing—is part of the code. Southerners are loath to criticize another individual directly, so often they'll instead take the opportunity to make an ironic joke. Self-deprecating humor is also much more common in the South than in other areas of the country. Because of this, conversely you're also expected to be able to take a joke yourself without being too sensitive.

Another key element in Southern manners is the discussion of money—or rather, the nondiscussion. Unlike some parts of the United States, in the South it's considered the height of rudeness to ask someone what their salary is or how much they paid for their house. Not that the subject is entirely taboo—far from it; you just have to know the code. For example, rather than brag about how much or how little they paid for their home, a Southern head of household will instead take you on a guided tour of the grounds. Along the way they'll make sure to detail: (a) all the work that was done; (b) how grueling and unexpected it all was; and (c) how hard it was to get the contractors to show up.

Depending on the circumstances, in the first segment, (a), you were just told either that the head of the house is made of money and has a lot more of it to spend on renovating than you do, or that they are a brilliant negotiator who got the house for a song. In part (b) you were told that you are not messing around with a lazy deadbeat here, but with someone who knows how to take care of themselves and can handle adversity with aplomb. And with part (c) you were told that the head of the house knows the best contractors in town and can pay enough for them to actually show up, and if you play your cards right, they might pass on their phone numbers to you with a personal recommendation. See? Breaking the code is easy once you get the hang of it.

Etiquette

As we've seen, it's rude here to inquire about personal finances, along with the usual no-go areas of religion and politics. Here are some other specific etiquette tips:

- **Basics:** Be liberal with "please" and "thank you," or conversely, "no thank you" if you want to decline a request or offering.

- **Eye contact:** With the exception of very elderly African Americans, eye contact is not only accepted in the South, it's encouraged. In fact, to avoid eye contact in the South means you're likely a shady character.

- **Handshake:** Men should always shake hands with a *very* firm, confident grip and appropriate eye contact. It's OK for women to offer a handshake in professional circles, but otherwise not required.

- **Chivalry:** When men open doors for women here—and they will—it is not thought of as a patronizing gesture but as a sign of respect. Accept graciously and walk through the door.

- **The elderly:** Senior citizens—or really anyone obviously older than you—should be called "sir" or "ma'am." Again, this is not a patronizing gesture in the South but is considered a sign of respect. Also, in any situation where you're dealing with someone in the service industry, addressing them as "sir" or "ma'am" regardless of their age will get you far.

- **Bodily contact:** Interestingly, though public displays of affection by romantic couples are generally frowned upon here, Southerners are otherwise pretty touchy-feely once they get to know you. Southerners who are well acquainted often say hello or goodbye with a hug.

Walter Edgar's Journal

He's originally from Alabama, but you could call University of South Carolina (USC) professor Walter Edgar the modern voice of the Palmetto State. From the rich diversity of barbecue to the inner workings of the poultry business and the charms of beach music, Edgar covers the gamut of South Carolina culture and experience on his popular weekly radio show *Walter Edgar's Journal*, airing on South Carolina public radio stations throughout the state.

Currently director of the USC Institute of Southern Studies, the Vietnam vet and certified barbecue contest judge explains the show like this: "On the *Journal* we look at current events in a broader perspective, trying to provide context that is often missing in the mainstream media." More specifically, Edgar devotes each one-hour show to a single guest, usually a South Carolinian—by birth or by choice—with a unique perspective on some aspect of state culture, business, arts, or folkways. By the time the inter-

view ends, you have a much deeper understanding not only of the topic of the show but of the interviewee as well. And because of Edgar's unique way of tying strands of his own vast knowledge and experience into every interview, you also leave with a deeper understanding of South Carolina itself.

In these days of media saturation, a public radio show might sound like a rather insignificant perch from which to influence an entire state. But remember that South Carolina is a small, close-knit place, a state of Main Street towns rather than impersonal metro areas. During any given show, many listeners in Edgar's audience will know his guests on a personal basis. And by the end of the show, the rest of the listeners will feel as if they do.

Listen to "Walter Edgar's Journal" each Friday at noon on South Carolina public radio, with a repeat each Sunday at 4pm. Hear podcasts of previous editions at www.scetv.org.

• **Driving:** With the exception of the interstate perimeter highways around the larger cities, drivers in the South are generally less aggressive than in other regions. Cutting sharply in front of someone in traffic is taken as a personal offense. If you need to cut in front of someone, poke the nose of your car a little bit in that direction and wait for a car to slow down and wave you in front. Don't forget to wave back as a thank-you. Similarly, using a car horn can also be taken as a personal affront, so use your horn sparingly, if at all. In rural areas, don't be surprised to see the driver of an oncoming car offer a little wave. This is an old custom, sadly dying out. Just give a little wave back; they're trying to be friendly.

THE GUN CULTURE

One of the most misunderstood aspects of the South is the value the region places on the personal possession of firearms. No doubt, the 2nd Amendment to the U.S. Constitution ("A well regulated Militia, being necessary to the security of a free State, the right of the people to keep and bear Arms, shall not be infringed") is well known here and fiercely protected, at the governmental and at the grassroots levels.

State laws do tend to be significantly more accommodating of gun owners here than in much of the rest of the country. It is legal to carry a concealed handgun in South Carolina and Georgia with the proper permit,
and you need no permit at all to possess a weapon in your house or car for
self-defense. However, there are regulations regarding how a handgun must
be conveyed in automobiles.

Both states now have so-called (and controversial) "stand your ground"
laws, whereby if you're in imminent lethal danger, you do not have to first
try to run away before resorting to deadly force to defend yourself.

In 2014, Georgia passed what is widely considered to be the most per-
missive new gun law in the country, allowing those with the proper license
to carry an open or concealed handgun into a bar (though if you do, you're
not supposed to drink alcohol). You can now even take your handgun into
a church service in Georgia unless the church specifically prohibits it.

FESTIVALS AND EVENTS

Savannah's calendar fairly bursts with festivals, many outdoors. Dates shift
from year to year, so it's best to consult the listed websites for details.

January

Floats and bands take part in the **Martin Luther King Jr. Day Parade**
downtown to commemorate the civil rights leader and Georgia native.
The bulk of the route is on historic MLK Jr. Boulevard, formerly West
Broad Street.

Straddling January and February is the week-long **PULSE Art +
Technology Festival** (www.telfair.org), an adventurous event that brings
video artists and offbeat electronic performance art into the modern Jepson
Center for the Arts.

February

Definitely not to be confused with St. Patrick's Day, the **Savannah Irish
Festival** (912/232-3448, www.savannahirish.org) focuses on Celtic music.

Hosted by the historically black Savannah State University at various
venues around town, the monthlong **Black Heritage Festival** (912/691-
6847) is tied into Black History Month and boasts name entertainers like
the Alvin Ailey Dance Theatre (performing free!). This event also usually
features plenty of historical lectures devoted to the very interesting and
rich history of African Americans in Savannah.

Also in February is the quickly growing **Savannah Book Festival** (www.
savannahbookfestival.org), modeled after a similar event in Washington
DC and featuring many national and regional authors at various venues
downtown.

March

One of the most anticipated events for house-proud Savannahians, the org) offers guests the opportunity to visit six beautiful sites off the usual tourist-trod path. This is a great way to expand your understanding of local architecture and hospitality beyond the usual house museums.

More than just a day, the citywide **St. Patrick's Day** (www.savannah-saintpatricksday.com) celebration generally lasts at least half a week and temporarily triples the population. The nearly three-hour parade—second-biggest in the United States—always begins at 10am on St. Patrick's Day (unless that falls on a Sunday, in which case it's generally on the previous Saturday) and includes an interesting mix of marching bands, wacky floats, and sauntering local Irishmen in kelly green jackets. The appeal comes not only from the festive atmosphere and generally beautiful spring weather but from Savannah's unique law allowing partiers to walk the streets with a cup filled with the adult beverage of their choice. While the parade itself is very family-friendly, afterward hardcore partiers generally head en masse to River Street, which is blocked off for the occasion and definitely not where you want to take small children. If you want to hear traditional Celtic music on St. Patrick's Day in Savannah, River Street also isn't the place to go, with the exception of Kevin Barry's on the west end. For authentic Irish music on St. Paddy's Day, wander around the pubs on the periphery of City Market.

The three-week **Savannah Music Festival** (912/234-3378, www.savannahmusicfestival.org) is held at various historic venues around town and begins right after St. Patrick's Day. Past festivals have featured Wynton Marsalis, Dianne Reeves, and the Avett Brothers. The jazz portion is locked down tight, thanks to the efforts of festival director Rob Gibson, a Georgia native who cut his teeth as the founding director of Jazz at Lincoln Center. The classical side is helmed by one of the world's great young violinists, Daniel Hope, acting as associate director. Other genres are featured in abundance as well, including gospel, bluegrass, zydeco, world music, and the always-popular American Traditions vocal competition. The most economical way to enjoy the Savannah Music Festival is to purchase tickets online before December of the previous year at a 10 percent discount. However, if you just want to take in a few events, individual tickets are available at a tiered pricing system. You can buy tickets to individual events in town at the walk-up box office beside the Trustees Theater on Broughton Street.

April

Short for "North of Gaston Street," the **NOGS Tour of Hidden Gardens** (912/961-4805, www.gcofsavnogstour.org, $30) is available two days in April and focuses on a selection of Savannah's amazing private gardens chosen for excellence of design, historical interest, and beauty.

Everyone loves the annual free **Sidewalk Arts Festival** (912/525-5865, www.scad.edu) presented by the Savannah College of Art and Design in

Forsyth Park. Contestants claim a rectangular section of sidewalk on which to display their chalk art talent. There's a noncontest section with chalk provided.

May

The SCAD-sponsored **Sand Arts Festival** (www.scad.edu) on Tybee Island's North Beach centers on a competition of sand castle design, sand sculpture, sand relief, and wind sculpture. You might be amazed at the level of artistry lavished on the sometimes-wondrous creations, only for them to wash away with the tide.

If you don't want to get wet, don't show up at the **Tybee Beach Bum Parade,** an uproarious event held the weekend prior to Memorial Day weekend. With a distinctly boozy overtone, this unique 20-year-old event features homemade floats filled with partiers who squirt the assembled crowds with various water pistols. The crowds, of course, pack their own heat and squirt back.

July

Two key events happen around **Fourth of July,** primarily the large fireworks show on River Street on July 4 but also an impressive fireworks display from the Tybee pier and pavilion on July 3. A nice bonus of the Tybee event is that sometimes you can look out over the Atlantic and see a similar fireworks display on nearby Hilton Head Island, South Carolina, a few minutes away by boat (but nearly an hour by car).

September

The second-largest gay and lesbian event in Georgia (only Atlanta's version is larger), the **Savannah Pride Festival** (www.savannahpride.org, various venues, free) happens every September. Crowds get pretty big for this festive, fun event, which usually features lots of dance acts and political booths.

Though the quality of the acts has been overshadowed lately by the Savannah Music Festival in the spring, the **Savannah Jazz Festival** (www.savannahjazzfestival.org) has two key things going for it: It's free, and it's outside in the glorious green expanse of Forsyth Park. Generally spread out over several nights, the volunteer-run festival draws a good crowd regardless of the lineup, and concessions are available.

October

The Savannah Symphony Orchestra is now defunct, but area musicians unite to play a free evening at **Picnic in the Park** (www.savannahga.gov), a concert in Forsyth Park that draws thousands of noshers. Arrive early to check out the ostentatious, whimsical picnic displays, which compete for prizes. Then set out your blanket, pop open a bottle of wine, and enjoy the sweet sounds.

The combined aroma of beer, sauerkraut, and sausage that you smell coming from the waterfront is the annual **Oktoberfest on the River** (www.riverstreetsavannah.com), which has evolved to be Savannah's second-largest celebration (behind only St. Patrick's Day). Live entertainment of varying quality is featured, though the attraction, of course, is the aforementioned beer and German food. A highlight is the Saturday morning "Weiner Dog Races" involving, you guessed it, competing dachshunds.

If pickin' and grinnin' is your thing, don't miss the low-key but always entertaining **Savannah Folk Music Festival** (www.savannahfolk.org). The main event of the weekend is held on a Sunday night at Historic Grayson Stadium in Daffin Park, but a popular Old-Time Country Dance is usually held the previous Saturday. Members of the Savannah Folk Music Society will help you learn how to do the dance, so don't be shy!

It's a fairly new festival, but the **Tybee Island Pirate Festival** (http://tybeepiratefest.com) is a fun and typically rollicking Tybee event in October featuring, well, everybody dressing up like pirates, saying "Arr" a lot, eating, drinking, and listening to cover bands. It may not sound like much, and it's really not, but it's typically very well attended.

Sponsored by St. Paul's Greek Orthodox Church, the popular **Savannah Greek Festival** (www.stpaulsgreekorthodox.org) features food, music, and Greek souvenirs. The weekend event is held across the street from the church at the parish center—in the gym, to be exact, right on the basketball court. Despite the pedestrian location, the food is authentic and delicious, and the atmosphere convivial and friendly.

Hosted by the Savannah College of Art and Design, the weeklong **Savannah Film Festival** (www.scad.edu) beginning in late October is rapidly growing not only in size but in prestige. Lots of older, more established Hollywood names appear as honored guests for the evening events, while buzz-worthy up-and-coming actors, directors, producers, writers, and animators give excellent workshops during the day. Many of these usually jaded showbiz types really let their hair down for this festival, because, as you'll see, Savannah is the real star. The best way to enjoy this excellent event is to buy a pass, which enables you to walk from event to event. Most importantly, the passes gain you admission to what many locals consider the best part of the festival: the after-parties, where you'll often find yourself face to face with some famous star or director. But whatever you do, don't ask for an autograph. The thing at these parties is to be cool—and if you can't *be* cool, at least act that way.

One of Savannah's most unique events is late October's **"Shalom Y'all" Jewish Food Festival** (912/233-1547, www.mickveisrael.org), held in Forsyth Park and sponsored by the historic Temple Mickve Israel. Latkes, matzo, and other nibbles are all featured along with entertainment.

CINEMA

The first high-profile film made in Savannah was 1962's *Cape Fear,* starring Gregory Peck and Robert Mitchum (who was arrested and briefly jailed years before for public indecency while wandering in a drunken state through Savannah). But 1975's *Gator,* directed by and starring Burt Reynolds, really put the city on the Hollywood map, due in no small part to the then-mega star power of Reynolds himself, whose filmmaking mission was, in his words, to "say some nice things about the South." In short order, parts of the landmark 1970s TV miniseries *Roots* were filmed in and around Savannah, as were parts of the follow-up *Roots: The Next Generation.*

Film aficionados fondly remember the 1980 TV movie *The Ordeal of Dr. Mudd,* starring Dennis Weaver. In addition to the infamous story from *Midnight in the Garden of Good and Evil* where Jim Williams unfurls a swastika banner to ruin a shot on Monterey Square, there are other reasons to remember the film. *Dr. Mudd* expertly uses interiors of Fort Pulaski to tell this largely sympathetic account of the physician accused of aiding Abraham Lincoln's assassin John Wilkes Booth. In an interesting bit of synchronicity, Booth's brother Edwin, the most famous actor in the United States during the 1800s, played in Savannah often.

A key chapter in local filmography came with the filming of 1989's *Glory.* River Street was the set for parade scenes, and as Colonel Shaw, Matthew Broderick delivered his address to the troops a block west of Mrs. Wilkes' Boarding House. The railroad roundhouse off MLK Jr. Boulevard stood in for a Massachusetts training ground.

Another brush with Hollywood came with the filming of 1994's *Forrest Gump* in and around Savannah. Look for Tom Hanks on a bench in Chippewa Square—and note how the traffic runs the wrong direction around the square! The bench itself now resides in the Savannah History Museum on MLK Jr. Boulevard. The steeple in the shot of the floating white feather is that of nearby Independent Presbyterian Church.

Ben Affleck and Sandra Bullock filmed many scenes of 1999's *Forces of Nature* on Tybee Island and in Savannah (yours truly's house is in the final scene for about two seconds). Longtime Hollywood producer and Savannah native Stratton Leopold, who also owns Leopold's Ice Cream on Broughton Street, helped Savannah land 1999's *The General's Daughter* starring John Travolta (look for the grand exterior of the main building at Oatland Island). Trotting out a serviceable Southern accent for a Brit, Kenneth Branagh came to town to play a disgruntled Savannah lawyer in Robert Altman's *Gingerbread Man.*

Though quite a few downtown art students had no idea what the fuss was about, Robert Redford still turned heads when he came to town to direct 2000's *The Legend of Bagger Vance,* with Will Smith as the eponymous caddie. In the film, watch for the facsimile of a Depression-era storefront specially built around City Market. Redford returned to Savannah in late 2009 to film *The Conspirator,* another locally shot film about the Lincoln assassination (Savannah stands in for Washington DC). Cate Blanchett and Katie Holmes starred in 2000's *The Gift,* one of the few movies to take full advantage of the beauty of Bonaventure Cemetery.

Ironically, considering the impact of "The Book" on Savannah, Clint Eastwood's *Midnight in the Garden of Good and Evil* (1997) is arguably the worst movie ever filmed here. Eastwood's famously laissez-faire attitude toward filmmaking—reportedly there were no rehearsals before cameras rolled—did not work well, perhaps because Savannah's already a pretty darn laissez-faire kind of place to begin with.

But the biggest stir of them all came in summer 2009, when Disney star Miley Cyrus of *Hannah Montana* fame came to Tybee Island to film *The Last Song.*

LITERATURE

The Savannah area has hosted some of America's most beloved literary figures, each indelibly influenced in some way by the charms and mystique of the area itself. Here are some literary highlights, with an eye toward soaking in the aspects of the Georgia coast that had such an impact on these authors' work.

In Savannah, visit the Flannery O'Connor Childhood Home and tour her church, the Cathedral of St. John the Baptist. Devotees of *Midnight in the Garden of Good and Evil* will enjoy the Mercer-Williams House Museum, Club One Jefferson, and Bonaventure Cemetery, which is also the final resting place of two of Savannah's most beloved native writers, Oscar-winning lyricist Johnny Mercer and Pulitzer Prize-winning author Conrad Aiken.

Darien, Georgia, is where Melissa Fay Greene set her best-seller *Praying for Sheetrock*. For fans of the classic comic strip *Pogo,* there's Okefenokee Swamp! A couple miles south of Darien, Georgia, is Butler Island Plantation, where English actress Fanny Kemble, married to the owner, was moved to write *Journal of a Residence on a Georgian Plantation,* one of the first antislavery books.

Essentials

Transportation

AIR

Savannah is served by the fairly new and efficient **Savannah/Hilton Head International Airport** (SAV, 400 Airways Ave., 912/964-0514, www.savannahairport.com) directly off I-95 at exit 104. The airport is about 20 minutes from downtown Savannah and 45 minutes from Hilton Head Island. Airlines with routes to SAV include American Airlines (www.aa.com), Delta (www.delta.com), JetBlue (www.jetblue.com), United Express (www.ual.com), and US Airways (www.usairways.com).

Taxi stands provide taxi transportation to Savannah at the following regulated fares and conditions: The cost is $2 for the first one-sixth of a mile and $0.32 per sixth of a mile thereafter, not to exceed $3.60 for the first mile and $1.92 per mile thereafter. Waiting charge is $21 per hour. No charge for baggage. The maximum fare for destinations in the historic district is $25.

Many travelers to the region are using **Jacksonville International Airport** (JAX, 2400 Yankee Clipper Dr., 904/741-4902, www.jia.com), about 20 miles north of Jacksonville, Florida. While it's a two-hour drive from Savannah, this airport's proximity to the attractions south of Savannah makes it attractive for some visitors, who can often find a good deal on airfare that makes it worth their while to make the drive.

CAR

Savannah is the eastern terminus of I-16, and that interstate is the most common entrance to the city. However, most travelers get to I-16 via I-95, taking the exit for downtown Savannah (historic district). Once on I-16, the most common entry points into Savannah proper are via the Gwinnett Street exit, which puts you near the southern edge of the historic district near Forsyth Park, or, more commonly, the Montgomery Street exit farther into the heart of downtown.

Paralleling I-95 is the old coastal highway, now U.S. 17, which goes through Savannah. U.S. 80 is Victory Drive for most of its length through town; after you pass through Thunderbolt on your way to the islands area, however, it reverts to U.S. 80, the only route to and from Tybee Island.

In Savannah, for quick access to the south, take the one-way streets Price (on the east side of downtown) or Whitaker (on the west side of downtown). Conversely, if you want to make a quick trip north into downtown, three one-way streets taking you there are East Broad, Lincoln, and Drayton.

When you're driving downtown and come to a square, the law says traffic within the square *always* has the right of way. In other words, if you haven't yet entered the square, you must yield to any vehicles already in the square.

Previous: ferry to Cumberland Island; Savannah tram.

Rental Cars

You don't have to have a car to enjoy Savannah, but to really explore the surrounding areas you'll need your own vehicle. Renting a car is easy and fairly inexpensive, as long as you play by the rules, which are simple. You need either a valid U.S. driver's license from any state or a valid international driving permit from your home country, and you must be at least 25 years old.

If you do not either purchase insurance coverage from the rental company or already have insurance coverage through the credit card you rent the car with, you will be 100 percent responsible for any damage caused to the car during your rental period. While purchasing insurance at the time of rental is by no means mandatory, it might be worth the extra expense just to have that peace of mind.

Some rental car locations are in Savannah proper, but the vast majority of outlets are at the Savannah/Hilton Head International Airport, including **Avis** (800/831-2847), **Budget** (800/527-0700), **Dollar** (912/964-9001), **Enterprise** (800/736-8222), **Hertz** (800/654-3131), **National** (800/227-7368), and **Thrifty** (800/367-2277). The airport locations have the bonus of generally holding longer hours than their in-town counterparts. Rental locations away from the airport are **Avis** (7810 Abercorn St., 912/354-4718), **Budget** (7070 Abercorn St., 912/355-0805), and **Enterprise** (3028 Skidaway Rd., 912/352-1424; 9505 Abercorn St., 912/925-0060; 11506-A Abercorn Expressway, 912/920-1093; 7510 White Bluff Rd., 912/355-6622).

Parking

Parking is at a premium in downtown Savannah. The city's Parking Services Department is extremely vigilant about parking violations. Traditional coin-operated meter parking is available throughout the city, but more and more the city is going to self-pay kiosks where you purchase a stamped receipt to display inside your car's dashboard. Bottom line: Be sure to pay for all parking weekdays 8:30am-5pm.

No matter what the printed information on the meter tells you, there is *no* enforcement of parking meters at all on weekends or any day after 5pm. That information has been on the meters for years and almost seems intended to bilk visitors.

Tybee Island is even stricter about parking regulations than Savannah. If the meter says to feed it until 8pm on the weekend, feed the meter until 8pm on the weekend.

The city operates several parking garages at various rates and hours: the **Bryan Street Garage** (100 E. Bryan St.), the **Robinson Garage** (132 Montgomery St.), the **State Street Garage** (100 E. State St.), the **Liberty Street Garage** (401 W. Liberty St.), and the new **Whitaker Street Garage** underneath revitalized Ellis Square.

TAXI

Taxi services in Georgia tend to be less regulated than in other states, but service is plentiful in Savannah and is generally reasonable. The chief local provider is **Yellow Cab** (866/319-9646, www.savannahyellowcab.com). For wheelchair accessibility, request cab 14. Other providers include **Adam Cab** (912/927-7466), **Magikal Taxi Service** (912/897-8294), and **Sunshine Cab** (912/272-0971).

If you're not in a big hurry, it's always fun to take a **Savannah Pedicab** (912/232-7900, www.savannahpedicab.com) for quick trips around downtown, or with the competing company **Royal Bike Taxi** (912/341-3944, www.royalbiketaxi.com). In both cases your friendly driver will pedal one or two passengers anywhere within the historic district for a reasonable price depending on the destination (ask your driver).

TRAIN

Passenger rail service in the car-dominated United States is far behind that of other developed nations, both in quantity and quality. Savannah is served by the New York-Miami *Silver Service* route of the national rail system, Amtrak (www.amtrak.com), which is pretty good, if erratic at times—although it certainly pales in comparison with European rail transit. Savannah's train station (2611 Seaboard Coastline Dr., 912/234-2611) is in a light industrial part of town, nowhere near the major tourist center. To get to the station on the west side of town, take I-16 west and then I-516 north. Immediately take the Gwinnett Street-Railroad Station exit and follow the Amtrak signs.

BUS

Chatham Area Transit (www.catchacat.org, Mon.-Sat. 5:30am-11:30pm, Sun. 7am-9pm, $1.25, includes one transfer, free for children under 41 inches tall, exact change only), Savannah's publicly supported bus system, is quite thorough and efficient considering Savannah's relatively small size. Plenty of routes crisscross the entire area.

Of primary interest to visitors is the free **Dot Express Shuttle** (daily 7am-9pm), which travels a continuous circuit route through the historic district with 11 stops at hotels, historic sites, and the Savannah Visitors Center. The shuttle is wheelchair-accessible.

If you're on River Street, a neat experience is to jump on the free **River Street Trolley** (www.catchacat.org, Thurs.-Sun.). This restored historic trolley moves on the old trolley lines on River Street, and while it only goes a short distance, serving six stops, it's certainly fun.

BOAT

One of the coolest things about the Savannah area is the presence of the Intracoastal Waterway, a combined artificial and natural sheltered seaway from Miami to Maine. Many boaters enjoy touring the coast by simply meandering up or down the Intracoastal, putting in at marinas along the way. There's a website for Intracoastal information at wwww.cruiseguides.com and a good resource of area marinas at www.marinamate.com.

TOURIST INFORMATION
Visitors Centers
Savannah

The main place for visitor information in Savannah is the downtown **Savannah Visitors Center** (301 MLK Jr. Blvd., 912/944-0455, Mon.-Fri. 8:30am-5pm, Sat.-Sun. and holidays 9am-5pm). **Visit Savannah** (101 E. Bay St., 877/728-2662, www.savannahvisit.com), the local convention and visitors bureau, maintains a list of lodgings and other visitors centers on its website. The revitalized Ellis Square features a small visitors kiosk (Mon.-Fri. 8am-6pm) at the northwest corner of the square, with public restrooms and elevators to the underground parking garage beneath the square.

Other visitors centers in the area include the **River Street Hospitality Center** (1 River St., 912/651-6662, daily 10am-10pm), the **Tybee Island Visitor Information Center** (S. Campbell Ave. and U.S. 80, 912/786-5444, daily 9am-5:30pm), and the **Savannah Airport Visitor Center** (464 Airways Ave., 912/964-1109, daily 10am-6pm).

Hilton Head Island

In Hilton Head, get information, book a room, or secure a tee time just as you come onto the island at the **Hilton Head Island Chamber of Commerce Welcome Center** (100 William Hilton Pkwy., 843/785-3673, www.hiltonheadisland.org, daily 9am-6pm).

The Golden Isles

The **Brunswick-Golden Isles Visitor Center** (2000 Glynn Ave., 912/264-5337, daily 9am-5pm) is at the intersection of U.S. 17 and the Torras Causeway to St. Simons Island. A downtown information station is in **Old City Hall**, at the corner of Mansfield and Newcastle Streets (912/262-6934, daily 8am-5pm).

The **Jekyll Island Visitor Center** (901 Downing Musgrove Causeway, 912/635-3636, daily 9am-5pm) is before you get to the island, on the long causeway along the marsh. The **St. Simons Visitor Center** (530-B Beachview Dr., 912/638-9014, www.bgivb.com, daily 9am-5pm) is in the St. Simons Casino building near Neptune Park and the Village.

The **Darien Welcome Center** is at the corner of U.S. 17 and Fort King George Drive (912/437-6684, Mon.-Sat. 9am-5pm). The **Sapelo Island Visitors Center** (912/437-3224, www.sapelonerr.org, Tues.-Fri. 7:30am-5:30pm, Sat. 8am-5:30pm, Sun. 1:30pm-5pm) is actually not on Sapelo but at the dock where you take the ferry, in Meridian, Georgia, on Highway 99 from Darien.

The **St. Marys Visitor Center** is at 406 Osborne Street (912/882-4000, www.stmaryswelcome.com, Mon.-Sat. 9am-5pm, Sun. noon-5pm). The **Cumberland Island Visitors Center** is at 113 St. Marys Street (912/882-4336, daily 8am-6pm).

There are several entrances to the Okefenokee Swamp, with the closest thing to a visitors center being the U.S. Fish and Wildlife Service's **Richard S. Bolt Visitor Center** (912/496-7836, daily 9am-5pm) at the eastern entrance near Folkston, Georgia.

Libraries

The **Live Oak Public Library** (www.liveoakpl.org) is the umbrella organization for the libraries of Chatham, Effingham, and Liberty Counties. By far the largest branch is the **Bull Street Branch** (222 Bull St., 912/652-3600, Mon.-Tues. 9am-8pm, Wed.-Fri. 9am-6pm, Sun. 2pm-6pm, closed Sat.), south of downtown Savannah. Farthest downtown and tucked away on Upper Factor's Walk is the charming little **Ola Wyeth Branch** (4 E. Bay St., 912/232-5488, Mon.-Fri. noon-3pm). In midtown Savannah is the historic **Carnegie Branch Library** (537 E. Henry St., 912/231-9921, Mon. 10am-8pm, Tues.-Thurs. 10am-6pm, Fri. 2pm-6pm, Sat. 10am-6am).

The **Georgia Historical Society** (501 Whitaker St., 912/651-2128, www.georgiahistory.com, Tues.-Sat. 10am-5pm) has an extensive collection of clippings, photos, maps, and other archival material at its headquarters at the corner of Forsyth Park in Hodgson Hall. Their website has been extensively revamped and is now one of the Southeast's best online resources for Georgia history information.

The **Jen Library** (201 E. Broughton St., 912/525-4700, www.scad.edu, Mon.-Fri. 7:30am-1am, Sat. 10am-1am, Sun. 11am-1am, shorter hours during school breaks), run by the Savannah College of Art and Design, features 3,000 Internet connections in its cavernous 85,000-square-foot space. Its main claim to fame is the remarkable variety of art periodicals to which it subscribes, nearly 1,000 at last count. It was built for the school's 7,000-plus art students, but the public can enter and use it as well with photo ID (you just can't check anything out).

MONEY

Automated teller machines (ATMs) are available in all urban areas covered in this guide. Be aware that if the ATM is not owned by your bank, not only will that ATM likely charge you a service fee, but your bank may charge you one as well. While ATMs have made traveler's checks less essential, traveler's checks do have the important advantage of accessibility, as some rural and less-developed areas covered in this guide have few or no ATMs. You can purchase traveler's checks at just about any bank.

Establishments in the United States accept only the national currency, the U.S. dollar. To exchange foreign money, go to any bank.

Generally, establishments that accept credit cards will feature stickers on the front entrance with the logo of the particular cards they accept, although this is not a legal requirement. The use of debit cards has dramatically increased in the United States. Most retail establishments and many fast-food chains are now accepting them. Make sure you get a receipt whenever you use a credit card or a debit card.

ACCESS FOR TRAVELERS WITH DISABILITIES

While the vast majority of attractions and accommodations make every effort to comply with federal law regarding those with disabilities, as they're obliged to do, the very historic nature of this region means that some structures simply cannot be retrofitted for maximum accessibility. This is something you'll need to find out on a case-by-case basis, so call ahead. The sites administered by the National Park Service in this guide (Fort Pulaski, Fort Frederica, and Cumberland Island National Seashore) are as wheelchair-accessible as possible.

Some special shuttles are available. In Savannah, Chatham Area Transit (www.catchacat.org) runs a **Teleride** service (912/354-6900). For people with visual impairments, there's the **Savannah Association for the Blind** (214 Drayton St., 912/236-4473).

TRAVELING WITH CHILDREN

The Lowcountry and Georgia coast are very kid-friendly, with the possible exception of some B&Bs that are clearly not designed for younger children. If you have any doubts about this, feel free to inquire. Otherwise, there are no special precautions unique to this area. There are no zoos per se in the region, but animal lovers of all ages will enjoy **Oatland Island Wildlife Center** in Savannah. Better still, take the kids on nature outings to the amazing national wildlife refuges in the area.

WOMEN TRAVELING ALONE

Women should take the same precautions they would take anywhere else. Many women traveling to this region have to adjust to the prevalence of traditional chivalry. In the South, if a man opens a door for you, it's considered a sign of respect, not condescension. Another adjustment is the possible assumption that two or three women who go to a bar or tavern together might be there to invite male companionship. This misunderstanding can happen anywhere, but in some parts of the South it might be slightly more prevalent. Being aware of it is the best defense; otherwise no other steps need to be taken.

SENIOR TRAVELERS

Both because of the large proportion of retirees in the region and because of Southerners' traditional respect for the elderly, the area is quite friendly to senior citizens. Many accommodations and attractions offer a slight senior discount, which can add up over the course of a trip. Always inquire about such discounts before making a reservation, however, as checkout time is too late to do so.

GAY AND LESBIAN TRAVELERS

Don't believe all the negative propaganda about the South. The truth is that the metropolitan area of Savannah is tolerant, and gay and lesbian travelers shouldn't expect anything untoward to happen. Outside the metro areas, locals are less welcoming to gay men and lesbian women, although overt hostility is rare. The best approach is to simply observe dominant Southern mores for anyone, gay or straight. In a nutshell, that means keep public displays of affection and politics to a minimum.

Visitors often find Savannah to be surprisingly cosmopolitan and diverse for a Deep South city, and nowhere is this truer than in its sizable and influential gay and lesbian community. In line with typical Southern protocol, the community is largely apolitical and more concerned with integration than provocation. But they're still very much aware of their growing impact on the local economy and are major players in art and commerce.

The **Savannah Pride Festival** is held every September at various venues in town. Top-flight dance-oriented musical acts perform, restaurants show off their creativity, and activists staff information booths. The chief resource for local gay and lesbian information and concerns is the **First City Network,** whose main website (www.firstcitynetwork.net) features many useful links. Another great Internet networking resource is **Gay Savannah** (www.gaysavannah.com).

TRAVELING WITH PETS

While the United States is very pet-friendly, that friendliness rarely extends to restaurants and other indoor locations. More and more accommodations are allowing pet owners to bring pets, often for an added fee, but inquire before you arrive. In any case, keep your dog on a leash at all times. Some beaches in the area permit dog-walking at certain times of the year, but as a general rule, keep dogs off of beaches unless you see signage saying otherwise.

Recreation

BEACHES

Some of the best beaches in the United States are in the region covered by this guide. While the upscale amenities aren't always there and they aren't very surfer-friendly, the area's beaches are outstanding for anyone looking for a relaxing, scenic getaway.

By law, beaches in the United States are fully accessible to the public up to the high-tide mark during daylight hours, even if the beach fronts private property and even if the only means of public access is by boat. While certain seaside resorts have over the years attempted to make the dunes in front of their properties exclusive to guests, this is actually illegal, although it can be hard to enforce. On federally run national wildlife refuges, access is limited to daytime hours, sunrise to sunset.

It is a misdemeanor to disturb the **sea oats,** those wispy, waving, wheat-like plants among the dunes. Their root system is vital to keeping the beach intact. Also, never disturb a turtle nesting area, whether it is marked or not.

The main beach in Georgia is outside Savannah at **Tybee Island,** with full accessibility from end to end. The beach on the north end is smaller and quieter, while the south end is wider, windier, and more populated. There are public parking lots, but you can park at metered spots near the beach as well.

Farther south, a very good beach is at **Jekyll Island,** a largely undeveloped barrier island owned by the state. There are three picnic areas with parking: **Clam Creek, South Dunes,** and **St. Andrew.** Nearby **St. Simons Island** does have a beach area, but it is comparatively narrow and small. Adjacent **Sea Island** is accessible only if you're a guest of the Sea Island resort.

The rest of Georgia's barrier islands are only accessible by ferry, charter, or private boat. Many outfitters will take you on a tour to barrier islands such as Wassaw or Sapelo; don't be shy about inquiring. The most gorgeous beach of all is at **Cumberland Island National Seashore.**

In South Carolina, **Hilton Head Island** has about 12 miles of beautiful family-friendly beaches, and while most of the island is devoted to private golf resorts, the beaches remain accessible to the general public at four convenient points with parking: **Driessen Beach Park, Coligny Beach Park, Alder Lane Beach Access,** and **Burkes Beach Road.**

SURFING

The only surfing of note near Savannah is on the south end of **Tybee Island** near the Tybrisa Pavilion. The key surf shop on Tybee is **High Tide Surf Shop.** For a surf report go to www.hightidesurfshop.com.

KAYAKING AND CANOEING

The Savannah area has rich kayaking and canoeing at **Tybee Island, Skidaway Island,** and the blackwater **Ebenezer Creek.** The best local outfitter and tour operator in this area is **Savannah Canoe and Kayak.** Farther south, down the Georgia coast, the richest kayaking and canoeing area is in the **Altamaha River** estuary, a hybrid blackwater-alluvial river. Good kayaking can be found in the **St. Simons Island** area. The best outfitter and tour operator in the area is **SouthEast Adventure Outfitters.** Kayaking to **Cumberland Island** is a special experience; contact **Up the Creek Xpeditions** in St. Marys.

The Hilton Head/Bluffton area has good kayaking opportunities at Hilton Head's **Calibogue Creek** and Bluffton's **May River.** The best outfitter and tour operator here is **Outside Hilton Head.** Nearby is **Port Royal Sound** near Beaufort; a good outfitter and tour operator in this area is **Carolina Heritage Outfitters.**

FISHING AND BOATING

Because of the large number of islands and wide area of salt marsh, life on the water is largely inseparable from life on the land in the Lowcountry and Georgia coast. Fishing and boating are very common pursuits here, with species of fish including spotted sea trout, channel bass, flounder, grouper, mackerel, sailfish, whiting, shark, amberjack, and tarpon. Farther inshore you'll find largemouth bass, bream, catfish, and crappie, among many more. While entire books can be and are devoted to the area's fishing opportunities, here is an overview.

It's easy to fish on piers, lakes, and streams, but if you're over age 16, you have to get a nonresident fishing license from the state. These are inexpensive and available in hardware stores, marinas, and tackle shops anywhere. In Georgia, a regular license is $9, a one-day license $3.50. A separate license is required for trout fishing. Go to http://georgiawildlife.dnr.state.ga.us for more information or to purchase a license online. In South Carolina, a nonresident seven-day license is $11. Go to www.dnr.sc.gov for more information or to purchase a license online.

The most popular places for casual anglers are the various public piers throughout the area. There are public fishing piers at **Tybee Island, St. Simons Island,** and **Jekyll Island.** The **Bluffton public landing** on the May River is a nice little public dock. Many anglers cast from abandoned bridges, unless signage dictates otherwise. Fishing charters and marinas are ample throughout the region, for both inshore and offshore trips.

GOLF AND TENNIS

The Ocean Forest Course at the **Sea Island Golf Club** on Sea Island is a gem—though you must be a guest at the club to play—as is the affiliated Seaside Course. For value, go in the off-season, in the colder months, when prices are lowest. Not all courses close, and most are in great shape because of the reduced traffic. **Harbour Town** on Sea Pines Plantation in Hilton Head is one of the finest courses in South Carolina. It hosts PGA events.

One of the top tennis destinations in the country, Hilton Head has over 20 tennis clubs, some of which offer court time to the public. Other key tennis facilities are at the **King and Prince Beach and Golf Resort** on St. Simons and **Jekyll Island Tennis Center.**

HIKING AND BIKING

Due to the flat nature of the Lowcountry and Georgia coast, hiking and biking here is not very strenuous. However, the great natural beauty and prevalence of a rich range of plant and animal life make hiking and biking very rewarding experiences. Probably the best trails can be found at state parks in the region, such as **Skidaway Island State Park.** Many national wildlife refuges (NWRs) in the area also feature excellent trails, such as **Pinckney Island NWR and Harris Neck NWR.**

The **McQueen Island Trail** on the way to Tybee Island outside Savannah is an appealing "rails to trails" project. Some areas are almost defined by the plethora of bike and pedestrian trails running nearly their entire length and breadth, such as Jekyll Island and Hilton Head Island.

Wide beaches, very conducive to biking on the sand, are one of the great pleasures of this area. Most bikes you rent in the area will have fat enough tires to do the job correctly. The best beach rides are on **Hilton Head Island, Jekyll Island, St. Simons Island, Cumberland Island,** and **Tybee Island.**

Media and Communications

NEWSPAPERS

The closest thing to a national newspaper in the United States is *USA Today,* which you will find at diverse locations from airports to gas stations. The national paper of record is the *New York Times,* which is available in larger urban areas but only rarely in outlying areas.

The local daily newspaper of record is the ***Savannah Morning News*** (912/525-0796, www.savannahnow.com). It puts out an entertainment insert, called "Do," on Thursdays. The free weekly newspaper in town is ***Connect Savannah*** (912/721-4350, www.connectsavannah.com), hitting stands each Wednesday. Look to it for culture and music coverage as well as an alternative take on local politics and issues.

Hilton Head's paper of record is the ***Island Packet*** (www.islandpacket.com). The main paper in the much more sparsely populated Golden Isles region is the ***Brunswick News*** (www.thebrunswicknews.com), but many people read the newspaper of record of nearby Jacksonville, Florida, the ***Florida Times-Union*** (www.jacksonville.com).

Two glossy magazines compete: the hipper ***The South*** magazine (912/236-5501, www.thesouthmag.com) and the more establishment ***Savannah*** magazine (912/652-0293, www.savannahmagazine.com).

RADIO AND TELEVISION

The National Public Radio affiliate is the Georgia Public Broadcasting station WSVH (91.1 FM). Savannah State University offers jazz, reggae, and Latin music on WHCJ (90.3 FM). Georgia Public Broadcasting is on WVAN. The local NBC affiliate is WSAV, the CBS affiliate is WTOC, the ABC affiliate is WJCL, and the Fox affiliate is WTGS.

INTERNET ACCESS

Visitors from Europe and Asia are likely to be disappointed at the quality of Internet access in the United States, particularly the area covered in this guide. Fiber-optic lines are still a rarity, and while many hotels and B&Bs now offer in-room Internet access—some charge, some don't, make sure to ask ahead—the quality and speed of the connection might prove poor. Wireless (Wi-Fi) networks are also less than impressive, but that situation continues to improve on a daily basis in coffeehouses, hotels, and airports. Unfortunately, many hot spots in private establishments charge fees. While Savannah does not yet have a citywide wireless network, you can get a list of free Savannah Wi-Fi hot spots at www.thecreativecoast.org/datainfo/hotspots.

Generally speaking, the United States is behind Europe and much of Asia in terms of cell phone technology. Unlike Europe, where "pay as you go" refills are easy to find, most American cell phone users pay for monthly plans through a handful of providers. Still, you should have no problem with cell phone coverage in urban areas. Where it gets much less dependable is in rural areas and on beaches. Bottom line: Don't depend on having cell service everywhere you go.

As with a regular landline, any time you face an emergency, call 911 on your cell phone.

All phone numbers in the United States are seven digits preceded by a three-digit area code. You may have to dial "1" before a phone number if it's a long-distance call, even within the same area code. The area code for the part of South Carolina covered in this guide is 843. The area code for the part of Georgia covered in this guide is 912.

Health and Safety

CRIME

While crime rates are indeed above national averages in many of the areas covered in this guide, incidents of crime in the more heavily trafficked tourist areas are no more common than anywhere else. In fact, these areas might be safer because of the amount of foot traffic and police attention.

By far the most common crime against visitors here is simple theft, primarily from cars. (Pickpocketing, thankfully, is rare in the United States.) Always lock your car doors. Conversely, only leave them unlocked if you're absolutely comfortable living without whatever's inside at the time. As a general rule, I try to lock valuables—such as CDs, a recent purchase, or my wife's purse—in the trunk. (Just make sure the "valet" button, allowing the trunk to be opened from the driver's area, is disabled.)

Should someone corner you and demand your wallet or purse, just give it to them. Unfortunately, the old advice to scream as loudly as you can is no longer the deterrent it once was, and in fact may hasten aggressive action by the robber.

If you are the victim of a crime, *always call the police.* Law enforcement wants more information, not less, and at the very least you'll have an incident report in case you need to make an insurance claim for lost or stolen property.

Remember that in the United States, as elsewhere, no good can come from a heated argument with a police officer. The place to prove a police officer wrong is in a court of law, perhaps with an attorney by your side, not at the scene.

For emergencies, always call 911.

POLICE

The city and county police forces recently merged to form the **Savannah-Chatham County Metropolitan Police Department.** For nonemergencies, call 912/651-6675; for emergencies, call 911.

AUTO ACCIDENTS

If you're in an auto accident where there's injury or damage to one or both cars, you must at minimum exchange insurance information with the other driver. It's always prudent to wait for police. Unless there is personal injury involved, you should move your car just enough to clear the way for other traffic if able to do so.

Since it's illegal to drive in these states without auto insurance, I'll assume you have some. And because you're insured, the best course of action in a minor accident, where injuries are unlikely, is to patiently wait for the police and give them your side of the story. In my experience, police react negatively to people who are too quick to start making accusations against other people. After that, let the insurance companies deal with it; that's what they're there for. If you suspect any injuries, call 911 immediately.

ILLEGAL DRUGS

Marijuana, heroin, methamphetamine, and cocaine and all its derivatives are illegal in the United States with only a very few select exceptions, none of which apply to the areas covered by this guide. The use of ecstasy and similar mood-elevators is also illegal. The penalties for illegal drug possession and use are quite severe.

ALCOHOL

The drinking age in the United States is 21. Most restaurants that serve alcoholic beverages allow those under 21 inside. Generally speaking, if only those over 21 are allowed inside, you will be greeted at the door by someone asking to see identification. These people are often poorly trained, and anything other than a state driver's license may confuse them, so be forewarned.

Drunk driving is a problem on the highways of the United States. Always drive defensively, especially late at night, and obey all posted speed limits and road signs—and never assume the other driver will do the same. You may never drive with an open alcoholic beverage in the car, even if it belongs to a passenger.

As far as retail purchase goes, in most parts of Georgia, no alcoholic beverages are sold at the retail level on Sundays, other than in restaurants that also sell food. In South Carolina you may buy only beer and wine, not hard liquor, on Sundays.

MEDICAL SERVICES

Unlike most developed nations, the United States has no comprehensive national health care system (although there are programs for the elderly and the very poor, as well as the new Affordable Care Act, or "Obamacare," for those who work but have no access to insurance). Visitors from other countries who need nonemergency medical attention are best served by going to freestanding medical clinics. The level of care is typically very good, but unfortunately you'll be paying out of pocket for the service. For emergencies, however, do not hesitate to go to the closest hospital emergency room, where the level of care is generally also quite good, especially for trauma. Worry about payment later; emergency rooms in the United States are required to take true emergency cases whether or not the patient can pay for services. Call 911 for ambulance service.

Hospitals

Savannah has two very good hospital systems. Centrally located near midtown, **Memorial Health University Hospital** (4700 Waters Ave., 912/350-8000, www.memorialhealth.com) is the region's only Level-I Trauma Center and is one of the best in the nation. The St. Joseph's-Candler Hospital System (www.sjchs.org) has two units, **St. Joseph's Hospital** (11705 Mercy Blvd., 912/819-4100) on the extreme south side and **Candler Hospital** (5401 Paulsen St., 912/819-6000), closer to midtown.

Pharmaceuticals

Unlike in many other nations, antibiotics are available in the United States only on a prescription basis and are not available over the counter. Most cold, flu, and allergy remedies are available over the counter. While homeopathic remedies are gaining popularity in the United States, they are nowhere near as prevalent as in Europe.

Drugs with the active ingredient ephedrine are available in the United States without a prescription, but their purchase is tightly regulated to cut down on the use of these products to make the illegal drug methamphetamine.

STAYING HEALTHY
Vaccinations

As of this writing, there are no vaccination requirements to enter the United States. Contact your embassy before coming to confirm this before arrival, however. In the autumn, at the beginning of flu season, preventive influenza vaccinations, simply called "flu shots," often become available at easily accessible locations like clinics, health departments, and even supermarkets.

Humidity, Heat, and Sun

There is only one way to fight the South's high heat and humidity, and that's to drink lots of fluids. A surprising number of people each year refuse to take this advice and find themselves in various states of dehydration, some of which can land you in a hospital. Remember: If you're thirsty, you're already suffering from dehydration. The thing to do is keep drinking fluids *before* you're thirsty as a preventative action rather than a reaction.

Always use sunscreen, even on a cloudy day. If you do get a sunburn, get a pain-relief product with aloe vera as an active ingredient. On extraordinarily sunny and hot summer days, don't even go outside between the hours of 10am and 2pm.

HAZARDS
Insects

Because of the recent increase in the mosquito-borne West Nile virus, the most important step to take in staying healthy in the Lowcountry and Georgia coast—especially if you have small children—is to keep **mosquito bites** to a minimum. Do this with a combination of mosquito repellent and long sleeves and long pants, if possible. Not every mosquito bite will give you the virus; in fact, chances are quite slim that one will. But don't take the chance if you don't have to.

The second major step in avoiding insect nastiness is to steer clear of **fire ants,** whose large gray or brown dirt nests are quite common in this area. They attack instantly and in great numbers, with little or no provocation. They don't just bite; they inject you with poison from their stingers. In short, fire ants are not to be trifled with. While the only real remedy is the preventative one of never coming in contact with them, should you find yourself being bitten by fire ants, the first thing to do is to stay calm. Take off your shoes and socks and get as many of the ants off you as you can. Unless you've had a truly large number of bites—in which case you should seek medical help immediately—the best thing to do next is wash the area to get any venom off, and then disinfect with alcohol if you have any handy. Then a topical treatment such as calamine lotion or hydrocortisone is advised. A fire ant bite will leave a red pustule that lasts about a week. Try your best not to scratch it so that it won't get infected.

Outdoor activity, especially in woodsy, undeveloped areas, may bring you in contact with another unpleasant indigenous creature, the tiny but obnoxious **chigger,** sometimes called the redbug. The bite of a chigger can't be felt, but the enzymes it leaves behind can lead to a very itchy little red spot. Contrary to folklore, putting fingernail polish on the itchy bite will not "suffocate" the chigger, because by this point the chigger itself is long gone. All you can do is get some topical itch or pain relief and go on with your life. The itching will eventually subside.

Threats in the Water

While enjoying area beaches, a lot of visitors become inordinately worried about **shark attacks.** Every couple of summers there's a lot of hysteria about this, but the truth is that you're much more likely to slip and fall in a bathroom than you are to even come close to being bitten by a shark in these shallow Atlantic waters.

A far more common fate for area swimmers is to get stung by a **jellyfish,**
or sea nettle. They can sting you in the water, but most often beachcombers
are stung by stepping on beached jellyfish stranded on the sand by the tide.
If you get stung, don't panic; wash the area with saltwater, not freshwater,
and apply vinegar or baking soda. A product called Jellyfish Squish is also
available and seems to work well.

Lightning

The southeastern United States is home to vicious, fast-moving thunder-
storms, often with an amazing amount of electrical activity. Death by lightning strike occurs often in this region and is something that should be
taken quite seriously. The general rule of thumb is that if you're in the water,
whether at the beach or in a swimming pool, and hear thunder, get out of
the water immediately until the storm passes. If you're on dry land and
see lightning flash a distance away, that's your cue to seek safety indoors.
Whatever you do, do not play sports outside when lightning threatens.

Resources

Suggested Reading

NONFICTION

Aberjhani and Sandra West. *Encyclopedia of the Harlem Renaissance.* New York: Checkmark Books, 2003. A brilliantly researched account of the great African American diaspora out of the South that eventually gave birth to the Charleston dance craze of the 1920s.

Calonius, Erik. *The Wanderer: The Last American Slave Ship and the Conspiracy That Set Its Sails.* New York: St. Martin's Press, 2006. A page-turning tale of the last illegal slave shipment to land in the United States, on Jekyll Island, Georgia.

Fraser, Walter J. Jr. *Savannah in the Old South.* Athens, GA: University of Georgia Press, 2005. An insightful and balanced history of Georgia's first city, from founding through Reconstruction.

Georgia Writers Project. *Drums and Shadows: Survival Studies Among the Georgia Coastal Negroes.* Athens, GA: University of Georgia Press, 1986. Arising from a government-funded research project during the Depression, this still ranks as one of the best oral histories ever assembled, using firsthand accounts from African American residents of Georgia's Sea Islands to paint a picture of a lifestyle gone by.

Greene, Melissa Fay. *Praying for Sheetrock.* New York: Ballantine, 1992. In this modern classic, Greene explores the racism and corruption endemic in McIntosh County, Georgia, during the era of the civil rights movement.

Kemble, Fanny. *Journal of a Residence on a Georgian Plantation in 1838-1839.* Athens, GA: University of Georgia Press, 1984. A famed English actress's groundbreaking antislavery account of her stay on a rice plantation in McIntosh County, Georgia.

Lewis, Lloyd. *Sherman: Fighting Prophet.* Lincoln, NE: University of Nebraska Press, 1993. Though first published in 1932, this remains the most thorough, insightful, and well-written biography of General William Sherman in existence.

Morgan, Philip, ed. *African American Life in the Georgia Lowcountry: The Atlantic World and the Gullah Geechee.* Athens, GA: University of Georgia Press, 2010. The best book I've come by on the history and folkways of Georgia's Gullah or Geechee people. Balanced, scholarly, yet still readable in the extreme.

Robinson, Sally Ann. *Gullah Home Cooking the Daufuskie Island Way.* Chapel Hill, NC: University of North Carolina Press, 2007. Subtitled "Smokin' Joe Butter Beans, Ol' 'Fuskie Fried Crab Rice, Sticky-Bush Blackberry Dumpling, and Other Sea Island Favorites," this cookbook by a native Daufuskie Islander features a foreword by Pat Conroy.

Seabrook, Charles. *Cumberland Island: Strong Women, Wild Horses.* Winston-Salem, NC: John F. Blair, 2002. An even-handed, journalistic look inside the tension between environmentalists and the residents of Cumberland Island.

Stehling, Robert. *Hominy Grill Recipes.* Charleston, SC: Big Cartel, 2009. This humble, hand-illustrated, self-published little tome (http://hominygrill.com) features 23 great recipes from one of Charleston's most respected Southern cooking joints, Hominy Grill.

Wood, Betty, ed. *Mary Telfair to Mary Few: Selected Letters, 1802-1844.* Athens, GA: University of Georgia Press, 2007. The revealing, chatty letters of a great arts patron and member of a major Savannah slave-owning family to her best friend, who left the city and moved north because of her abolitionist leanings. We know that Mary Few replied, but her letters remain undiscovered.

FICTION

Berendt, John. *Midnight in the Garden of Good and Evil.* New York: Vintage, 1999. Well, not exactly fiction, but far from completely true, nonetheless this modern classic definitely reads like a novel while remaining one of the unique and readable travelogues of recent times.

Caskey, James. *Haunted* Savannah: The Official Guidebook to Savannah Haunted History Tour. Savannah: Bonaventture Books, 2012. The author may quibble with this being in the "fiction" section, but this is an entertaining and also quite educating look at Savannah's various paranormal tales.

Conroy, Pat. *The Lords of Discipline.* New York: Bantam, 1985. For all practical purposes set at the Citadel, this novel takes you behind the scenes of the notoriously insular Charleston military college.

Conroy, Pat. *The Water Is Wide.* New York: Bantam, 1987. Immortal account of Conroy's time teaching African American children in a one-room schoolhouse on "Yamacraw" (actually Daufuskie) Island.

Hervey, Harry. *The Damned Don't Cry.* Marietta, GA: Cherokee Publishing, 2003. The original *Midnight,* this bawdy 1939 potboiler takes you into the streets, shanties, drawing rooms, and boudoirs of real Savannahians during the Depression.

O'Connor, Flannery. *Flannery O'Connor: Collected Works.* New York: Library of America, 1988. For a look into Savannah's conflicted, paradoxical soul, read anything by this native-born writer, so grounded in tradition yet so ahead of her time even to this day. This volume includes selected letters, an especially valuable (and entertaining) insight.

Internet Resources

CUISINE AND ENTERTAINMENT

Savannah Foodie

www.savannahfoodie.com

An insider's look at the Savannah restaurant scene, with an emphasis on breaking news.

HISTORY AND BACKGROUND

New Georgia Encyclopedia

www.georgiaencyclopedia.org

A mother lode of concise, neutral, and well-written information on the natural and human history of Georgia from prehistory to the present.

NATURE AND ENVIRONMENT

Ocean Science

http://oceanscience.wordpress.com

A blog by the staff of Savannah's Skidaway Institute of Oceanography, focusing on barrier island ecology and the maritime environment.

RECREATION

Dozier's Waterway Guide

www.waterwayguide.com

A serious boater's guide to stops on the Intracoastal Waterway, with a lot of solid navigational information.

www.gadnr.org

This site has lots of great information on the wildlife and geology of Georgia's beautiful and largely undeveloped barrier islands.

Georgia State Parks

www.gastateparks.org

Vital historical and visitor information for Georgia's underrated network of historical state park sites along the coast, including camping reservations.

Savannah Bicycle Campaign

www.bicyclecampaign.org

The clearinghouse for routes and rides by Savannah's most dedicated cyclists.

TOURISM INFORMATION

Visit Savannah

www.visitsavannah.com

Savannah's Convention & Visitors Bureau is particularly adept at social media.

Index

Restaurants Index

Nightlife Index

Shops Index

Hotels Index

Photo Credits

title page: detail of fountain in Forsyth Park © Rolf52 | Dreamstime.com; page 2 (top left) Forsyth Park © Jim Morekis, (top right) Leopold's Ice Cream courtesy of Leopold's Ice Cream, (bottom) Savannah's waterfront at night © Natalia Bratslavsky | Dreamstime.com; page 14 (top left) © Meanmachine77 | Dreamstime.com, (top right) © Marshall Turner | Dreamstime.com, (bottom) © Natalia Bratslavsky | Dreamstime.com; page 15 © David Davis | Dreamstime.com; page 16 (left) © Bgrant814 | Dreamstime.com, (right) © Anthony Aneese Totah Jr | Dreamstime.com; page 17 © Nickolay Khoroshkov | Dreamstime.com; page 19 (both) © Jim Morekis; page 21 courtesy of Elizabeth on 37th; page 22 © Jim Morekis; page 24 © Jim Morekis; page 25 © tomcat2170/123rf.com; page 26 © Smvphotos | Dreamstime.com; page 27 (top) © Jim Morekis, (bottom) © David Davis | Dreamstime.com; pages 31 - 81 © Jim Morekis; page 82 (top) courtesy of B. Matthew's Eatery, (bottom) courtesy of Vic's on the River; page 86 (top left) courtesy of B. Matthew's Eatery, (top right) © Jim Morekis, (bottom) © Benjamin Nehrig; page 91 (top left) courtesy of Leopold's Ice Cream, (top right and bottom) © Jim Morekis; page 97 (top) courtesy of The Coffee Fox, (bottom) courtesy of Foxy Loxy Cafe; page 101 (top) © Peter Marra, (bottom) courtesy of 24e Design Co.; page 105 (top left and right) © Jim Morekis, (bottom) © Geoff L Johnson Photography; page 108 (top left) courtesy of 24e Design Co., (top right) © Jade + Matthew take pictures, (bottom) courtesy of the Savannah Bee Company; page 112 (top) © John Hix | Dreamstime.com, (bottom) courtesy of Savannah Fly Fishing Charters; page 121 (top left and right) © Jim Morekis, (bottom) © Kevin Rose/Telecaster Charters; page 124 (top left) © Benkrut | Dreamstime.com, (top right) © Kevin Rose/Telecaster Charters, (bottom) courtesy of Savannah Fly Fishing Charters; page 130 (top) © Hyatt, (bottom) © Cindy Roberts, Bed & Breakfasts of Savannah; page 135 (top left) © Jim Morekis, (top right) courtesy of Inn at Ellis Square, (bottom) © Jim Morekis; page 137 (top left) © Green Palm Inn/Adam Kuehl, (top right) © Jim Morekis, (bottom) © Cindy Roberts, Bed & Breakfasts of Savannah; page 140 (top) © Jim Morekis, (bottom) © Susan Gottberg | Dreamstime.com; page 149 (top left) © Peter Lakomy | Dreamstime.com, (top right) © Zachary Dalzell | Dreamstime.com; (bottom) © Denise Kappa | Dreamstime.com; page 172 (top left) courtesy of Georgia State Parks & Historic Sites, (top right) courtesy of Blythe Island Regional Park, (bottom) © Jim Morekis; page 174 © Jim Morekis; page 179 (all) © Jim Morekis; page 188 (all) © Jim Morekis; page 199 (all) © Jim Morekis; page 213 © Katie Smith/123rf.com; page 214 (all) © Jim Morekis; page 224 (top) © Jim Morekis, (bottom) © Heatherc123 | Dreamstime.com; page 227 (top left) Brian Lasenby/123rf.com; (top right) © Jim Morekis, (bottom) © Travisowenby | Dreamstime.com; page 249 (top left) © Jim Morekis, (top right) © Oseland | Dreamstime.com, (bottom) © Benkrut | Dreamstime.com; page 272 (top) © Jim Morekis, (bottom) © Wiktor Wojtas | Dreamstime.com

MAP SYMBOLS

≈≈≈ Expressway	○ City/Town	✈ Airport	⚓ Golf Course
— Primary Road	⊛ State Capital	✗ Airfield	🅿 Parking Area
Secondary Road	⊛ National Capital	▲ Mountain	⬮ Archaeological Site
Unpaved Road	★ Point of Interest	✦ Unique Natural Feature	⛪ Church
- - - Trail	• Accommodation		⛽ Gas Station
⋯⋯ Ferry	▾ Restaurant/Bar	⬙ Waterfall	◯ Glacier
-•- Railroad	▪ Other Location	⬙ Park	▨ Mangrove
Pedestrian Walkway		◨ Trailhead	⬚ Reef
▭▭ Stairs	△ Campground	⛷ Skiing Area	▭ Swamp

CONVERSION TABLES

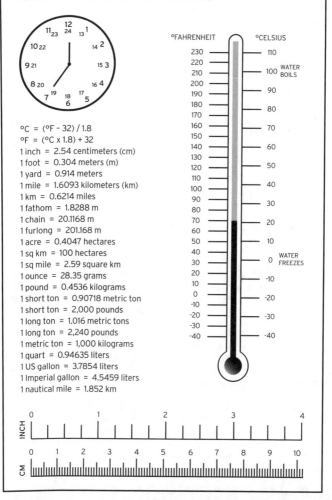

°C = (°F − 32) / 1.8
°F = (°C x 1.8) + 32
1 inch = 2.54 centimeters (cm)
1 foot = 0.304 meters (m)
1 yard = 0.914 meters
1 mile = 1.6093 kilometers (km)
1 km = 0.6214 miles
1 fathom = 1.8288 m
1 chain = 20.1168 m
1 furlong = 201.168 m
1 acre = 0.4047 hectares
1 sq km = 100 hectares
1 sq mile = 2.59 square km
1 ounce = 28.35 grams
1 pound = 0.4536 kilograms
1 short ton = 0.90718 metric ton
1 short ton = 2,000 pounds
1 long ton = 1.016 metric tons
1 long ton = 2,240 pounds
1 metric ton = 1,000 kilograms
1 quart = 0.94635 liters
1 US gallon = 3.7854 liters
1 Imperial gallon = 4.5459 liters
1 nautical mile = 1.852 km

MOON SAVANNAH

Avalon Travel
a member of the Perseus Books Group
1700 Fourth Street
Berkeley, CA 94710, USA
www.moon.com

Editor: Leah Gordon
Series Manager: Erin Raber
Copy Editor: Deana Shields
Graphics Coordinators: Kathryn Osgood, Elizabeth Jang
Production Coordinator: Elizabeth Jang
Cover Design: Faceout Studios, Charles Brock
Moon Logo: Tim McGrath
Map Editor: Kat Bennett
Cartographer: Stephanie Poulain

ISBN-13: 978-1-63121-069-3
ISSN: 2377-1461

Printing History
1st Edition — May 2015
5 4 3 2 1